Hollow Victory

Angela Young

New Generation **Publishing**

Angela Young

Angela Young worked as a researcher in London's dynamic advertising scene during the late 1970's and '80's. Today, she lives and works in Buckinghamshire.

Acknowledgement

My sincere thanks go to Dick Thompson. His enthusiasm and encouragement kept me writing.

For Joe

Life is what you make it

One

Balloons and Talc

The Toby Ales sign was creaking in the wind and soggy rubbish circled around Maureen's ankles as she rang the doorbell. It was a cold December afternoon and her toes were frozen. She stared at her distorted reflection in the wavy surface of the green wall tiles surrounding the pub and willed her father to hurry up. Despite being a teenager, she still wasn't allowed a key – Cyril seeing his daughter as an easy target for bandits to gain access to his Aladdin's cave.

A blast of foghorns from the river made her jump. Peering down Hardy Street, the end of the pier was dissolving into the surrounding greyness and she could just about make out the flashing lights signalling the suspension of the Tilbury ferry. A recent collision off

Northfleet Hope, between three vessels in thick fog, was making everyone extra cautious. Zipping up her nylon diamond-quilted anorak, she rang the bell again then bent down to remove a couple of dog-ends that had somehow managed to get stuck to the sole of her shoe.

The bolt finally slid across and the door swung open.

"Sorry Sook. Been there long? Just 'avin' me forty winks before stockin' up."

Nick-named Sookie or Sook for some reason by her father, Maureen was only too pleased to get inside to the familiar smell of stale beer and cigarette smoke. This was 1964, when going to the pub for a pint of mild or bitter - sometimes twice a day - was still the norm for the working man. As for smoking, well, you were considered anti-social if you *didn't* light up with your pint. There was always 'one on the go' smouldering on the edge of an ashtray, or resting behind your ear in waiting. Filter tips were gaining popularity, not for health reasons, but because they were cheaper - the space taken up by the filter being free of tax.

"Fashion fad for the tarts," was Cyril's take on it. "Less fag, more packin', ta keep lipstick off the real fing." Not that Florrie, Maureen's Mum, would have anything to do with them. As far as she was concerned, she 'wasn't gunna lose an inch of her ciggie for no one.'

Maureen was the only child of Cyril and Florrie, esteemed landlord and landlady of *The Victory* - a Kent town pub within spitting distance of the Thames across from Tilbury docks. She had lived in this establishment all her life and knew it like the back of her hand. In fact she took it all for granted; just as she did the twinkling lights of the power stations and the huge paper and cement mill chimneys that straddled the river. It was all strangely comforting. There was always a big ship or two, guided by the river tugs, making their way in and out of the Docks that she could watch from her bedroom window.

"Nuffink like as many as there used to be," was Cyril's constant lament. "River's nearly dead now. Once upon a time you could walk to Tilbury from 'ere, deck to deck."

As a child Maureen imagined herself doing that.

"Reckon this winter's gunna be like the last one," he said gloomily as he slammed the front door, reinstating the bolt. "Boxing Day, d'ya remember? Blizzards started early 'n we 'ad twelve inches of driftin' snow. Kept fallin' till March. Big Freeze they called it. Bloody bitter it was. Two 'undred ships 'ad to drop anchor round 'ere. Devastatin' fer me takin's!"

Maureen certainly remembered the days she *couldn't* go to school that year and the snowman she made in the yard that lasted for two months. But then the winters throughout her childhood always seemed pretty cold, mounds of snow piled up on the pavement, icy fog and her father moaning about having to drag the coal scuttle up the stairs.

"At least the old Thames didn't freeze... not like '47."

Sensing an epic on its way, Maureen scurried across the bar, heading for the stairs. Cyril could tell he was losing his audience.

"Gi'us an 'and wiv the pale ales, luv, and then we'll get on with the decorations, eh?"

"In a minute, Dad," she yelled back, squeezing under the bar flap. Anything to escape one of his long-drawn-out reminiscences. Surfacing the other side she spotted the age-old flimsy paper lanterns and icicle-shaped glass baubles laid out on the counter. "You got the talc?"

3

"No, yer Mum won't let me use 'er Imperial Leather, so she's gone down the Price Reduction Stores to get a cheap one".

Storage space was at a premium in the Victory. On the way up to dump her school stuff, Maureen had to negotiate mountains of cigarette packets stacked on the stairs. Multipacks of 200 were delivered 'fresh' every week with the steady seller, Rothmans King Size, towering over the rest - *'The best money can buy',* according to the adverts. Aimed at the affluent smoker, Cyril saw himself in this bracket. The new Embassy brand disappeared off the stairs as fast as Florrie could stack them. They appealled to both sexes equally and women were catching up with men, apparently because they found smoking liberating. As yet, Maureen had no desire to join the congregation. Unlike others in her class at school she didn't even fancy trying one. She could have done; Cyril and Florrie wouldn't have been surprised, being big time smokers themselves. She'd posed in the mirror, before now, demurely holding one between outstretched fingers, but that's as far as it went. Maybe it was those 'mimic' cigarette sweets Cyril kept giving her till she was old enough for the real thing, or because she knew how just how bad her clothes smelt, that put her off. No-one wanted to hang their coat next to hers in the juniors' cloakroom. Her Mother had smoked since she started factory work at fourteen. Maureen doubted *she* felt liberated. Addicted, more like it. Further up the stairs were the new mild cigarettes, Silk Cut. Cyril was adamant he wasn't going to stock up with loads of new brands. Tastes were fickle. He'd been left with too many unsold packets of Strand after the *You're never alone with...* campaign famously flopped. "'Ardly surprisin'," was his take on it. "Fags for loners - what's the point of that?"

As it was, cigarette packets were only part of the obstacle course. There were large tins of Smiths crisps with their little blue salt bags, odd boxes of dry biscuits that the ladies seemed to like feeding to their dogs, Rizla cigarette papers, matches and - balanced precariously on the bannisters - cardboard peanut dispensers which exposed ever-increasing areas of a scantily clad beauty as each packet was ripped off. In fact a serious storage crisis was looming. News had just arrived that Smiths were spicing up their range - tins of cheese and onion, salt and vinegar and smokey bacon varieties were on their way. Cyril was sceptical about their take up, but had reluctantly agreed to give the new fad a try.

At some point on the way up Maureen must have scraped her leg on the aforementioned coal scuttle waiting to be filled from the coal bunker in the yard, because there was a ladder forming on her stocking. Blast, she thought, no amount of nail varnish is going to stop this run. Much to her Father's dismay she'd recently made the transition from long white socks to seven-denier stockings. They could be quite draughty and the suspenders left marks on her thighs but these were small sacrifices to make in the name of fashion. There was massive all round relief that seamless versions were becoming available. Stopping the seams from helter-skeltering round your calves was a full time job, besides they were so old-fashioned.

An athletic limbo on the landing got her round the massive old English Electric fridge which grunted its usual welcome. There was simply nowhere else for it to stand. Full bottles of Britvic and Babycham clanked together on the shelves in an unceasing rhythm. This area had also come into its own as a 'cloakroom' for the barmaids. Encouraged not to stray into the private living quarters of their employer, Cyril had generously fixed hooks to the fridge sides for their coats and cardies. An inside shelf provided storage for chilled *4711 eau du cologne*. Florrie supplied this on the house, considering it 'suitably restrained' for the women to splash on when they needed it. (Previously, bottles of *Possession* and *Intimate* had caused sleepless nights.) A clothes brush was tethered to the handle and a large mirror had recently been bolted to the top to facilitate the smearing on of bright red last-minute lippie. It was a bizarre sight to behold, for most. For Maureen just the norm.

There was no central heating of course, so the glowing coal fire in the living room was extremely welcoming. Moving the fire guard to get some heat to her toes prompted Ricky, the pub poodle, to raise his head appreciatively before falling back into his slumber. The dog had originally been bought as company for Maureen when she was eight, but he quickly became Florrie's faithful companion. In fact he would growl and bare his teeth whenever Cyril got within an arm's length of his wife.

Clearing a space between the vinegar and HP brown sauce bottles, permanently on the table in readiness for the hurried meals, was the next task before starting her homework. But this time it was going to have to wait.

"'Ello luv, doing yer 'omework?" Florrie was back and having trouble with the zips on the front of her new ankle boots. "Put the kettle on, I'm gasping. 'S'pect you are too, Ricky?"

Ricky would burst into life on hearing the water spurting into the kettle, followed by the sound of a match being struck. Florrie was adept at igniting the gas on the ring whilst still having enough heat left in the dying match to light the Players Weight dangling from the side of her mouth.

It has to be said, a cup of 'Rosie' in the Victory was

an acquired taste. Very strong - the teapot rarely washed out - then sweetened with condensed milk and two sugars. Never a saucer. Florrie would then slump into the armchair, kick off her shoes and relax for a precious few minutes, her loyal companion sitting by his mistress's toes waiting patiently. As soon as she'd had enough the cup would be put down for him to lap up the sugary tan sludge left at the bottom. It was routine and quite a sight – this white fluffy dog with brown teeth and a permanent tea stain encircling his mouth.

"Yer dad's on about 'is balloons," Florrie shouted from the kitchen. "I've got the talc. It says it's fer afflete's foot on the side, but can't see it matters. Take it down when you go luv. Oh an' I spoke to Ken. 'E was sticking a price ticket on every single can on the shelf. Thankless job if yer ask me. Anyway, 'e says 'e'll be in later to *continue negotiations*. I'm guessing yer know what 'e's on about."

Maureen nodded. She was in the middle of doing a deal with Ken - one of the Victory's regulars and chief shelf-stacker at the new self-service Price Reduction Stores across the road. It had quickly become Florrie's favourite after she found she could get a plastic daffodil with every packet of Persil. Mind you, you had to watch how much you put in the trolleys. The building had originally been the Plaza cinema and still had sloping floors so the final stretch to the tills was uphill all the way. Anyway Ken, a left-over Teddy Boy, right down to his crepe-soled, suede brothel creepers, fancied himself as *Rebel without a cause*, James Dean even though he still lived with his Mum and regularly travelled by bus. Florrie and the barmaids gossiped about never seeing him out courting, but Maureen liked the fact that he spent his money on records rather than flowers and chocolates - that way she got to hear about his rock and roll collection. Ken was keen to share his knowledge and enjoyed laying out his singles in their paper sleeves on the bar, his favourite being *Shakin' all over* by Johnny Kidd and the Pirates. Against his better judgement he'd bowed to pressure from Maureen and bought the first Long Player of The Rolling Stones. Despite his sister knowing someone who had been to Dartford Grammar with the band's flamboyant lead singer, Ken didn't rate them. He told Maureen, with some certainty, that they were going nowhere and that he was sticking with Elvis. Now it looked like he was about to sell her the album for ten bob.

Glancing at the clock, Maureen realised there was only an hour to go before her dad opened up for Curly and Wink, the two six o'clock *regulars*. Curly, a Tilbury docker would chain his bike to the railings at 5.50, light up a Navy Cut and wait for Wink the Dustman to flee the council depot on the 496 bus, arriving just in the nick of time at 5.57. If Cyril was a minute late they'd be tapping on the Public Bar window. After downing a pint each - concentrating hard on the task - they'd be gone by 6.15, their wives none the wiser. Mind you they'd be back again most nights after tea. They seemed an unlikely duo given their different backgrounds, but they clearly enjoyed standing together at the bar exchanging quips. After all they'd been doing it for as long as anyone could remember.

Homework postponed, Maureen set to work. Cyril had brought up the crates of Toby pale ales so she set about stocking the shelf under the counter in the Saloon. Rule of thumb meant that the Public Bar customers - all solid working class men from the surrounding factories and river - drank Mild or IPA bitter, or indeed a mild and bitter mix (mild in first). These were on draught and pulled by traditional,

8

gleaming, long-handled pumps. The shelves in the Public were mostly for pint glasses which had to be filled to the point of overflowing into the drip tray, as no regular would pay for froth.

Any self-respecting female wouldn't be seen in the Public Bar, nor indeed be welcome there - except of course for Molly, wife to Jim and mother to the small group of gypsies allowed in there. "Give 'em their due," Cyril would grudgingly acknowledge, "Didicoys, they might be, but they know 'ow to be'ave. Besides they're 'andy to 'ave on yer side if there's any trouble brewin'." Actually, Molly didn't bat an eyelid at being the only female in that bar. She knew she would stand out like a sore thumb in the Saloon and Florrie certainly wouldn't let her in anyway. Many's the time, when Maureen was small, her mother would drag her across the road to avoid Molly's colourful language around the market.

The Saloon Bar clientele was *very* different - tradesmen, office workers and professional people - some coming off the commuter trains from London, others like lecturers and students from the college across the road and even the vicar from the Church opposite. Much to Cyril's chagrin, a slightly *better class* of person meant having to provide a greater variety of drinks and that meant keeping up with trends and changing his stock accordingly. The popular bottled beers were known by their inimitable catch-phrases: Double Diamond ...*works wonders*, Mackeson ...*looks good, tastes good and by golly does you good* and, of course, Guinness ...*is good for you*, which featured an unfathomable toucan. An inflated plastic free sample was propped up behind the soda syphon on the bar.

Then he had to cater for the women who fell prey to the many beguiling adverts on television. Maureen

9

particularly loved the one for Babycham, demand for which was driving Cyril mental. It meant getting in special flimsy glasses as well as those infuriating bottles with their foil wrappers. Ripped-off bits lay everywhere. The ad showed a cartoon yellow deer with a blue bow leading a young couple through a waterfall to a hidden grotto full of sparkling drink. "I'd *love* a Babycham," simpers the girl. A seductive voice tells her there's a *world of difference* waiting for her when she drinks it. "That'll never catch on," Cyril said. "What the 'ell's a deer gotta do wiv it?"

But the one that really got up his nose was the French bloke, Fernandel, with huge teeth, who seduced all the ladies with his sultry *Do 'ave a Dubonnet* line. "Now they're asking for a bleedin' wine glass," Cyril moaned. Luckily Florrie found a dusty half dozen in Woolworths and all was well. Advocaat, which looked like egg yolks and brought back childhood memories of medicine, made Cyril feel sick. So it was up to Florrie to make the 'Snowballs' with lemonade, and then pop to the Price Reduction stores to purchase glacé cherries and cocktail sticks to put in them.

The Landlady herself wasn't taken in by the drinking fads of the female customers and stuck religiously to her Guinness. "After 'alf past eight and only when a customer offers you one fer yourself", she used to say. By the third, Maureen could hear her mother's forced laughter above all the other racket coming from down below.

Cyril was still holding out against fresh lemon slices and ice (though there was a jar of candied lemon peels for emergencies.) On being asked for a glass of wine by an intrepid Spanish visitor who had made it across the river by ferry from his ship docked at Tilbury, the poor man got short shrift. Cyril wasn't keen on foreigners, the only exception being the occasional influx of

Russians, who arrived the same way from the *Baltika* as part of their sixteen-day round trip from Leningrad. After disembarking its passengers at Tilbury, the ship continued on to Surrey Docks to switch to cargo. The Soviets had four days before its return. They liked Marks and Spencer and drinking IPA with a shot of Smirnoff on the side. Despite his reservations about the Cold War – which had really hit home when a bunker was erected in Woodlands Park – the *communists* turned out to be 'enthusiastic drinkers'. However much the Daily Express might go on about the Cuban Missile Crisis or people trying to climb over the Berlin Wall, Cyril managed to hold his tongue when a round was being ordered.

The opening of the Dartford Tunnel, the previous year, had created extra problems for the Victory as it diverted the traffic heading for the Tilbury-Gravesend car ferry. Passing trade had disappeared almost overnight. The much-loved *Tessa*, which had been carrying vehicles across the river since 1924, had been replaced by a downgraded foot ferry. If you had any sense you didn't raise the subject since *Mimie*, her sister ferry, introduced three years later, had just had her last sailing, sealing the fate of the Ford Anglia drivers with their old road maps and hot water bottles. Transport developments in the early 1960s constantly unsettled Cyril. News of a Channel Tunnel hadn't gone down well ("What 'appens if there's anuvver war?") and motorways were opening up all over the country with no speed limits. People were tasting freedom with their cars and abandoning old-fashioned train travel in their thousands. "It'll all end in tears," Cyril warned. "That Beeching bloke's axing everyfink. Won't be nuffink left soon. You wait."

Maureen stopped stacking, knelt up and looked across

11

to the corner which, at lunchtimes, was home to Mrs Price, Mrs James, Miss Knight and Queenie Frost. Two port and lemons, one gin and 'it' and a large sweet sherry. Such was their private club-like huddle that no-one else dared sit there. Even the occasional stranger seemed to know instinctively to leave it well alone. Maureen knew little about them and it was hard to picture them now, but some things stick in the memory: a navy felt hat with a huge hatpin, an anchor-patterned headscarf, an unruly heap of agéd fur coats smelling of mothballs and a rather large mole on a chin with hair growing out of it.

During the evenings some of the men would bring their wives. Never referred to by their Christian names by staff, they would sit patiently at a table while their husbands lingered at the bar socialising before bringing the drinks. The women seemed quite prepared to put up with the lack of male company between refills, occasionally leaning across to discuss Ena Sharples abrasive tongue, or the arrival of Hilda Ogden in her curlers on the '*Street*'. But in the main they stayed put. The female sex knew its place, Maureen noted. Even the superior Mrs Jenkins. It was quite funny really. She and her husband lived in Khartoum Crescent. Maureen didn't know anyone who lived there. He always wore a suit, even on a Saturday; she three rows of *real* pearls (not the plastic Poppit interlocking ones that everyone else wore), and they spoke with posh accents. Florrie seemed greatly vexed by Mrs J's manicured fingernails. "She gets 'em done every week, falsies stuck on and painted, and 'er 'air's set by that Mau*reece* bloke at Tramps." Florrie's nails, by contrast, were ragged and yellow with tar stains. Worse still, no amount of Nivea could improve her rough hands, damaged by so much washing up.

Recently retired, Mr Jenkins, who had worked *in*

London, now had the time and they clearly had enough money to do whatever they wanted. Why they spent so much time in the Victory was a mystery to Maureen. As soon as they made their grand entrance, Florrie would come scurrying over to greet them, overflowing with platitudes.

"Been *abroad*...ooah, how loverly." "On *holiday*... that must be nice for you." And what's more, they had the tans to prove it.

"Canaries," Mr Jenkins added snootily.

A holiday in the sun surrounded by canaries. They must be *very* rich, Maureen thought. The only canary she'd ever seen was in a cage on Aunt Lil's windowsill.

"Come on luv, we've gotta get these up in the next 'alf hour." Cyril's words brought her sharply back to the job in hand. He was manhandling a packet of assorted balloons, the talc and a small funnel.

"I'll stick up the rest, you get going on these."

Maureen blew up her first balloon, tipped in the talcum powder with the aid of the funnel, and then tied a knot. After twenty of these her head was spinning and there was an unusual medicinal whiff in the air. Soon the entire bar was festooned with the things, slotted in between the paper chains.

"Got plennya talc in 'em?" Cyril enquired, answering his own question by squeezing one. "Feel 'eavy enough. Bloody 'ell, smell funny don't they. Still, might work in me favour."

The balloons were nothing compared to the intense odour of cigarettes at the top of the ladder as the ceiling was coated in a thick sickly yellow layer of nicotine and tar. Surveying the Public Bar from this vantage point Maureen wondered how it managed to keep a large crowd of regulars happy every day. Depressingly off-white net curtains, peppered with burn holes,

13

covered the windows, which were too high to see out of, even assuming one wanted to. Then there was the lino. Or at least what was left of the dark red lino with its multiple burn holes. Years of having fag ends stamped out on it had taken its toll. Mind you, it was in a better state here than in the Saloon. There it had been machine gunned by stiletto heels as well.

Below the windows ran wood panelling, varnished with numerous coats of light oak, courtesy of Cyril. The main part of the bar had nowhere to sit, not even stools. It was standing room only for these regulars, mostly factory labourers. Maureen had an inkling that her father considered them unworthy of a seat. Men from the cement works arrived caked in a fine film of grey dust. Maureen could feel their powder-coated, leathery hands as they took the pints from her and their coins would need dusting before putting into the till. She would listen to them cough violently after their first drag on a Woodbine - the last straw for their already clogged lungs. These men didn't cross the class barrier into the Saloon - the 'Great Divide' was firmly in place.

There were just two small round tables and chairs for the group of flat-capped pensioners to play cribbage, draughts and shoveha'penny, and then at the far end was the dart board. Flanked on either side by blackboards, a central spotlight announced its importance within the bar. The Victory darts team had held a lofty position in the league for many years and a high shelf displaying cups, medals and trophies bore testament to their success. Cyril supplied Toby Ales ties in the brewery colours to all the team and gave regular lectures on solidarity. There were fortnightly practice evenings and, of course, home matches. On these nights Florrie came into her own. Out would come the cheese sandwiches, saveloys and home-pickled onions kept in big screw-top jars that had been donated by the sweet shop next door but one. Maureen always knew when a match was imminent; the smell of lingering vinegar would make her eyes water.

The dart board itself was treated with reverence. It had to be taken down every night after closing and kept in a tank of water in the yard to keep it supple. That stopped the darts doing all those irritating 'bounce offs' that left pin holes in the floor and panelling. Maureen used to play by herself quite often in the afternoons. She was good at getting doubles and the mental arithmetic helped with her sums at school.

The constantly flashing fruits of the Victory's latest addition caught Maureen's eye. Over by the main door, a huge one armed bandit stood looking gormless and out of place. This was Cyril's concession to the modern age. He absolutely hated it, but was only too aware that all the pubs in the vicinity had one, so he had reluctantly acquiesced. It was there to tell passers-by that the Victory was 'up there with the rest of them' and could compete with the neighbours. Luckily Maureen knew where Cyril kept the key to the monster and would surreptitiously retrieve her pocket money from its innards after a losing streak.

The truth is that Cyril felt much more comfortable clinging to the past, hence the dusty old piano tucked away in an alcove under a sign saying 'This way, GENTS'. It (the piano, not the Gents) was rarely used now but Cyril couldn't bring himself to get rid of it. So it served only as a reminder of the old *Saturday Night is Talent Night* which had finally been consigned to history a couple of years earlier. He played piano and drums well and had been in a number of local bands during his youth. Talent night had been a huge success throughout the 1950's, with singers like Johnny Ray, the American heartthrob, a regular favourite to impersonate.

Nicknamed 'The Prince of *Wails*' and 'Mr Emotion', his act included tearing at his hair, falling to the floor and crying on stage. Ken could do a fantastic version of his first hit *Cry,* shaking and cavorting in an original long drape jacket with velvet trim and bootlace tie. The audience, issued with sheets of toilet paper from the Ladies, would chuck them at him when he reached the tragic bit. And if anyone was brave enough to try *Just walking in the rain,* Cyril would be standing in the wings armed with a water filled ice bucket in readiness.

Wink was known for his rendition of Frankie Vaughan's *Give me the moonlight.* Turning up the collar on his donkey jacket, donning an old straw boater and cane for props made him look the part, but he had an unfortunate problem with Frankie's trademark left leg kick. With one eye permanently shut due to an air gun accident as a child, his spatial awareness wasn't up to much and he'd developed some rather jerky head movements to help him focus. It didn't do to be too close to him when he was attempting a kick on the blind side. Thankfully, his other half, Reenie, would arrive, after washing up the tea things, to make sure he didn't do himself any permanent mischief. She wouldn't stop long though, always leaving well before closing time to warm up the electric blanket in their flat above the fish shop close by.

The demise of Talent Night had left a nasty taste in Cyril's mouth. Some of the younger set started turning up with Vox AC15 amplifiers – built just down the road in Dartford. The Shadows had featured them on their No.1 hit *Apache* and now just about every British group was using them. Trouble is, the Victory wasn't cavernous enough for that kind of output and the feedback would leave the regulars wincing in agony. So Cyril called it a day. After that, whenever 'talent night' came up in conversation, it would always be about the 'good old days' and someone would inevitably re-tell the story of when a loose black ivory flew off the piano and landed in Stripey Watkins mum's stout.

Having put the ladders back out in the yard Cyril returned to admire their handiwork. "That'll do," he said. "Should put the buggers off!"

Years of having balloons burst prematurely by over-zealous drinkers holding their cigarettes aloft, had spurred the Victory's ever-inventive landlord into action. The chance of a liberal dousing of talc on ones shoulders, or worse still, in your pint, would prolong the life of the balloons until New Year's Eve, when everyone expected to get plastered anyway at the stroke of twelve.

Two

Ready Steady Go

Back upstairs, Maureen finally finished her homework and went to her bedroom. This took some courage as it was usually damp or dripping with condensation. Smoke and nicotine had permeated the walls to such an extent that no self-respecting wallpaper would stay up. Even trusty Evo-stik couldn't win the battle. Still, at least the smell of the glue overpowered that of the mildew, even if it left you a little light-headed. There was a fireplace, but Cyril had never let a fire be lit in it due to the flammable nature of the newly-invented brushed nylon nighties. According to him, they were lethal because they gave off sparks when you turned over in bed in the dark which could be seen through the pink candlewick bedspread. To top it all, the windows had been sealed shut by paint as a security measure, with the result that no fresh air found its way inside.

There had been an unfortunate incident with the windows which made Maureen wary of trying to open them. Lorraine, Maureen's best friend from school, overcome with the need to wave at some boys heading for the Wimpy one summer's evening, had tried to do exactly that. The Victory was on a corner of a busy high street with Sid the butcher - a firm friend, always to be seen in a crisp white apron - next door. An old fashioned Bata shoe shop and the Super were in the other direction. One of two cinemas in the town, the Super had recently been turned into a bingo hall. Cinema audiences had dwindled, the only busy time being Saturday morning pictures when the kids would queue up to watch westerns and cartoons. Not that Maureen had ever been allowed to go. Cyril wasn't keen on the language he could hear from beneath his bedroom window. Indeed the only time he'd taken her to a matinee himself was to see an old silent Laurel and Hardy black and white picture. Irritatingly, she came away with her hood filled with bubble gum wrappers, thanks to the kids sitting in the row behind.

Anyway, in those days queues for the Bingo were made up of blue rinse ladies stretching right round the corner, blocking the entrances to both bars of the pub. This tested Cyril's tolerance to the limit. Lorraine, convinced she could see Clive Mont in the gang, approached the window in desperation just as the bingo queue was at its height. Feeling resistance, she leant on the glass to get a firmer grip on the frame.

"It's definitely 'im, Mo. Come and see. Ooah, 'es wearing drainpipes. Blimey, they're tight. Gotta let 'im know we're up 'ere."

"Lorr, I don't think you should lean on the window..." That was all it needed. The sound of broken glass hitting the ground was nothing compared to the sound of scattering bingo ladies.

The girls stood in stunned silence waiting for the inevitable. They didn't have to wait long before a furious Cyril barged into the room.

"There's three women lying dead down there... in pools of blood," he raged. "What am I gunna tell their 'usbands, eh? It'll be *my* neck on the block!"

It was virtually opening time and Maureen was brought back to reality by the sound of her Father on the stairs.

"Bloody 'ell, I look like the Wreck of the Hesperus." Cyril had caught sight of himself in the mirror. "Paper chains 'ave messed up me partin'. Where's me Brylcreme? Florrie... Gotta freshen up this shirt too. Where's the Odorono? Florrie…"

"Try the fridge," came a suggestion from the kitchen.

Since Woman's Own and Titbits had started going on about the dreaded *B.O*, the state of one's armpits had suddenly become a matter of national concern. Unfortunately this coincided with the invention of the miraculous non-iron, drip-dry, Rael Brook polyester shirt, which only served to make matters worse. Cyril had never used deodorant before and was sceptical about spraying it directly onto his skin. Besides, time was of the essence, so why not just apply it to the shirt? This meant that going to the toilet involved negotiating a route past an army of shirts drip-drying themselves over the bath. Trouble is that after a while they'd take on a life form of their own, arms outstretched rigid from a crusty chemical residue that no amount of Omo could shift.

Not to be left out, Florrie's gesture to fashion was wash and wear wrinkle-resistant, Crimplene shift dresses. These new synthetic yarns came in an alarming variety of colours, patterns and bobbly textures - even embossed rainbow arches - which finished up joining the shirts on the drip-dryer. When you looked closely at them, every garment had little holes here and there where the wearer's fag ash had dropped. Cyril, in fact, had recently experienced a nasty moment when, in the dark, he'd bumped into a stiff sleeve with a cigarette in his mouth and narrowly avoided incinerating himself.

Buttoning up his faithful beige knitted waistcoat, he made his way downstairs again, finally leaving Maureen to change out of her school clothes. The waistband on her skirt took some time to flatten out after being rolled up and down to adjust the length several times that day. Skirts were beginning to get shorter, but neither her school nor Cyril had caught on to it yet.

Settling for her denim hipster slacks with their slimming chunky plastic belt and a turtle neck jumper, she stuck back the pictures of the Beatles from her weekly Fabulous 208 magazine which regularly fell off the wall due to the effects of damp on sellotape. A yellowing picture of old heartthrob Kookie - from the American TV show *77 Sunset Strip* – was finally consigned to the bin. As her mind wandered she saw... The Fab Four popping into the Saloon on a detour from Lewisham Odeon. George enters first, their eyes meet across the crowded bar and he declares he's willing to wait for her... all this to the chorus of *Love me Do.*

'Who's your favourite Beatle?' was the main topic of conversation at school, and whenever Maureen saw them on television she knew she was going to cry.

Back in real time she rearranged her herd of yellow Bakelite Babycham bambis sporting their regulatory blue bows on the mantelpiece. As orders increased at the pub, so did the number and size of the promotional gifts. Wandering back into the living room to warm up, she found Florrie making tea, only this time it was deliberately being left to get cold.

"Mo," she said "come and 'old this bottle for me, I need three 'ands."

Maureen obliged by pouring the weak brown liquid into an empty whisky bottle.

"I'm on to 'er game, this'll be on the optics after closing time, ready for 'er early morning tipple," she said with a snigger.

Maureen knew only too well what this was all about. Gert, the cleaner, had started her campaign of having a drink for Christmas early in November. Apart from the amount of alcohol she was managing to get through even before breakfast, Brasso was being far too

21

liberally applied to all surfaces and was becoming a danger to life and limb.

As the bells rang from the Church opposite, a gasping Curly Campbell was already banging on the window. Florrie had given her growing bunch of plastic PRS daffodils their weekly wash. It was Opening Time. Cyril straightened his Toby Ales tie, restored the centre parting in his slick short back and sides and after removing some stray tinsel from his shoulders, unlocked the door. This was Friday, the busiest evening of the week. The Public Bar would be bursting at the seams, with tickets for the meat raffle on offer, courtesy of Sid the butcher next door. Delivered by hand, Sid would proudly demonstrate his meat's finer qualities by laying the carcass on the counter, which meant Cyril having to shield his eyes for fear of being sick. The more sedate Saloon would be the scene for courting couples congregating on the green vinyl benches or the almost-matching chairs and tables, under the red flock wallpaper. Cyril wouldn't allow any over-zealous canoodling of course. Bad for business. If they got too distracted they wouldn't refill their glasses.

Maureen had worked out the town's weekend dating ritual, watching, as she often did, from the living room windows. The couples would meet up either outside the Church, the Ritz café, or under the awning of Kentons furniture shop if it was raining - most arriving by bus. A quick peck on the cheek, a sharing of cigarettes, they would then cross the road and come into the pub. On a Saturday - as seen from the bedroom window on the other side - they would bypass the pub and head down Hamilton Road to watch the latest picture from the back row of the Majestic, possibly stopping on the way for a Wimpy beefburger if the bloke still felt flush.

"Coming down at closing then?" asked Florrie, pushing open the door with her bottom. She was carrying a steaming washing up bowl. Undoing her suspenders through the Crimplene, she rolled down her stockings and, sitting on the armchair near the fire, plonked her feet into the bowl.

"Ahh," she sighed, "just enough time to soak me bunions before things get going. I swear me varicose veins are getting worse. Pluck me eyebrows luv? That Miss World's got nuffink on me." Maureen shuddered at the thought of her Mother in a swim suit parading on a cat walk in front of a panel of male judges. She had recently joined the millions who watched scantily-dressed Ann Sidney, become Miss World on TV. Listening to the girls espousing their visions for 'world peace' whilst adjusting vital elastic, was a special treat.

"Ta luv," winced Florrie after Maureen had extracted several sprouting hairs. Licking the end of an eye brow pencil, she proceeded to draw on two dark semi circles in the vacant space.

"Is one 'igher that the other, Mo? Can't see in this light."

Inspired by Lucille Ball, Florrie had sported a look of mild surprise since *I Love Lucy* was first beamed to our TV from America.

At weekends Maureen was encouraged to go down into the bar when the first bell was rung. So at ten to eleven, she looked at herself in the mirror and was mortified to find a new spot emerging on her forehead. Arranging her fringe in a clump to hide it, she brushed her long, straight hair whilst toying with the idea of enraging Cyril by applying some black eye make-up, like Cathy McGowan.

Maureen liked *Juke Box Jury,* with its bell and hooter signifying a 'hit' or a 'miss,' but her favourite television programme was *Ready Steady Go.* The first real teenager show she'd ever seen, it came on at 6pm on a Friday, with the catchphrase *The weekend starts*

23

here. Manfred Mann's *5-4-3-2-1* would herald the appearance of Cathy. She was Maureen's idol, barely out of her teens herself and seemingly as awe-inspired at introducing the groups as Maureen would have been. Her fashion sense earned her the title 'Queen of the Mods'. She made trouser suits acceptable and when she launched her own fashion range at British Home Stores, Maureen was over the moon.

Locating her shoes, she descended into the smog below and began her chores. Her first job was to go round the tables emptying the ashtrays - this would enforce the message that it was time to go home. Then, to make it even more obvious, she'd take away empty or near empty glasses. Lastly she'd wipe the tables with a wet cloth, not forgetting the underside at the edges which were always sticky and liable to give the ladies soggy skirts. On this particular night it was a bit embarrassing as several of the couples were still courting, oblivious to all around them and not taking the hint. Cyril rang the curfew bell furiously to make them shift. That got the message through alright and *en masse* they gathered their belongings and wandered out into the freezing, foggy night. Eddie the barman, Theresa and Sylvia, the evening barmaids, washed and dried the glasses knowing that Florrie wouldn't give them the signal to go until everything was back on the shelves. Theresa was mindful of the time as she had to catch the last 888 bus to the new Riverview Park estate. Cyril didn't share her enthusiasm for new houses – confirmed for him that summer when a plague of earwigs invaded the estate. It was even on the local news.

Theresa was Maureen's favourite. She was quite young and pretty with an amazing Jacqueline Kennedy bouffant hairstyle held in place by sticky hair lacquer which always left a cloud circling round the fridge.

Maureen would pop out to talk to her while she made her final *teasing* adjustments. Occasionally it would be subtly different, without any loose hair at the sides. This beehive, by all accounts, took around two hours to achieve with even more backcombing than the bouffant. She usually wore a straight skirt with inverted pleats front and back, called kick pleats. Theresa said they allowed her to do the twist properly and the two of them would have a little go on the landing, whilst singing Chubby Checker's *Let's twist again.* Apparently it was great doing the twist at parties as you didn't have to wait to be asked to dance.

Other tricks of the trade staggered Maureen. You could wrap your newly washed lambswool jumpers in tissue and brown paper and then put them under the carpet for two days. The more they were trodden on the flatter they became. Toilet paper had its uses too - keeping the beehive stable when wrapped around your head at bedtime, just so long as you remembered to pick out any fragments left behind in the morning.

Besides her fashion and dance sense, Theresa had a wry sense of humour, particularly about current affairs. She shared snippets from *That was the week that was* with a select few around the bar and was always well up on the scandals of the day. Watching Mrs Jenkins lapping up her salacious stories about Russian spies, prostitutes and Government ministers, was highly entertaining. The story of Christine Keeler being paid £23,000 by the News of the World for details of her affair with John Profumo - a fortune in anyone's book – meant it *had* to be true. Luckily, Cyril was impressed with Theresa too. She was polite, quick around the bar and did more than her fair share of a barmaid's duties, plus she was studying typing and shorthand at the college.

Sylvia had her fans on the other side of the counter,

25

causing Florrie to keep a beady eye on her, well aware of her pros and cons. A fair bit older - at least 30 - Maureen thought she was rather old fashioned and still wearing styles from the '50s. The jacket of her collarless, tight fitting Chanel-type suit was always undone. You couldn't fail to notice the Triumph bra - its circular stitching creating a pointed conical shape through her angora sweater. Constantly checking and straightening her stocking seams, Maureen reckoned she wore a really tight suffocating roll-on too. She was always making Theresa get the bottles on the lower shelves, since bending was out of the question. With peroxide blonde hair and solid make up, it was clear she thought she looked like a glamorous American film star. Gushing and flirty, there was always a queue for her attention. She tolerated the ogling and leering, but her smile left with the last customer.

By all accounts there was an ex-husband somewhere - a bus conductor on the 'Maidstone and District' – not that anyone ever saw him. When she tried to leave her two daughters upstairs one evening as playmates for Maureen, the suggestion went down like a lead balloon. But the real problem was that there'd been talk of an *understanding* between Sylvia and Curly. He would often walk her home during the week. As far as Florrie was concerned, this sealed her fate. Curly's reputation, on the other hand, remained unsullied.

A few regulars were still hanging around, vying for position, hoping to be invited to stop behind for a drink. This was Cyril's prerogative. He enjoyed his position of power deciding if, and then who, could remain after the doors were locked. He would play host for a couple of hours more. Florrie, for her part, would have none of it. As soon as the last tea towel was hung over the pumps, she'd be off upstairs with the contents of the till and the dregs of her last Guinness, to put her hair up in overnight curlers, held in place with a thick hairnet.

"Gunna stop too, Sook?" Cyril asked Maureen, pouring her out a Dubonnet and lemonade. 'Yes' was the answer and Maureen joined her Dad, Bryn – a travelling salesman from who-knows-where, wearing his weekend mop-top Beatle wig that no-one was supposed to notice, and Sid the butcher – *sans* apron, with their Johnny Walker whiskies and a squirt of soda, all lined up on stools at the Saloon Bar counter. She listened to the World being put to rights for a while until the conversation turned yet again to the old chestnuts of the Labour Government and race relations.

"Bein' told I *'ave* to serve 'em, that's what I can't get over. They'll soon be crawlin' all over us. Game was up when first lot got a council 'ouse this year. Sod it, I'm not lettin' 'em in the Saloon. Public maybe, but that's it."

Maureen had watched her father, many times, screaming "Out" to those he didn't want. A colour bar was common practice and Cyril certainly wasn't the only landlord to exercise his 'rights'.

The first immigrants from India and Pakistan had started arriving in the town about eight years earlier. Maureen thought it was going to be a long while before attitudes changed and, not being sure how she felt about the conversation, decided it was time for bed.

By the late 1950's Britain's industry was running at full strength. It was a boom time and a high demand for skilled labour in this heavily industrialised local area meant full wage packets. The post-war years of austerity seemed to have been left behind and, at last, ordinary people were beginning to sense a bit of hope. Prime Minister Harold McMillan cleverly captured the new sense of optimism when he told the nation that "most of our people have never had it so good" which, for Cyril and Florrie, was true. Pubs were playing a hugely important part in peoples' social lives. It was very hard work, but they both enjoyed the life. They were fully occupied, which is why Maureen's memories of spending time with them were so few and far between.

By the Sixties, however, things were happening in the country that looked set to derail Cyril's dream. The 1964 General Election, held that October, brought an end to thirteen years of Conservative rule. Back came the Labour Party, returned to power with the slimmest of majorities – just four seats, Gravesend being one of the sixty three seats to switch allegiance. Cyril was disgusted at the town's disloyalty. Harold Wilson seemed bent on changing everything that people like him held dear. He was going to abolish capital punishment, legalise homosexuality and abortion, increase taxes on beer and cigarettes, hike commercial rents, test people for 'drink driving'… it was all too much. If 'modernising' Britain meant stacking the odds up against running a pub profitably, who wanted it?

Cyril and Florrie started to argue a lot around this time, often about these sorts of things, but mainly about Florrie not pulling her weight. "You've only got 'er to look after and a few sandwiches to make," he'd carp with his usual disdain for the female sex. "I'm the one shoulderin' the responsibility for this place."

The rows would take place upstairs, so as to keep up appearances in the bar, which meant Maureen would always be caught in the middle of them. In her eyes her Mother was rarely the one found lying in bed dangerously close to opening time.

Customers were demanding new things - the fruit machine being a classic example. The latest rumblings around the bar were about getting in a juke box. Now *that* really rubbed Cyril up the wrong way. Another monster taking up drinking space. Far worse, customers being able to choose the music... not bloody likely. Cyril had even thought seriously about dusting off the old piano. That's where the conversation had got to as Maureen neared the top of the stairs.

"Trouble is, me little finger's completely bent over inta me palm, see. Can't tickle the ivories like I used to. Course, if I 'adn't've broke me arm, I wouldn't 'ave this wanky finger."

"Oh no, not again," she winced. "Why won't someone *tell* him? He's so embarrassing". Thankfully reaching the top, she could barely hear him anymore.

Cyril had broken his arm very badly as a small boy playing football. There was some awful story about the local doctors threatening to amputate, but Maureen's Grandad would have none of it and had taken him by train to the Royal Orthopaedic Hospital in London - quite something since this was in the 1920s. Anyway they'd operated and poor Cyril was forced to wear a metal splint at night for two years. As a result, his arm was always slightly twisted, and the little finger, seemingly fine at the time, had slowly bent inwards throughout his adult life. This was what Cyril charmingly referred to as his 'wanky finger'. He seemed totally oblivious to any other usage of the word.

Indeed, when a slightly modified version of it appeared sprayed on the tiles outside, he genuinely thought someone was paying homage to the musical legend residing within.

Three

Gone up Brookies

"You'll let me know if he's up to a visit then Mum. Busy time for me though." Cyril was talking to Dot on the phone. "Cheerio for now."

Maureen was standing behind him on the bottom stair waiting for news of her Grandfather. Without making eye contact Cyril hung the receiver back on the wall, grabbed a packet of Rothmans from above her head, opened the door into the bar and shot off down the cellar steps. She heard a match strike as he exited.

Bert, Cyril's Dad, had been ill for a bit. Maureen hadn't been given a clear answer as to what was wrong, just a lot of face-pulling and hushed tones, so she suspected the worst. Neither of her parents discussed serious illness and she knew better than to pry.

Sinking onto the stairs she pondered her Christmas, which was now only a week away. Things were obviously going to be different this year. Maureen had spent the two-week Christmas school holiday with her Grandad and Nanna - Bert and Dot - for as long as she could remember. Not this year it seemed. They were going to be looked after by Aunty Ethel, Cyril's sister, which meant Maureen having to stay at the Victory. She shuddered to think what it was going to be like.

Living only a ten minute walk away, Maureen had got used to spending weekends and most of her school holidays in their company. She had her own bedroom which looked out on to the garden and would lay in bed listening to the wood pigeons, something she *never* heard in the Victory.

There were so many happy memories in that garden. Hot summer days dangling her feet in a tiny paddling pool, her Nanna's feet alongside hers cooling between the bugs in the water. Maureen would be in her blue, ruched-all-over swimsuit which everyone seemed to wear in the Fifties; Nanna, as always, wearing her wrap-around pinnie, her long hair tightly rolled around her head, shelling peas into a colander, the heady, spicy, clove smell of carnations wafting their way as Grandad selected a perfect specimen for his button hole before he headed off to the pub.

Maureen remembered the way he liked to look smart in his funny old shiny brown suit, trousers just that little bit too short, due to the pull from heavy elasticated braces. Always wearing his huge rabbit-hair felt fedora, he would walk arm in arm with Dot, equally elegant, on their annual day trip by ferry and train to Southend. It was the nearest Maureen got to a summer holiday and she always looked forward to it. Disembarking from the packed train at the end of the line, the salty sea air and screeching seagulls would swamp their senses as the crowd spilled out of the station. Heading straight for Woolworth's creaking floorboards on the High Street, the trio would stock up on essentials – straw hats, plastic sandals for walking on the stony beach, and spangles to suck whilst there. Then, to really get in the seaside mood, it was next door to Rossi's ice cream parlour for a dish of their beautiful white ice cream with chunks of ice still in it.

In a mix of fear and excitement, it was on to the famous Kursaal Amusement Park - along the promenade watching the waves crashing onto the stones and hearing the sound of the daredevil motorcyclists on the *Wall of Death* getting louder by the minute. By the time they were walking down the sloping tunnel into the Kursaal grounds Maureen would have her hands over her ears. She'd be hoisted on to Grandad's shoulders to watch the bikers perform their amazing tricks - standing on their heads on the saddle, riding backwards at breakneck speed around a spinning vortex with only the force of gravity to stop them plunging to their death. It wasn't for the fainthearted that's for sure.

Dot generally wouldn't go on the rides, reckoning that she'd sink the tub on the *Tunnel of Love* or squash someone to death on the *Waltzer* when it tipped, but she'd accompany her grandaughter on the *Caterpillar* so she wouldn't be too scared when its green skin enveloped them half way through. They'd both be in hysterics trying to hold their skirts down when a blast of air blew them up over their heads.

Bert was partial to a turn on the dodgems - the nearest he ever got to driving a car - and he loved to torment Maureen on the boating lake as he disobeyed the call to 'come in number three.' He'd pretend he'd forgotten how to row, causing a tidal wave as they circled round and round, Maureen's ponytail dripping and his buttonhole drooping in the spray. Dot would get her much needed cuppa in the Dolphin Cafe at the end of the longest pier in the world, reached by draughty train, while Bert and Maureen watched the sea whooshing between the planks underfoot.

At dusk they would stroll through *Never Never Land* - a magical wonderland of illuminated mythical castles, goblins, dragons and things that made you jump when they moved as you went past them. They'd eat fish and chips out of the paper on the prom and wait until completely dark before coming home so they could see the fairy lights switching on all along the seafront. Every day was a perfect day.

Before she was able to walk home by herself, it was always her grandparents she'd look for at the school gates and talk to about what she's been up to. Grandad would pretend he'd forgotten where they lived and go into strangers front gardens, sometimes up to the front doors, causing Maureen to squeal with a mixture of horror and delight. Finally reaching home, she was able to spend an hour or so before Florrie collected her, looking at a set of huge books called *Peoples from around the World* that Bert had picked up for a song from Smokey Fishmans' junkyard under the railway arches. They were very old and from another era, but she loved sitting at the table poring over them with her Grandad. He wore small round glasses, supposedly to help with reading, but more often than not they would be buried in his thick, pure white hair. Instead he struggled to see the small print with a tiny magnifying glass propped against one eye like a monocle. Every time he spoke it fell out, usually landing under the table.

Nanna found time to play endless card and board games and didn't mind cricket so long as she could sit on a chair and always bat. She taught Maureen to sew, knit and crochet and would send her off to the local shop to buy them both ice creams in wafers.

Maureen loved the relationship between Bert and Dot too. He called her Jim, no idea why. They were a great double act, teasing one another and laughing most of the time. Bert was a hoarder - old newspapers, junk post, bric-a-brac, you name it. Dot regularly had a clear out. Needless to say, Bert would forever be searching for something. "What's 'appened to … Where's that…" and Dot's reply would always be the same: "Gone up Brookies, I expect." *Brookies Dust Hole,* to give it its full name, was an imaginary place where all lost items went. "All manner of me gubbins ends up Brookies," Bert would sigh.

The truth is that Maureen had been loved,

supported, educated, entertained and indulged by them all her childhood, and because of that she loved them as if they were her parents.

But why hadn't her *real* parents made her feel that way? "Don't have the time", was her Father's usual justification, to which, more often than not, Florrie would add, "Pub's no place for a nipper". Or the excuse would be: "It's a twenty-four-hour, seven-days-a-week job. Can't 'ave an 'oliday, not even a day out." It was always the same, bedtime stories, family chat, or even family meals, just didn't happen in the Victory.

The thing that confused her more than Cyril's apparent lack of interest was his over-protectiveness towards her. He saw danger in everything, which prevented her from doing normal things with her friends.

"If I could wrap you in cotton wool and keep you in a glass case I would," was how he'd couch his reason for saying no.

"We'd like to ask you to come," embarrassed Aunts and Uncles would say, "but we're going by car," or, "we'll be near water," or, "we're cycling." So no visits or school trips for Maureen, no outings to the swimming pool, no trips to the woods. The list was endless and got longer as she got older.

At this time of the year the fog made things worse. Cyril was always on high alert that there would be a repeat of the *Great Smog of '52*. The Clean Air Act was actually beginning to make things a little better, but 'better safe than sorry', was Cyril's motto and most mornings when Maureen was little he could be seen leading her across the road to the bus stop, hurricane lamp in hand, dripping paraffin as he went.

Smog was weird. Everything looked hazy yellow under the streetlights and you could hardly see your hand in front of your face. The bus took forever to get to school and the whole time she had to wear a cotton *peasouper protection mask* specially made (and named) by Dot. It made her feel stupid, but at least it stopped Cyril insisting on her being smothered in Vick's vapour rub to prevent wheezing. It was bad enough that she had to wear a fleecy liberty bodice over her vest from November 1st onwards. Not only did it have rubber buttons which became sticky after being boiled to keep the undergarment white, but Florrie would chant, "Do not cast a clout till May is out", as a justification for it to remain in place for months on end.

Bert and Dot on the other hand were made of sterner stuff, but even they didn't want a lecture from their son, so would find ways to outwit him. Next to Bert's *dunegan* - his outside privy - with its newspaper toilet sheets hanging from an old shoelace, was a lean-to where roller skates, stilts and a scooter (all from Smokey's) were hidden behind a rabbit hutch. *Pinkie* had been bought by Bert from a supposed rabbit breeder at the pub. White with pink eyes, he'd turned out to be quite a hoodlum. No one besides Bert would go anywhere near him - certainly not Cyril - so the stash remained a secret.

On a Sunday afternoon, Cyril would take a trip to visit his parents and collect Maureen, a perky Ricky alongside him, escorting the Master on his long-distance mission. Maureen's heart would sink when she heard his steel-toe-capped shoes coming round the corner of Sudan Street, putting an end to her weekend fun. Everyone would be on tenterhooks if there was a grazed knee, hoping upon hope they'd get their stories straight. Worse still, on a Saturday evening, Cyril would send a customer to walk back with her. He saw no harm in it despite it always being a man and, more often than not, someone Maureen hardly knew. She didn't like it and her Nanna was obviously uncomfortable about letting her go. However the practice stopped abruptly when Maureen was twelve.

Lionel - actually one of Maureen's favourites - was a kindly old man, with a bow tie, pipe held in the corner of his mouth and a jaunty cap, who tried his best to keep the conversation going on the walk. Most of the collectors would start out well, but by Trafalgar Street would run out of ideas. Anyway, one day, after reaching the Victory, there were more whispers than usual between Cyril and Florrie. Her Father shot out of the room leaving Florrie to ask strange questions about Lionel and his hands. Maureen had no knowledge of hands being anywhere other than in pockets, nevertheless Lionel was promptly crossed off the collector list. From then on he seemed to be absent from his usual standing spot at the Bar.

It was only when Maureen overheard her parents discussing Lionel's demise that she discovered what had been going on. Apparently, getting a taste for walking young girls, Lionel had - on Cyril's recommendation by the way - taken Sylvia the barmaid's two daughters to the annual circus on the 'rec'. Maureen had been desperate to go too, but Cyril was worried about tropical diseases. Anyway, there was an accusation from the older girl that Lionel had put his hand in her knickers. He vehemently denied it of course, but it was enough for him to be barred from the Pub. In truth, the barring was to stop Sylvia going to the Police.

"Couldn't afford a scandal, especially since it was my idea," Cyril admitted sheepishly. "Still can't believe it of old Lionel Lee though. 'Ave yer seen the way that girl dresses now? 'Ow old was she at the time Flo?"

"'Bout thirteen, well developed though," was Florrie's conspiratorial reply as they sucked on their cigarettes and tapped the ash in unison into the Canada

Dry ashtray on the dinner table.

"Mmm," concluded Cyril. "Barmaid's daughter an' all". Florrie nodded knowingly, thinking that that was the end of it.

But there was more to come, Curly took the law into his own hands and made sure that Lionel wouldn't be visiting the Victory or indeed any other hostelry again in a hurry. Cyril made discreet enquiries at the hospital and was quietly relieved to hear that Lionel would make a full recovery, certainly in time to move to Dover where his brother lived.

"Knocked 'is bleedin' 'ead off, didn't 'e," Cyril spluttered on his return. "'Good fing 'e's not pressin' charges. Let's 'ope it all blows over. Best not say anyfink to Curly, eh"

"Not on yer nelly," agreed Florrie. "Wonder what Sandra makes of it though?"

Cyril had sampled Curly's temper on many occasions, so he was keen to keep the peace over this. There was enough to argue about over the *unions*. Things were hotting up again at the docks and it looked like things were about to boil over. Curly, a stocky, square-jawed, heavily-tattooed and balding man was an active member of the Dockers union, the TGWU. According to Cyril, the fact that he could be relied upon to regularly return on the 5.35pm ferry, regardless of the arrival of a container ship, was 'a sign of the bloody times'. As an ex-Thames man himself, Cyril blamed the unions for the demise of the commercial river and the loss of his previous way of life. It could only get worse now that modern machinery was being installed in the new extension at the docks. Rumours of sixteen men unloading timber in half the time previously taken by sixty were spreading like wild fire. The TGWU was already flexing its muscles over predicted lay-offs. Despite all this there was just about enough common ground to keep the conversation on an even keel, and Cyril secretly admired Curly's doggedness.

Maureen liked him too. Often slipping her half a crown for her money box, lemonade and favourite crisps would be sent upstairs on his behalf when his wife Sandra, handbag always hanging in the crook of her arm, was treated to a night out in the Saloon on a Saturday. Meeting up with Reenie, the ladies would sip their 'snowballs' and wait patiently for their men to join them from the Public when they were ready.

The memory of the whole 'Lionel' event made Maureen shiver and she quickly turned her thoughts back to Christmas and happier times – in particular the family year-end celebrations *chez* Bert and Dot in Gordon Street when the house would be full of guests enjoying a raucous time, enlivened by Grandad's practical jokes and Nanna's festive cooking.

It would start on Christmas Eve, the excitement almost too much to bear. With no central heating there would be hot water bottles for little Maureen, Grandad sitting at the end of her bed softly playing his harmonica to lull her to sleep. Waking up on Christmas Day she'd find her stocking full of presents and she'd brave the freezing air above the eiderdown to tear the paper off to get to them - then run to join her grandparents in bed, warming her feet on theirs. "Father Christmas must like you", they'd say with a knowing look. Bert would be first to get up, he'd deal with the po, or *gazunder* as he called it, then get busy lighting the coal fire in the bedroom so that Dot and Maureen could get dressed in the warm.

Dot having cooked the chicken (turkey was too posh) and a small piece of beef, they would wait, somewhat impatiently, with Aunt Betsy from Bedford or Aunt Daisy from Stratford, whichever one had come to stay. At about three o'clock - just in time for the Queen's speech - Cyril and Florrie would arrive having cleared up after the lunchtime revelry at the Victory. "No chicken for me," Cyril would regularly say as his contribution to the Yuletide meal and, after downing some food and a bit more present-opening, both parents would return to where they both felt most comfortable - the pub. Well, not quite. Having taken the momentous decision, a few years earlier, not to open for both sessions on Christmas Day, you'd have found Florrie asleep in her chair in front of the TV while her husband was off scouring the town for a pub that was still open.

It was much the same with Maureen's birthday parties, held in the same week. Florrie and Cyril would walk round after lunchtime closing, but were usually gone before it started – missing out on the banana and sugar sandwiches. Party games were fun, but what everyone waited for was Grandad entertaining with his array of magic tricks and practical jokes involving exploding caps and soot – the mothers fully expecting that they and their children would go home in a mess. The holiday was finished off in riotous fashion on New Year's Eve at Aunt Ethel's prefab.

The idea that none of this was likely to be happening again was deeply depressing. Maureen wondered if her parents realised how much they'd missed out on over the years. Maybe, just maybe, she thought, there was something that could be done to keep the family tradition going. She looked at her watch and decided there was just enough time to collar her Father who she could hear whistling and hammering in the cellar below. Descending the steps into the alcove, where the barrels rested on a wooden rack, she found him thumping a tap into the bung at the end of one of them, readying it for connection to the pumps upstairs.

"Can we have the family party here?" she asked a note of perceived panic in her voice.

"Not bloody likely!" Cyril rasped back without looking up. "Don't get on wiv most of 'em now. Not since I turned down Effel's tropical fish tank. Besides don't want that nutter Charlie 'ere wiv 'is antics. Fire Brigade's not up for much over Christmas. You only need someone to open the door unexpectedly and the bloody optics'll go up!"

Uncle Charlie, Cyril's cousin, was known for a party trick that was a bit of show stopper. Bert and his brothers and sisters had been born in the East End of London and were all amateur party entertainers in one way or another. There was George the One Man Band, Harry on spoons, Bert on Jews Harp and Ukelele, Joe on drums, using a selection of kitchen implements including saucepan on head, Daisy on piano and Betsy on washboard. But it was always Charlie who stole the show. Without any prompting from anyone, he'd eat fire.

Lampshades in the immediate area were removed, an old blanket thrown down to protect the carpet and small children told to stay in their seats on pain of death. The show would last several minutes until Great Aunt Ada would be overcome by heat and fumes. From an early age Maureen had learned not to engage Uncle Charlie in conversation straight after the performance for fear of being rendered unconscious by the noxious vapours emanating from his mouth.

Then, whilst he was dousing himself down, someone would start up the Dunkirk discussion. At fifteen, he had been the youngest apprentice to take part in the beach rescue. His tug, *Sun 1V*, had helped save several hundred Tommies on two return trips by plucking them out of the water whilst under constant fire. Dodging mines, he said, had made him adopt a cavalier approach to life – hence the party trick. At least, that was his excuse.

As it transpired the family made their own arrangements without her and so Maureen resigned herself to spending her first Christmas at the Victory. Luckily, the festive red and white check gingham dress she'd ordered from page ten of the Daily Mirror had arrived in time. Seeing as it was a BIBA design costing just over three pounds, she was more than happy.

To her surprise Christmas Day turned out much better than she had expected. The pub was extremely busy at lunchtime with customers full of seasonal spirit. Even the ladies in their 'snug' bundled their coats under the table so that Sandra and Reenie could budge up alongside them. All the barmaids, along with Eddie the barman, were working in unison and there was great camaraderie between them.

In fact, Maureen couldn't take her eyes off Eddie. This unassuming little man, who lived on his own, didn't have another job and hung on Cyril's every word, rarely said boo to a goose. But there he was, his red face glowing, his equally red wavy hair bursting out from under a Lincoln green felt elves hat complete with bell, lurid green tights and dangerously short tunic, producing an occasional blast from the bugle hanging across his shoulder. The latter - clearly from past boys' brigade days – got him a steely glare from Florrie. Normally it would have frozen him to the spot. For someone who raced around all the time shifting crates and clearing glasses, barely visible to the world, Eddie's performance was a crowd puller, securing him *Star of the Show*. Under normal circumstances Cyril wouldn't let him change a barrel. That was the Landlord's job. But on this particular Christmas Day, probably because they were so busy, Eddie's bell was

41

to be heard jangling from beneath the cellar steps. The Landlord was never far behind though, hammer in hand, double-checking everything.

Despite the hectic pace Maureen could see they were all enjoying themselves and she felt the buzz. Florrie produced chipolatas balanced precariously on ritz crackers and, on Mrs Jenkins' recommendation, bought several jars of gherkins. Not that she had a clue what they were, but stuck on a cocktail stick with a bit of red Edam they looked colourful enough. Soon Maureen, too, was enjoying herself, despite the overflowing ashtrays and super-sticky tables.

It took quite some time to get the crowds to go home to their simmering sprouts. Brothers Chalky and Snowy White staggered out with the 17lb Bernard Matthews's turkey they'd won the day before in Sid's meat raffle and forgotton to take home. Florrie was very tired but she still managed to rustle up some lamb chops and roast potatoes. The three of them even sat at the table at the same time. It really *was* Christmas. Mind you, it wasn't long before Florrie was asleep in the chair, with Ricky, full of meaty left overs, curled up on her lap. Cyril wiped the beer stains from his trousers, polished his sticky shoes, donned his trilby and headed off down Hamilton Street whistling.

It's always a disadvantage to have a birthday so close to Christmas, because no one takes any notice of it with all the other festivities going on, so Maureen was chancing her arm with the next request when Cyril got back. She'd waited up, practicing her speech.

"Can I have a birthday party here - upstairs, Dad?"

Perhaps it was because he'd had a few pints that the expected negative response left room for negotiation. He pondered the idea for a minute then shook his head.

"Don't think so, not keen on it up 'ere. No-one to

keep an eye on ya."

Indignant, Maureen ploughed on.

"But we're fourteen, or near enough - and all girls!"

"No, not wiv bedrooms close by. I can't take on the responsibility."

Sensing an opportunity, Maureen had a brainwave.

"What about an afternoon tea party in the Saloon then? You'll be in earshot in the cellar."

"Gotta be over by six though," sniffed an uncertain Cyril.

A hollow victory it may have seemed, but at least she'd gained some ground.

"Blimey, didn't expect that. D'ya reckon we could use a cocktail shaker to rustle up some dry Martinis?" Lorraine was chancing her luck on the phone later.

"Shaken, not stirred, no doubt." Maureen quipped excitedly. "Don't think we possess one. Anyway, it's good news isn't it? Can you help ringing round with the invites?"

"Will do. Everyone'll come to a party in a *bar*, even Clive Mont. Can we at least have shandy and use the beer mats?"

"Can't invite boys, Lorr. That'll push my Dad over the edge. Just make sure they get to know what they're missing".

Lorraine was right; the invites were accepted with no one unavailable. Maureen now felt this was going to be a party at the very height of sophistication, and she was determined to make the most of it. Cyril was allowing the babycham glasses to be used for lemonade, and Florrie, caught up in the excitement, had bought proper paper serviettes from the Price Reduction Stores to be professionally folded and stood in them beforehand.

The birthday started with a morning spent in the

bathroom making full use of her presents from Aunt Ethel who'd become one of the *Ding Dong... Avon calling* army of ladies. This new phenomenon of selling make-up, perfume and toiletries door to door meant that the 'modern' housewife could try the samples then place an order in the comfort of her own home. Maureen got the benefit of Pretty Peach soap *on a rope* in the bath, Miss Lollipop body lotion with her sailor hat screw top, as well as Tinkerbell wiff n' puff cologne and dusting powder. It was a heady mixture and a pity she couldn't open the window.

By the afternoon it was time to get dressed. After some deliberation and another phone call to Lorraine, Maureen chose her new geometric black and white shift dress with a zip all the way up the front and long, wide trumpet sleeves which scooped up food from the plates if you weren't careful. There'd already been rows about hem lengths, but a consensus of two inches above the knee had been agreed. She'd had some black patent shoes with kitten heels from Florrie and Cyril and a black and white check raffia-knit bag from Bert and Dot. A pair of large shiny disk earrings completed her *op-art* look. Taking a risk on her overly long fringe covering a multitude of sins, Maureen surreptitiously applied white eye shadow framed with heavy duty mascara at the last minute.

As predicted, her friends thought a party in a pub was quite novel, even if they were the only ones there. Some entered clearly hoping that the bar was still in full swing, only to be disappointed by the welcoming committee of Florrie and her barmaids. Still things livened up when the music got underway and they were able to dance the twist for a bit. Sid the butcher had kindly lent his G-Plan teak radiogram and Ken, some long players. Maureen had wondered earlier if it was worth going to all the trouble, having listened to her

Father complaining for most of the day about putting his back out struggling to get it through the various doors. Thankfully he forgot all about it once he'd clocked the fashions on display.

"What's that Lorraine wearin' then?" His eyes were on stalks. "She looks like an all-in wrestler in plastic boots. And as fer that one…"

Some of the girls were more advanced than others.

"Surely her muvver don't know she's out like that! It's got more 'oles than our net curtains."

Jacosia was wearing a skinny rib-fitting sleeveless sweater and a white crochet knitted skirt. It was quite short, very see-through and figure-hugging and came with a matching beret. The outfit was finished off with white thigh-high go-go boots.

Cyril was so shocked that he had to go next door to get Sid to come and take a look at what the entertainment had revealed. But it wasn't a look of shock on Sid's face. It was certainly a *look*, but it wasn't shock. Maureen, for her part, was just relieved he had changed his apron.

Luckily, Bob Dylan came to the rescue. *Blowin' in the wind* produced a moment of solemnity allowing Maureen to announce it was time for tea. The girls pulled the tables together while Florrie, Sylvia, Theresa and Joyce, the lunchtime barmaid (called Miss Stiffstarch by Bert), who had surprisingly stayed after her shift was over to help, tripped upstairs to get the egg and cress sandwiches. The girls chinked their glasses and tucked their serviettes into their waistbands. Maureen glowed as she revelled in her new role as party hostess. Time seemed to race by and soon Cyril was up from the cellar raising his eyebrows at the clock. The birthday cake was hurriedly cut, wrapped and given to the girls along with momentos - a silver pencil with *Compliments of the Victory Public House* written on the side and some flip top matches with a miniature photo of the pub on the flap. The gaggle of girls single filed out of the Saloon bar door just as a stunned Curly was chaining his bike to the railings.

Next day was New Year's Eve. The lunchtime session was quite quiet, the punters saving themselves for the evening, so Cyril and Eddie dragged the piano out of its alcove into the Bar. With microphone and amp connected and a quick dust of the keys, all was set for a memorable evening - Maureen's first in the Victory – and it turned out to be just that.

In a flurry of excitement in front of the fire, Florrie changed into her striking stretchy gold fabric dress with matching sandals. In retrospect it might have been a better idea not to have been wearing the shoes when Cyril sprayed them gold that afternoon, but luckily her feet were hidden behind the bar most of the time, stripes unseen. Cyril had borrowed Bert's vibrating bowler and flashing tie, so Maureen, giving her Christmas Day outfit another airing, felt somewhat underdressed.

Later, whilst they were spearing the cocktail cherries in readiness for the rush, Eddie arrived with a carrier bag and disappeared upstairs to the fridge. After much rustling through the kitchen drawers for double sided tape he made his entrance behind the bar. Sporting a wobbly goatee and having switched his knitted waistcoat for a striped one, Eddie (aka Acker Bilk) whistled a few bars of *Strangers on the shore* whilst pretending to play a plastic penny whistle. Overall, this guise met with Florrie's approval.

As the evening took shape, Cyril was on particularly good form. Pints were lined up on the top of the piano as he played as best he could with his wanky finger. He'd bought sheet music of Lonnie Donegan's hits and had been practicing a medley including *Puttin' on the style* and *My Old Man's a dustman,* which were enthusiastically received. There was a bit of singing, lots of swaying and some impromptu dancing, of sorts. Wink and Ken cajoled Maureen and Theresa into attempting a few jive moves in a confined space, while everyone screeched *That'll be the day* in unison. It would have made Buddy Holly proud. Even Joyce let her hair down, clicking her fingers in time with the beat.

Throughout all the revelry Maureen caught glimpses of her Mother continuously serving the thirsty crowds. Occasionally she'd stop to light herself a cigarette, blowing smoke into the cloud near the ceiling that slowly descended as the evening wore on. A gulp of Guinness to wet the whistle, smile reinstated, and she was back. After the *Okey Cokey* and *Knees up Mother Brown,* a spontaneous conga line curved its way out of the Public bar door into the road and back into the Saloon with Maureen in the middle holding on to Mrs Jenkins fur stole for grim death. Avoiding the priceless pearls thrashing about over Mrs J's shoulder was quite a feat. The class barrier lifted, the two bars became one.

A loud cheer went up as the Church bells rang the first of its twelve chimes and a spontaneous performance of *Auld Lang Syne* began *en masse* in the Public. Back they all rushed, arms linked, singing at the tops of their voices. Balloons burst, talc filled the air and the kissing seemed to go on forever, certainly between Sylvia and Bryn, his wig wobbling as he got hotter and hotter under the collar. Maureen's eyes followed Florrie's to seek out Curly at the bar, downing his pint rather too quickly and inhaling hard as he watched those two still locked together long after everyone else had gone back to their beer. Sandra, deep in conversation with Reenie, appeared not to notice.

Drinks were served for a little longer until Florrie rang time, her feet killing her. "Best bloody night ever Cyril!" someone yelled from amongst the staggering masses. "You're the greatest."

Maureen watched her Father swell with pride, revelling in his own self-importance, and in that moment she realised what, for him, it was all for.

One by one the crowd spilled onto the street, the cold air sucking out the fog from inside. Cyril had nobly ordered a taxi for the staff, but Sylvia preferred to walk off the excess alcohol with her new beau. Eddie was mightily relieved too as he was usually Sylvia's reluctant walking companion on the nights when Curly's wife was there.

Maureen swore Bryn's wig looked glossier as they left arm in arm.

Four

One Buzz or Two?

During the weeks after Christmas the pub was quiet, snow and ice conspiring to keep people away. Only the stalwarts ventured out to brave the elements. Cyril himself hardly poked his nose outside the Saloon Bar door until the end of January, and then only because Sir Winston Churchill had died. Deciding it was their duty, he and Bert joined the thousands paying their respects at the State Funeral in London – one of the largest assemblies of world statesmen ever seen. At Tower Hill they stood, Bert proudly wearing his medals, watching the dockers lower their crane jibs in a salute as the coffin was piped aboard the launch *Havengore* for the voyage up the Thames to Waterloo. Later they counted the nineteen-gun salute and watched the RAF fly-past as the coffin was placed on a train en-route to Sir Winston's final resting place near Blenheim. Father and son remained silent all the way home. As they thawed out by the Saloon Bar gas fire Maureen poured them both a warming whisky. After a while, Bert lifted his glass in the air. "To the greatest of 'em all," he said.

For much of the Winter Cyril set his mind to tackling the thorny issue of the juke box. "Flamin' Beatles 'ave a lot to answer for," he moaned. "Long-'aired layabouts. Should 'ave thrown them *five minute wonders* in the Tower for that Palladium caper…"

Maureen was fed up with listening to this story. What had happened was that at the end of 1963 the Fab Four had appeared before the Queen as part of the

49

Royal Variety Performance at the London Palladium. You could barely hear the music for the screaming. Just before launching into *Twist and shout* John Lennon said, "For our last number I'd like to ask your help. Would the people in the cheaper seats clap your hands? And the rest of you, if you'll just rattle your jewellery." The audience loved it. Cyril was incensed. To him the younger generation had no respect for anything sacred.

Funnily enough, even Florrie, who, up until then, regarded Perry Como's *Magic moments* as top of her hit parade, had taken a shine to Paul. Mother and daughter had actually gone together to the Majestic to watch *A Hard Days Night* - something unheard of since Hayley Mills was *Pollyanna*.

Bert was getting 'wiv it' too. He especially liked Susan Maughan singing *I wanna be Bobby's girl* and would belt out Kathy Kirby's *Secret love* whilst making a cuppa in the scullery. Cyril, however, was unmoved by this camaraderie. "As fer that mob yellin' *Do wah diddy diddy dum diddy do* - what the bleedin' 'ell's that all about then?"

Music reflecting modern teenage life particularly needled him. As far as he was concerned it all started in the 1950's with *Blackboard Jungle*, a film featuring classroom 'Teddy Boy' bravado set against Bill Haley's *Rock around the clock*. "Wha'd'yer expect?" he'd rage. "If yer gunna let 'em run wild at school, what 'ope 'ave we got?" Then there was Twinkle singing about her *Terry* getting killed on his motor bike, which seemed to glorify the teenage death-wish. But there was one musical experience, closer to home, which left a particularly bad taste in Cyril's mouth, and it came up in conversation at least once a year.

The Victory had an annual outing – traditionally a 'no passport' day trip to France on the *Royal Daffodil*. Not that much time was spent there, after all there weren't any pubs, the public toilets were suspect, and the food was deeply suspicious. The entire population reeked of garlic and it was impossible to walk the streets without treading on dog poo and discarded empty snail shells. Sailing on the Daffodil, however, was truly special. She was no ordinary boat to Cyril. He held her in deep reverence and needed everyone to show respect, so every year he'd give a lecture prior to embarkation. The men would assemble very early in the Public Bar, to hear him hold forth on her exploits during World War Two. Florrie, who had been up even earlier, had already been to the Co-op florists to pick up white carnations ordered for button holes. Strong, sugary cups of tea laced with a wee dram of whisky would be downed to line their stomachs for the choppy seas ahead, while Cyril spoke in hushed tones.

"Course she's twin-screw, built in 1939. Took 9500 men off Dunkirk, in seven trips. And to top it all, on the last one, a bleedin' bomb went right through her hull and exploded outside. Phew.... bloody lucky that was. Never believe it, hole was patched up wiv a mattress and she limped 'ome."

Suitably impressed the men would then set off for 'the Continent', and once across the gangplank, headed straight for the bar. Being *at sea* there were no restrictions on licensing hours and the duty free shop was well stocked.

After some very successful trips, the pub crowd found themselves increasingly surrounded by groups of 'young people'. In an effort to revive dwindling passenger numbers, the Daffodil started holding 'Rock across the Channel' events. They began with a Disk Jockey playing records like Marty Wilde's *Why must I be a teenager in love* – bound to get Cyril going on the subject of teenage 'morals' – and came to a head when another outing was ambushed by a *live* performance featuring some 'oink' called Gene Vincent.

"Young delinquents, that's all they are," was the general consensus. "Made it bloody difficult to get to the bar".

But the final straw came when the 'Outing Committee' heard that Jerry Lee Lewis - the Yank who'd married his *thirteen* year old cousin - had been booked for the next summer. That was it. An extraordinary meeting was immediately held after closing where they reluctantly voted in favour of horse racing at Lingfield Park. To make up for the disappointment of losing the boat trip they hired a coach large enough to hold two barrels of IPA and nine dozen of Florrie's pickled eggs. The rest is up to your imagination.

By the second year, Cyril had bought some binoculars and surprised himself with his undisputed talent for spotting the winners. Coming back flush with his earnings he developed a taste for the gee-gees and would send Eddie out to buy Sporting Life as soon as he arrived to study 'form'. While the bar was quiet, Cyril took to phoning the local bookies to have a daily flutter. This led to a mostly unhappy phase lasting several months, until he conceded that the oddsmakers couldn't be beaten and threw in the towel.

Anyway, returning to music, despite his prejudices Cyril knew it was important to have some kind of background noise at the Victory and started experimenting with an old Roberts radio balanced on a high shelf in the Saloon Bar. However, re-tuning it to stop Radio Luxembourg fading in and out, proved hopeless as it involved Eddie standing on an upturned crate, inevitably in Cyril's way, pointing the aerial in every conceivable direction. It was when one of the boys from the college mentioned a *pirate* radio station broadcasting from Shivering Sands that Cyril came up with the answer. *Radio Sutch* was operating from the south tower of an abandoned wartime anti-aircraft fort in the Thames Estuary. Cyril knew its location well having circled around it on his motor boat just after the War. Originally made up of seven connected towers, one had been destroyed when a ship collided with it, leaving the northernmost tower isolated. The other five were linked by catwalks. Low-powered and low-budget, relying on a transmitter from an old bomber, a plethora of old car batteries and a scaffold pole with a skull and crossbones flag serving as an antenna, the station was *local* and, as far as Cyril was concerned, worth giving it a go.

Mind you, having been set up by someone called *Screaming* Lord Sutch was never likely to impress Cyril. There was too much so-called comedy and talking for his liking. A forum for listeners to complain about anything that annoyed them annoyed Cyril far more. The incessant advertising was irritating too. But Cyril was canny. He'd noticed that a few of the regulars, as well as Sylvia the barmaid, were quick to join in with the jingles he so hated. By osmosis they could quote all the quips and catch phrases in no time.

"I'm 'avin' summa that," he informed a perplexed Florrie as she prized out her curlers. "If ya can't beat 'em, join 'em."

They were all in the kitchen, Maureen standing at the worktop eating her Rice Krispies (there being no room for a stool) with the new-fangled mustard suedette transistor radio blaring away on the draining board.

"What the devil are you on about?" she asked. "Thought you 'ated it. You ain't stopped moaning since twiddlin' yer knob and findin' it."

Maureen lurched forward, almost choking on her

53

cereal.

"That's enough of that, Mo!" Florrie snapped, realising what she'd just said.

Cyril was having a shave with his new Gillette slim-handled 1-9 adjustable, used by James Bond in *Goldfinger* according to the Price Reduction Stores. He was standing in his vest and trousers, his belt undone with its buckle clinking on the side of the sink. The lower half of his face was hidden by thick lather, yet he still managed to have a lit cigarette dangling out of the side of his mouth. The Victory kitchen was tiny, but with the oven door open and the gas lit, it was warm. They all got washed and dressed in relays in there, including hair washing and teeth cleaning. Mind you, only Maureen had all her own teeth. Florrie had had all hers removed when she was just forty. Best thing she ever did, she said. Teeth were just a nuisance. No more toothache now. Cyril had tombstone teeth. Not many in number and black round the edges. He never went to the dentist as far as Maureen knew. He and his daughter only brushed their teeth in the morning, whilst Florrie put hers in Steradent to get that *perfectly clean feeling.* Funny thing was, none of them used the bathroom sink, not even in the summer.

"Listen", Cyril continued, oblivious to the innuendo, "I've phoned up that screamin' bloke and we're gunna be on the radio. It's called an Ad Slot or summink like that. Ten seconds, every couple of hours, next weekend. See, I know about 'uman nature."

He was very proud of his enterprising idea. He wrote and rewrote his precious message, timing his ten seconds with a stop watch bought from local rogue, Spud Murphy ("Ask no questions Cyril. Suffice to say, it belonged to Mary Rand at the Tokyo Olympics.") Mr. Jenkins checked the grammar and gave it his seal of approval.

Finally, down in the pub, his congregation waited with baited breath for the appointed first break.

"Shhh! Shhh! 'Ere it comes. After *You've got your troubles* by the Fortunes."

You could have heard a pin drop. If the Queen had abdicated it couldn't have been quieter.

"Come to the Victory Public House, High Street, Gravesend, for a relaxing drink in a convivial atmosphere. You'll get a warm greeting from mein hosts, Cyril and Florrie, too!"

Spontaneous applause.

"D'ya like it then?" Cyril said, grinning from ear to ear as the clapping and jeering died down. "Made it up meself."

"Reckon you'll 'ave to issue tickets to get in Cyril," laughed Curly. "Can I 'ave yer autograph? 'Ere sign me Navy Cut packet."

He was a proud man that night. Mightily proud.

Over the next couple of weeks Cyril happily lectured anyone who made the mistake of showing interest that although the station's output never exceeded 2kW, the antenna's efficiency *over water,* gave it the "same sorta range as one of them more powerful land-based stations, right…"

"Why over water?" someone would always ask.

"'Cos it reflects radio waves better," he'd reply, full of himself.

When the campaign was over, with no new customers, a salesman from the Radio convinced Cyril that he needed more *exposure.*

"We're goin' fer more impact. They've dunna demagrafick breakdown of me weekly reach. Needs some *cluster scatterin'* during the dayparts."

Curly, Ken, Wink, Bryn and Sid the butcher nodded in dubious agreement.

For a while the pub continued tuning into the

station, by this time known as Radio City, or 'The Tower of Power', the regulars politely listening until the novelty wore off. Soon it was only Cyril stopping what he was doing to get his money's worth. Sadly no new people, desperate for conviviality, came through the doors.

"Bleedin' waste of money!" he was heard to say as he rang the closing time bell. And when a Port of London Authority pilot, who was popping in for a pint, told him that the PLA had registered a complaint against the station, Cyril's suspicions about 'that screamin' bloke' were confirmed.

What happened was that the PLA had placed wind and tidal gauges on the isolated North Tower and argued that the radio station's signal was interfering with the radio link to the mainland - potentially placing shipping at risk. Cyril, a man of the river with many years' experience, wasn't going to let himself be seen to support this, so little was said when the pirate radio was unceremoniously switched off.

Meanwhile, unbeknownst to Cyril, Maureen was secretly listening to Radio Caroline, *The Sound of the Nation,* upstairs in her bedroom. She would snuggle under the bed covers with her transistor radio to feel closer to the poor lonely DJ's stranded out there on the high seas. At one point, her favourite, Johnny Walker, even asked motorists to park on the seafront at Frinton and flash their headlights in the direction of the music pirate.

Looking back, it would have been so much easier just to accept a juke box as being the way forward. But not Cyril. He reluctantly agreed to trial a small counter-top version which had a compendium of ten singles to select from at any one time. The company sent dozens of records to feed into it, but he wasn't happy with any of the selections.

"Elvis… Elvis and some uvver gyratin' Yanks. No thanks… not right for the Victory!"

It was summarily dispatched to from whence it came.

Not to be defeated, Cyril hatched another plan. During a precious gap between opening times, he visited the Co-op, returning with a small suitcase – at least that's what it looked like.

"*This...,*" he announced with a flourish, "is a Bermuda four-speed autochanger - top of the range - cost 13 guineas!"

Opening the case Maureen realised it was something she'd been dreaming of, and foolishly imagined that this vivid red and white leatherette Dansette record player had been bought for her. Having been unable to play the copy of *She loves you,* left behind by a careless customer, a whole new opportunity now lay before her. With singles costing six shillings and eight pence, she began totting up how many more records her stash of pocket money would buy.

That's when reality kicked in. Out of a bag Cyril produced all the LP's he'd just bought and in a reverential tone proceeded to read out the titles

Pack up your troubles - Russ Conway

Songs to sing in your bath - Russ Conway

Party time - Russ Conway

Family favourites, including Side saddle and Toy balloons - Russ Conway

Mrs Mills medley, parts 1&2

Hoe down party - Mrs Mills

We're gonna throw a little party - including Ten green bottles - Mrs Mills

Family favourites, part 1&2 - Mrs Mills...

"Ten see. You can put ten records on at once."

Delicately removing all the LPs from their sleeves, he balanced them one by one on the central arm. They wobbled precariously. Cyril pressed the red button and the turntable leapt into action. Down dropped the first record, the stylus automatically aligning itself. A high-pitched sound resembling *Pinky and Perky* - the kids' favourite singing pigs - issued from the built-in speaker.

"Whoops must be on the wrong speed." Adjustments made, Russ started banging out his distinctive piano tunes.

"Hey," said Florrie excitedly, grabbing her glossy Green Shield Stamp catalogue that she kept on her bedside table, "I've seen just the thing to keep 'em in." Licking the end of her finger she flicked through the pages. "Look, 'ere," she said, waving the music page under Cyril's nose and reading out the caption: "Wire record rack equals one book. I've got two full books since the Price Reduction Stores 'ave been giving out stamps."

"Fought you were savin' up for a television." he replied with a sneer.

"Nah, given up all 'ope for that. You need eighty eight books. I worked it out. You 'ave to spend sixpence to get one stamp. A full book's got one fousand, two 'undred an' eighty stamps. That means the telly costs two fousand, eight 'undred quid. You can buy an 'ouse for that!"

And she wasn't wrong. Certainly not in 1965 anyway.

For a couple of weeks the Dansette blared out its honky tonk load from behind the bar. You could really only hear it in the Saloon and with staff rushed off their feet; turning over the pile of records quickly became a chore. With long gaps between renditions and dripping bitter taking its toll, the final straw came when a few stray metal bottle caps ended up spinning round with the records, scratching them beyond use. A fresh

58

strategy was called for.

"What are you doing Dad?" Maureen, just home from school, had located Cyril's legs half way up a ladder wedged behind the bar.

"Minor adjustments. Actually, while yer 'ere, 'ang on to this wire. When I yell, push it through the ceiling."

The Dansette was re-sited to the living room above, its dulcet tones blaring out at full volume both upstairs and down thanks to loud speakers hanging in both bars. There were wires trailing everywhere, hooked up with string back to the hole in the ceiling.

"Ya won't notice it after a while," Cyril said. "Just turn the pile over when ya see it's finished. Not much to ask is it?"

About 7 o'clock it started. That was when there were enough customers to entertain. That was also when homework had to be finished. Dansette duty, Maureen called it.

She learned all the tunes and got to know the order of play so well that she reckoned she could have played *Side saddle* on the piano in her sleep. Not that she was getting any. Unlike her friends who never wanted to go to bed, Maureen sought sanctuary from the noise as early as possible. Once off duty, there was this short delicious gap at the end of each playing pile before Florrie's footsteps would be tripping up the stairs to turn them over again, at which point Maureen would be contemplating slitting her wrists. Ricky no longer hogged the chair next to the fire, preferring instead to take his chances on the bottom stair. Luckily Florrie noticed that her daughter was lacking sleep which led Cyril to refine the system.

"Just 'ang on to this wire, push it through when I yell."

Somehow he had found a way to create a 'silence

59

upstairs' facility.

"Now all ya gotta do is give it a *butchers* every now and then, so you don't miss the moment."

Turning the stack over was a small price to pay for being able to watch Rowdy Yates (the young Clint Eastwood) driving the cattle herds on the never ending trail in *Rawhide,* before getting off to sleep.

Sanity restored.

Unfortunately, what she didn't know was that a new LP dropping down on many predecessors had a tendency to slip, which was painful on the downstairs ear. With her now being totally engrossed in exciting series like *The Avengers* she was blissfully unaware when the stack was exhausted, or when, sticky with beer, the auto changer would drop five or six records at the same time. Cyril's 'moment' between albums must have seemed like an age downstairs, and it generally led to Florrie being dispatched upstairs to sort it out again.

"This needs more thought," Cyril declared one day, reaching for his trusty tool kit. More holes in the ceiling, more wires passing up and down before he revealed his fullproof (and unexpectedly drastic) remedy – an eardrum-busting buzzer blaring out in the living room.

"Bloody brilliant! Should've fought of this in the first place."

Finally he was satisfied. Someone behind the bar could now press the buzzer to alert Maureen to attend to the Dansette when it fell silent.

It wasn't long before the buzzer became Cyril's favoured mode of communication with his daughter:

One buzz - sort out music

Two buzzes - come down, now, for ashtray duties

Three buzzes - dog needs letting up/down

'Whatever next', Maureen thought.

Five

The Bottle Shunter

"Hold on to the pipe and feed it through the 'ole. Then when I grab it, stop, but whatever you do, don't let go."

This time Cyril had Maureen helping with the plumbing. Not the mains water, the beer. He was installing keg beer on tap and was calling out instructions from the depths of the cellar. She did as she was asked and after a lot of "left a bit, right a bit," the pipe was successfully attached and she tripped down the steps to join her Father in the 'engine room'.

"'Ope yer got a fick cardy on, it's subzero down 'ere," Cyril said tapping the thermometer. The brewery insisted that this new beer should be served *cold,* which meant the cellar temperature had to be lowered. There was a box full of laboratory equipment that had to be mastered even before a drop had been spilt.

"What d'ya make of this then, Sook?" he yelled, waving a cylinder marked CO_2 in the air. "Like a bleedin' science lab, it is. I've gotta play wiv this chemistry kit before I can pull the first pint." Apparently, this was what was going to force the beer up to the tap. He gingerly attached it to the keg as per the instructions, half expecting an explosion. "Right, it's in, 'ere goes." And with that they both rushed up the steps to watch the Victory's first frothy pint erupt. Despite much excitement at this new development, Cyril had only placed a small order as he was absolutely certain that no self-respecting beer drinker was going to want it fizzy.

Every week, the draymen delivered the mild and the

bitter in huge wooden barrels which were rolled down the delivery shute directly into the cellar. The new beer, however, had to be stored in metal kegs and was too volatile to be rolled. It got dumped in the yard, much to Cyril's disgust. Also, now that bottled beer was catching on, crates were being delivered and stored in the tiny yard too, as it wasn't practical to keep fetching them up the cellar stairs.

"This ain't progress, it's bloody congestion," he grumbled.

It was just as well that Maureen was no longer interested in playing one-person tennis against the yard wall anymore - there were now too many obstacles in the way.

While Cyril was finishing off in the cellar, she opened the back door to see how the 'garden' was doing. The usual overpowering smell of disinfectant hit her senses first, followed by the sound of the water running through the urinals in the Gents. Men could get to the toilet direct from the Public Bar, but from the Saloon they had to cross the yard. Not that they'd get too wet if it was raining; it was only a few feet. On the opposite side was a tiny brick-built Ladies, part of the coal bunker lean-to. Cyril had tried his best to improve the scene for the female visitors by placing a half barrel filled with geraniums by the door. Sadly his efforts were in vain as it was always full of cigarette butts, the poor flowers either choked or incinerated. The water tank for the dart board (which tennis balls had an uncanny knack of landing in) took up the last bit of space. Maureen no longer found the mass of wriggly wormlike creatures that co-habited in there fascinating. To give the place a more verdant air, Cyril had painted the yard surface leaf green. Nice touch. Unfortunately the sound of meat being chopped on the wooden slab from Sid's next door rather destroyed the ambience.

Maureen could tell that Cyril was in a state back in the bar. As well as having to contend with the whims of the brewery, he had a big night ahead getting the pub ready for the Liston v Ali re-match. The men were looking forward to it. Even Bert, now feeling better, was coming. He'd gone a few rounds himself as a youngster growing up in the East End. Discussions had been taking place in both bars for some time as to the likely outcome and Maureen had lost count of how often she had heard "float like a butterfly, sting like a bee" mentioned.

Such was the evening's significance that Florrie had retrieved a cookery page from *Ideal Home* that Mrs Jenkins had given her featuring foreign frozen vol-au-vents filled with prawns. She'd had to pull strings at the Price Reduction Stores to get in a supply.

There was always a flurry of interest when a heavyweight boxing match was being televised, particularly when Sonny Liston was in the ring. He'd lost his crown on a technical knockout to twenty two year-old "I'm the greatest" Cassius Clay, but the World Boxing Association promptly stripped Clay of his title, forcing a re-match.

Thanks to London's Henry Cooper having made his mark by nearly knocking Clay out in an earlier fight, passions at the Victory had heightened. Indeed a practice glove supposedly worn by Cooper had been bought from Spud and was now on permanent display. The general view was that *Our 'enry* and Sonny had both previously lost to Clay under 'questionable' circumstances. What's more Clay, by this time, had changed his name to Muhammad Ali, which didn't go down at all well with Cyril.

Occasionally, a couple of trusted regulars had been allowed to stray upstairs to watch the matches in the living room, which Maureen rather enjoyed. It was

63

nice, for once, to have a bit of company. As the time for the re-match neared, Cyril had a brainwave. He decided to let everybody have the opportunity to go upstairs, as, he argued, this would stop him and the staff having to run up and down between rounds to report the news. (Besides, *The Bell,* round the corner, now had a TV *in the bar.*)

Looking up at the leaden grey sky, Maureen found herself wondering if her parents regretted not being able to spend more time upstairs with her. Ever since she could remember, virtually every evening was a lonely one. Florrie would pop up now and again to see if she was OK, but more often to take the weight off her feet for a few precious minutes. But that was about it. Maureen's evening consisted of watching television, disappearing into her own imaginary world and then taking herself off to bed. She didn't even have Ricky for company as he, too, preferred life behind the bar. In fact Cyril had built a tiny bench for him, at counter height, where he could sit watching who was coming in to admire him in his custom-made papier mache hat and scarf. Being just out of reach of the customers, Ricky could remain aloof, until he spotted a potential sucker. Then he'd jump down and whimper at the door like a lost puppy so he'd be let into the bar. Doe-eyed, few could resist stroking him and feeding him their crisps.

Of course, there wasn't much hope of knowing what her parents really felt about anything personal. Opinions, declarations, statements, yes, particularly in the case of Cyril, but feelings were kept firmly under wraps. For all she knew, *not* spending time together as a family could have been a deliberate choice. Nothing made a lot of sense. Cyril often said he'd left his job on the river and took the pub to be able to be with his new daughter. Said he knew it the minute he first laid eyes on her at the hospital. As it turned out, the distance up the staircase was further than any ocean he'd crossed.

Racking her brains, Maureen couldn't dredge up anything of significance about her Mother. She was a mystery. All the things that go into making up a person – stories, childhood memories, experiences, relationships – were missing. Maybe she'd put them aside thinking that Cyril had enough for both of them. He'd talk constantly about his idyllic childhood, showing Maureen his school book prizes and photos and where there were gaps, Bert and Dot filled them in. Not so Florrie. The only snippets gleaned were about scouring coal waste heaps for clinker in the harsh winters and the whole family hop-picking when the factories shut down in the summer. Her childhood didn't sound at all idyllic.   Maureen had a photo of herself aged about two holding a teddy, which apparently had been given to her by Florrie's Mum just before she died. She could vaguely remember her Grandfather being in the Public Bar, but he was just one of many dusty, flat-capped, tweed-jacketers standing with their pints. She must have been about eight when he died. Anyway, Cyril never had a good word to say about him. Working all his life in the cement factory, as well as living next door to it, put him on the wrong side of the Great Divide. That was all it took with Cyril.

Maureen wished she could go back in time and see her parents meeting and falling in love. But that wasn't a word *ever* used in the Victory. Not between them and certainly not to her. It was a word that got pursed lips from Florrie and caused Cyril to jangle the coins in his pockets. Maureen would instinctively look over her shoulder to check when she was even thinking about that *frowned upon* word. So what had happened? They must have courted for some years if the dates on the photos were right. To be honest though, most of Cyril's photos were of him and another girl, Eileen. He often spoke of her, causing Florrie to raise her eyebrows and reach for her fags.

"Could 'ave been a beauty queen. Miss Gravesend and Northfleet, 'er. Couldn't wait while I was fightin' the war. Jilted me and went off wiv anuvver bleeder. Me Mum 'ad to send me the wedding picture from the *Reporter* while I was in Greenock docks. Broke me 'eart she did."

Still, he'd had plenty of time to get over it. There was seven years between the end of the war and the date on Florrie and Cyril's register office wedding photo. Maureen had often looked at it amongst the collection on top of Bert and Dot's piano in the parlour. Florrie in a suit with fluffy ear muffs amidst a sea of white chiffon and long veils worn by the other blushing brides. The reception had been held in that very room, and everything looked exactly the same despite thirty or so people squashed in around trestle tables.

He must have had time to get over Eileen. To decide that Florrie was the one for him, to marry, have a daughter and take on the Victory... maybe it was the pub that changed everything between them? Or maybe it was *Maureen*. After all, it was her they never wanted to spend time alone with. Perhaps if Cyril had built a matching bench for a tiny Maureen to sit alongside Ricky, all might have been well. She could have been on hand to show off her skills without having to be summoned from upstairs.

Pulling a pint as soon as she could reach the pumps was the one Cyril was most proud of. "Look, she can do it, watch...," he would boast. "Come on luv, don't forget to put in that extra drop after the froth goes - just like I've shown ya."

Maureen excelled at removing bottle tops and

tipping a glass perfectly whilst pouring in the beer. She could be counted on to shout at the top of her voice: "Time Ladies and Gentlemen, please," whilst standing on a crate, pulling on a rope which rang the ship's bell hanging from the ceiling. The assembled crowd loved it.

"Gawd Cyril, you've got 'er well trained." "Start 'er off young and she'll be a great barmaid." "She's a credit to yer, Cyril." "Can I 'ave mine pulled by little Mo…" The comments may have been well-intentioned, but sometimes they went a bit too far.

While Ricky loved being on show, especially after a trip to the poodle parlour when he'd get extra crisps, Maureen grew to hate it. The only way to the flat upstairs was through the Saloon Bar, when she'd have to run the gauntlet of customers every time she came home. They'd all ask the same questions about school, what she was wearing and now, heaven forbid, boys. All the attention was cringingly embarrassing, but she couldn't be rude. Try to look Wink in the one eye that was looking at you. Comment favourably on Ken's quiff if asked, but don't stare at Bryn's wig. Say Good Morning to the three mothballers in the snug. Smile but don't stare at Curly's tattoos. In a nutshell, always be polite and never answer back.

Thankfully, Cyril's keenness to show his daughter off gradually diminished, but Florrie's insensitivity didn't. Maureen still hadn't forgotten when her Mother gave away her toys to customers. Even from a very young age, things were handed over the counter in front of her.

"No, she don't play wiv it anymore, take it," would be the first Maureen knew that something was going. The weirdest thing though, was that she would stand rooted to the spot without showing any emotion even when one of her favourite's time had come. Despite

67

being upset, she'd never question why it happened. She had plenty of toys after all.

There was worse to come. Nothing was sacred. As puberty took hold, Maureen put on a little bit of weight. It was all in the right places, but she was very conscious of it. Florrie obviously felt she needed to explain to the customers what the excess flesh on her daughter's hips was all about, so she pinched at it and pointed while mouthing to the assembled crowd "Puppy fat... tut tut." By that time Maureen would be bright red with embarrassment.

Florrie had noticed that her child was growing up, but found it difficult to come to terms with it. Anything to do with physical changes and, heaven forbid *sex,* brought on a mild form of apoplexy. For that generation it was a case of 'don't talk about it and it will go away.' Weirdly, when Maureen started developing breasts, bits of the newspapers started disappearing. Florrie bought the Mirror and the new one (the Sun) every day, yet when Maureen went to look at them she found Page Three, or whatever, ripped out. At first she thought that her Dad was collecting pin-ups until she noticed the ashes in the fire.

Then aged twelve, something cataclysmic happened. She woke up one morning and thought she was dying. Blood was on the sheets and, scarily, it was coming from her internally. Having no alternative, she told Florrie that she needed a doctor. Her Mother went very pale and tight lipped. Returning from a trip to her bedroom she dragged on her cigarette almost to the end, ash dropping all over the carpet, and said: "No yer not dying. This will 'appen every month and yer can't have a bath or wash your 'air."

A paper bag containing a collection of strange bandage-like items was thrust into Maureen's hand.

"You'll 'ave to wear these and then we'll burn 'em

on the fire." Florrie now needed a cup of tea and another cigarette. Maureen, visibly shaken, with a billion questions racing around in her head, was then given the benefit of her Mother's infinite wisdom on the matter. "And by the way, this 'as to be a secret - don't tell yer Dad."

Maureen stayed awake all that first night; there was a lot to come to terms with. Not least of which was the realisation that her ignorance must have caused huge embarrassment to a classmate in a packed corridor some weeks before. On noticing a bright red patch on the back of Dorothy's dress, Maureen called attention to it by yelling out that she must have sat on a red pen. What a bitch she must have seemed. The thought of it made her cringe. But she soon found out for herself what periods were all about, taking comfort in the fact that they were *normal* and then upsetting Florrie by washing her hair. Despite this, no matter how many times she tried to talk to her Mother, Florrie would have none of it. It was another closed book and the defining reason for Maureen's retreat into silence at home.

After mulling it all over, she concluded that she had to be an all-round disappointment to her parents. Cyril looked disgusted most of the time at her long loose hair and ever shortening skirts. The mini had well and truly arrived. Thankfully so had tights - doing away with stockings and suspender belts. The first pair Maureen bought cost £1 and she had to rinse them out at night, desperate to make them last at least a week. Luckily Marks and Spencer had caught on to the trend and had started offering cheaper multiple packs which provided Maureen with permanent American Tan legs. She'd also started to wear a little make up, getting away with Miners' *Strawberry Meringue* 3/9d pearly lipstick and a thin coat of pancake foundation. But her attempt at thickly-lined eye sockets *a la Julie Christie* had tipped Cyril over the edge. *Sixties chick with chic* cut no ice with him. Florrie wasn't much help either. Having ignored her blossoming daughter's need for a bra, she finally condescended, amid much tutting, to take her to Woolworths underwear counter.

To top it all, Maureen had recently become short-sighted. Florrie put off making an appointment with the optician on the grounds that "glasses'll spoil yer chances." Pity really as she was not only struggling to see the bus number, but the bus itself. Eventually her mother relented. The optician was staggered at how Maureen had coped; prescribing a pair of trendy 'winged' framed spectacles. The relief of being able to see clearly was wonderful and more than made up for being called 'four eyes' at school. Cyril's only comment was predictable: "Told yer that 'air danglin' in yer eyes would do yer damage. It'll be yer 'earin' next, what wiv 'avin' chandeliers dangling off 'em."

The sound of her Father hurtling up and down the cellar steps finally brought Maureen back in from the yard. She helped with his last minute checks, just in time before the familiar thump came on the door.

"Betta let Curly in," Cyril said, nodding in that direction, "it's not the bleedin' knocker of Newgate."

Maureen went upstairs to arrange the furniture to let as many as possible get a clear view of the TV.

"Reckon we'd better move Joey out luv," Florrie said, "make more room. Besides his chirping might be a nuisance. Stick 'im in me bedroom."

Maureen steadied the swinging cage while Florrie pulled the base. Joey the budgie tried to maintain his balance and squawked furiously as his mirror swayed to and fro.

"Course Mrs Jenkins 'as a cockatoo," Florrie said

wistfully, staring out the window in the direction of Khartoum Crescent. Joey was left shivering and wondering what he'd done wrong. This was the third Joey to Maureen's knowledge, his predecessors having all succumbed to passive smoking. So far this Joey seemed well enough, though he hadn't much appetite for his Trill, which remained in his IPA drip-tray for days. Worryingly, he seemed to perk up after Florrie lit her first one in the morning.

"Still, I s'pose you'd need a much bigger cage... and probably tropical food."

As the boxers entered the ring, Cyril put his plan into action. Like the Pied Piper he led a trail of customers, pints in hands, up the stairs to join Maureen in the living room. As a result, the Public Bar was deserted – all the Liston supporters having brought their own fold-up chairs to sit on. Sadly, the fight was somewhat short-lived. Midway through the first round Liston hit the canvas following a blow that Ali didn't seem sure he'd thrown. Chaos and mayhem followed with Ali standing over the prostrate Liston yelling "Get up and fight, sucker." It was all a bit of an anti-climax. A shame really, because Florrie had warmed up the sausage rolls nicely. (The *vol au vent* delicacies had fallen by the wayside when pilchards, used in place of prawns, made the pastry soggy.)

Next day, Cyril and Maureen were loading crates with bottles emptied during the previous night's excitement and stacking them as usual in the yard.

"Gotta do summink wiv these buggers, Sook. The Ladies were complainin' last night, snaggin' their stockin's on the way to the toilet. I'm gunna get me catalogue out in a mo' and find the answer."

Maureen puzzled over what kind of answer a catalogue could possibly provide for reducing stocking damage. But Cyril found one, on page ten. A bottle shunting device - the very height of modern technology. Within a few weeks a bottle-sized shute was fitted behind the bar which went through the floor and down to a massive metal tray-like contraption in the cellar. Empties could be dropped down, bottoms first and one at a time. The shute was a tight fit with rubberized sides which prevented them from reaching the speed of sound. Instead of hurtling down they had a gentle, steady journey. As one reached the end, the next one pushed it out onto the tray, and so on, until they shunted round and filled all the space. It reminded Maureen of those penny machines in seaside arcades where your coin might be the one that tipped the pile over the edge and into your pocket.

It was a great novelty at first, watching the machine in action. Unfortunately technology didn't cover the unloading - manual labour being required for that.

"It'll be fun," said Cyril persuasively. "We can do it in the afternoons. Won't take long if we do it together."

And so it was another little job for Maureen. Separate crates for different beers, mixers and soft drinks, the full ones stacked by Eddie, ready for the draymen to lift out of the hatch. Unfortunately, when the pub was really busy, the shute would jam if the tray was full. That was when Cyril's patent buzzer system came into its own – a four-buzz alert having been added. This one meant 'stick on a pullover and head for the cellar'.

"D'ya mind 'avin' a go down there by yerself, Mo?" Cyril said one day. "Got summink I wanna do in the yard."

On this occasion he was standing in the doorway with a tin and paintbrush in hand. "Gotta take advantage of a sunny afternoon, 'aven't ya?"

"What are you up to Dad?"

"Wait'n see, you're gunna like it."

Reserving judgement, she opened the cellar door, turned on the lights and headed down into the depths. Thankfully the tray was only half full and after pulling the empty crates up next to it, she started the monotonous task of loading. The cellar was a strange place to be on your own. The tunnel-like walls were distempered white which gave them a distinctive musty smell. This, mingling with the yeasty beer and numerous other bottled drinks, produced a sweet, overpowering, though not unpleasant aroma. She walked around shouting *Hello* to see if her voice echoed. It did, everywhere, except under the wooden trap door to ground level. Here all she could hear were the voices of the matinee Bingo queue and the passersby. Not that she really minded being down there. It was fine until it got too chilly for comfort. Cyril's voice faded in and out of range as he walked past the cellar steps, but she could pick out the odd word and guessed that he was telling Eddie how Ted Heath, the new Tory leader, was going to kick Harold Wilson into touch.

She'd just finished filling the last crate when she heard her Father yelling excitedly up and down both sets of stairs.

"Florrie, Maureen! Come an' 'ave a *butchers*."

Mother and daughter obediently congregated by the back door. No more crates meant that the yard could have a facelift. Cyril had wired up a powerful spotlight. Maureen's mouth dropped open. A huge framed mural was bolted to her tennis wall. A hilly waterfall scene now greeted toilet-goers, to which Cyril was applying a third and final coat of yacht varnish, giving it a surreal appearance.

"What d'ya reckon on me muriel then, eh?"

"Luverly," enthused Florrie.

73

"Me piece de resistance," said Cyril, standing back to admire his masterpiece.

Maureen studied it with as much enthusiasm as she could muster.

"Impressive, Dad, impressive."

Six

Sindy was my downfall

"Are ya comin'," Cyril yelled up the stairs. "We gotta get down the pier and see this up close... quick bring me binos."

Maureen ran to catch up with her Dad as they rushed down Hamilton Road following the excited crowd. Florrie stayed put, dozing in her chair. As far as she was concerned this was just another one of Cyril's exaggerated stories, like his supposed sighting of Ronnie Biggs, the Great Train Robber, who'd escaped from Wandsworth jail after scaling a wall with a home-made rope ladder. Mind you, since Diana Dors had opened Kentons the furniture shop the previous summer, the slightest whiff of anything unusual going on sent the locals into a spin.

Sure enough, as they got near the front, they could clearly see whales. Not just one, but around thirty sunning themselves in the river.

"Bloody 'ell," a stunned Cyril exclaimed. "No wonder I 'ad to sell me shrimpin' boat."

Actually, he'd stopped shrimping in 1949, not because of the 'bleedin' whales eating me catch,' as he was now telling everybody, but, more likely because of river pollution from detergents and other chemicals. Cyril's sister Ethel, and her husband Fred, had taken on a fish shop after the war, so Cyril, ever the entrepreneur, bought a shrimping boat which he kept on Bawley Bay and would go out early in the morning on the estuary to trawl for something to sell them. Unfortunately, shrinking catches soon put paid to that

75

venture. It was during the Victorian era, when Gravesend enjoyed huge popularity as a resort, that the passion for brown shrimps - the local delicacy - first caught on. Up to seventy 'Bawley boats' worked from this side of the river and would moor up alongside the row of cottages and small boatyard named after them.

Standing on a breaker by the Old Seaman's Mission, Maureen marvelled at the display, whilst trying to watch out for tar. Many's the time a dress would be hanging on Dot's washing line, tar smears around the hem, with Bert making matters worse by trying to rectify the situation with turpentine. White socks were a dead loss at such times.

News spread amongst the whale watchers that an animal trainer had arrived from Billy Smart's Circus who was attempting to catch one of the animals. He hadn't got far before an army of uniformed PLA officials arrived from Trinity House to read him the riot act and send him packing. Apparently, attempting to catch a whale in the Thames constituted a contravention of Port of London Authority laws.

As people slowly started drifting away Cyril looked at his watch and sighed. "Better be gettin' 'ome. Bottles don't empty 'emselves, ya know."

With that, father and daughter jumped down onto the pebbles, made their way off the prom and sauntered back through the town in the sunshine.

"So, do you think Grandad will be up to celebrating then?" Maureen knew her innocent question risked being ignored out of hand. Cyril sniffed, reached into his pocket for his cigarettes and struck a match, motioning to Maureen to cup her hands as a wind shield.

"Dunno," came the eventual judgement.

Bert and Dot had been married fifty years, and were due to celebrate their golden wedding anniversary in

October - which was only two weeks away. Bert was determined to have a party in his own house and had foolishly wallpapered the front room in readiness for it. Maureen had helped him, but he really wasn't well enough and had paid the price by falling ill again. No one dared tell him that the paper was upside down. Bunches of grapes were defying gravity by hanging upwards on the vines.

"They're both looking forward to it and loads of people have been invited," she added tentatively.

"We'll just 'ave to 'ope he's alright. I'm gunna phone the Reporter anyway. Yer Grandad's a local 'ero. First Kent man to be awarded the George Medal. They're bound to wanna put it in the paper. S'pect they'll come and interview me too. Well-respected Landlord of a well-respected 'ostelry"

The last bit perplexed Maureen, but she let it go, knowing how proud the whole family were of Bert. He had retired in 1956, the day after he was sixty five, following fifty years working afloat on the Thames. The longest serving PLA tug master at Tilbury Docks, he'd been a skipper for thirty six years, eighteen of which were as Captain of the *Sirdar*. During the London Blitz he was stationed at King George V Dock where, on two consecutive nights, he and his crew extinguished major fires caused by incendiary bombs and risked their lives moving barges and other craft out of the danger zone. For these acts he was awarded The George Medal for gallant conduct.

Dot often told Maureen how she hadn't recognised him when he returned home after those two nights. His face was red, with peeling skin. He had no hair below his hat line and no eyebrows. After continuous bombing with incendiaries and high explosives, the quay where thousands of vats of Navy rum were stored had become a raging inferno. At one point the firestorm created such a vortex of air throughout the dock that the *Sirdar* was sent spinning.

Looking her absolute best in a new hat and gloves as she watched her husband having his medal pinned on by King George VI at Buckingham Palace, Dot was completely tongue-tied when they were invited to tea with Winston Churchill.

Maureen knew a little about her Grandad's early life, he sometimes talked about it when they were sitting next to the range in the kitchen, but he found it hard to fight back the tears. His childhood memories were not happy ones. He'd had to cope with a lot of poverty and tragedy which made his achievements all the more impressive.

Born in 1891, Bert was one of eight surviving children who lived close to the Royal Victoria Dock in East Ham, London. It was the first dock specifically built to take steam ships and its opening in 1855 not only created employment, but a huge demand for housing to accommodate workers and their families.

"Used to be no more than cattle grazin' on Plaistow Marshes in eighteen 'undred," Maureen remembered him telling her, "and only one 'ouse between Bow and Barking Creek, and what's more, when they started diggin' the Dock, up came a twenty seven foot canoe and whale bones!"

Bert had a fascination for the history of East Ham and the urban sprawl the Docks generated. Maureen would sit transfixed listening to stories like that of George Bidder: "That bloke knew a good thing when he saw it - bought up all the marshes. Made a million he did, selling it off for the docks and factories."

The demand for land for factories here had been encouraged by the 1844 Building Act which prohibited 'harmful trades' in inner London. One of the first factories to arrive was Samuel Silver's waterproof clothing works, from which Silvertown got its name. Then there was Henry Tate and Abram Lyle's sugar refinery which made them their fortunes. Soon the area was a major industrial centre, attracting people from all over Britain to work in the factories, docks and gas works.

Bert's own Grandad, Henry, a farm worker, left Cambridgeshire in search of a new life in the capital. Finding a job in the docks, he married a servantgirl and had seven children. All of them shared a small house in Canning Town with yet another family. As the population rocketed, doubling every ten years, families like these found themselves crowded into long terraces, lacking a proper water supply and sewerage system. It wasn't long before these new housing settlements became breeding grounds for diseases such as cholera and smallpox.

Bert's Father, Joe, hauled coal from the docks for the Gas Light and Coke Company, Europe's largest gas works. Opened in 1870 by Simon Adams Beck it served the whole of London. As a result, the district was named after him. Joe, his brothers and brothers-in-law worked at Beckton gas works, and lived close by in Cyprus, a squalid estate so- named when the Union Jack was raised over the Mediterranean island. Unfortunately, the area was the destination for all the sewage coming from north of the Thames, which meant living alongside the largest treatment works in Europe.

"Can yer believe it Mo? Eight of us kids living in three rooms. With another family *and* a lodger in the rest. We 'ardly ever went to school, so I couldn't read or write then. And the pong... when the wind blew the wrong way, it was disgustin'! What wiv the sewage, the gasometers, coal tar disinfectants and sulphuric acid for making fertilizer, not sure which was worse. Me Dad 'ad to work twelve hours a day, seven days a week. If 'e couldn't do it, 'e'd 'ave got the sack. Bloody dangerous too, I can tell ya. Will Thorne was our 'ero. Made a speech at Canning Town Hall. Eight hour day, six days a week, that's what 'e demanded. Organised a union. Said "it's easy to break one stick, but when fifty sticks are together in one bundle it's much 'arder". Eight 'undred joined on the first day alone. So Company started laying off the workforce. Bloody 'ard times I can tell ya, but Union won 'em an eight hour day."

Dockers were forced to fight one another for low paid casual work, often in brutal conditions, many dying as a result. They had to carry three hundred pounds on their backs and when their 'tanner' an hour raise was rejected – a measly sixpence in the old money - they were forced to strike. The 'Great Dock Strike' of 1889 spread like wildfire. Within three days, ten thousand workers had joined. Soon the whole Port of London was at a standstill. Sixteen thousand dockers and a hundred thousand other workers across East London picketed the fifty mile stretch of docks.

"Fings went from bad to worse in our 'ouse. None of us kids 'ad any shoes. I can remember me Dad getting real bad moods when he wasn't earnin'. Then 'is sister Eliza got pregnant at seventeen and went in Union Work'ouse. Don't know what 'appened to the baby - boy it was. Then they come to take us *all* to the Work'ouse. I was only fourteen. But me and me older brother 'id behind the door of Aunt Nancy's grocery shop in Cyprus Place and escaped."

Bert wouldn't talk any more about his Mother and Father. Luckily he remained close to his brothers and sisters despite them dispersing in all directions as they became old enough to leave the workhouse. Maureen had studied the sepia photo of Bert and Dot's wedding day and noticed that neither of his parents was there.

After asking why many times, Cyril eventually told her the truth - to keep her from badgering Bert. It was shocking news. Joe, Bert's Dad, had tried to hang himself on Beckton Marshes, such was his despair. He was taken to an asylum for the insane, where he died aged only thirty three. Bert's Mother was forced to leave her children in order to become a servant to a Jewish tobacconist in Spitalfields. Whether this was by choice or not, it resulted in all the younger children finishing up in West Ham Workhouse. The youngest, Ada, died there from influenza. Two other sisters eventually went into service. The younger boys were sent to the National Nautical School for the Homeless and Destitute in Portishead. As for Bill and his younger brother Bert, they carried on lodging with Aunt Nancy, managing to get themselves apprenticeships with a tug company on the River. Somehow they taught themselves to read and write along the way. Cyril told Maureen that Bert didn't have much to do with his Mother after that. She married again when she was in her sixties and had sent a photo to Bert with kisses all over the back of it. Bert threw it in a drawer.

"Me and me bruvver were all we 'ad when we were your age," Maureen remembered her Grandad telling her one day. "I was on the *Dunera,* he was on the *Britannia*. Then when 'e was nineteen and me seventeen, his tug collided with the sludge steamer *Bazalgette*. Five of 'em lost their lives, Bill included. Still got 'is pocket watch they brought up wiv the wreck."

"Thanks Mr Cooke, think we've got all the details. Just need a photo of you both. Can you stand behind the cake?"

The boy from the *Reporter* was putting the finishing touches to his piece. Maureen could see the puzzled look on his face as the topsy-turvy grapes came into focus through his lens.

"Think we'll put the Golden Wedding details in with the stuff about the George Medal and the Brightman Cup; make for good reading that will. Paper comes out on Friday just in time for the Shrimper's Regatta and your party."

Bert, wearing his three medals, and Dot with her corsage, obliged happily.

"Just a quick word with your Son and I'm done." And with that he was off to get his story filed.

The article, with several photos, filled almost a whole page, right next to photos of the opening of the new Post Office Tower in London. Details of Bert's bravery were described alongside his earlier sporting achievements - part of the winning *choc fours* rowing crew in the 1920s at the PLA regatta in Putney, and a glowing report about his football talents at Gravesend Hotspurs. But it was the final paragraph that took the biscuit. Asked whether Bert would be watching the Regatta on Sunday, his son *"Mr Cyril Cooke, licensee of the Victory,"* replied, *"We will have to see what the weather's like first."*

Maureen set off early on Saturday afternoon to help with party preparations. As she arrived Dot was sorting out the flowers and getting the table ready to receive the tongue sandwiches and sausage rolls being prepared by Ethel. Bert was bringing in scaffolding planks and balancing them on upturned crates for extra seating in the front room.

"Just like old times, Mo. We've 'ad some good knees ups in 'ere."

The green Old Holborn tobacco tin, Rizla papers and lighter were laid out on the top platform of the stepladder. Bert methodically began the process of rolling his own cigarette then running his tongue up and down the paper. With a final tap it on the tin lid to settle the tobacco it was ready to rest in the corner of his mouth and be lit.

"Had we better move the sewing machine, Grandad?" Maureen tried to pull it towards her, but the chunky ironwork and wooden frame were too heavy.

"Yes, luv, but I think we'd better get some 'elp. I'd better not try; doctor's orders…" Bert winked over in Dot's direction.

The old *Singer* held pride of place in the bay window, as it afforded Dot as much light as possible when her right foot was pumping away furiously on the treadle. Numerous children's outfits had been exquisitely sewn here, from Cyril's sailor suits and Ethel's sack dresses in the 1920s, to Maureen's own smocks and pinafores – not forgetting everyone's *make do and mend* clothes during the War.

"Tell you what, we'll move it, along with the pedestal and the aspidistra into the parlour when me brothers get 'ere. Better get on and light the fire. Get us some newspaper, Mo."

Bert was determined to have everything just right. After all, the party had been on and off so many times. Maureen cast her eyes around the parlour. No one went in there much, so finding a newspaper wasn't likely. Glancing at the empty brown velvet sofa she was reminded of *Dot's dolls,* an enterprising chapter in her Grandma's middle age.

The streets all around her Grandparents' home were residential, yet in the middle of the one next to theirs (Sudan Street) was a small factory. It seemed very out of place, with nothing on the outside to tell you what treasures lay within. Its windows were too high up to give any clues and there was no smell, smoke or noise when the door was shut. But at 5.30 the doors flew open and two dozen women would race out and thunder down a flight of wooden steps. Maureen often watched them tying their headscarves and lighting fags as they disappeared in various directions.

Dot knew, of course, that it was a ladies underwear factory. In the 1950's petticoats were big, both in size and demand. Multiple layers of nylon net with satin binding on each tier, sitting on an organza under-skirt, was required wearing under the rockabilly style skirts of the day. These materials, along with foam for the padded bras, and lace by the acre, were manipulated with great dexterity within the factory. A far cry from Maureen's own underwear collection of navy blue knickers, vests and plain cotton petticoats.

From a very young age she would reluctantly climb the steps of the factory, carrying a basket, practicing her speech as she did so. Dot would remain at the bottom whispering encouragement. Banging on the door as hard as she could, it would open to reveal a regiment of women sitting behind rows of modern sewing machines. Maureen was mesmerised by the scene. "Can I have some scraps from the floor to play with please?" a little voice would plead. A bemused employee would then take the basket and, passing by every work station, bend down and scoop up handfuls of discarded material. In no time at all it was filled with an assortment of pastel coloured off-cuts of all shapes and sizes, none bigger than a handkerchief.

"'Ere ya go luv, can't imagine what you're gunna do wiv 'em." And with that the door would slam shut.

"Been to The Sudan again?" Bert would laugh on their return.

The basket of gems was not for Maureen of course. They were for Dot's dolls and this exercise would be repeated about every two months or so to build up a good stock. Bert's brother, Joe, had done well for himself despite his humble beginnings. He'd worked for the Hong Kong and Shanghai Police Force and still had his contacts in China, one of whom was an exporter supplying cheap plastic 'teenage' undressed dolls about eight inches tall, with fixed stares and shoulder-length, wavy blonde hair. Dot's initial idea was to use the tiny bits of white netting and organza to make fairies and angels for the tops of Christmas trees. These were finished off by Bert with tinsel and pipe cleaners for wings and halos and every member of the family got a prototype to test out.

Cyril, keen as always to seize on a business opportunity, started to take orders from the Victory's customers and, following suit, Bert would hawk them round his locals in November. Business soon grew and diversified. As fashions became more risqué, the material fragments gleaned from the factory floor started to include black and red satin. Dot produced a troupe of French can-can girls complete with frilly knickers. Very popular in the Public Bar they were too. Occasionally the garden shed took on a macabre air as three dozen dolls lay sawn in half, their lower portions discarded in a pile, as Bert sandpapered their midriffs. Dot had found that cutting the thin foam into squares and then joining them by the corners into an igloo shape made a wonderful crinoline skirt for the legless girls. Adding an organza top with leg-of-mutton sleeves and a net ruff, topped off with lace and beads in their hair and... Voilá! - A perfect Elizabethan toilet roll cover. These proved so popular that Dot struggled to satisfy demand.

On hearing from Maureen that everyone these days wanted to be *with it*, Dot hit upon another money spinner. Little girls didn't just want dolls as babies; they wanted them to be teenagers as they imagined themselves to be. So Dot made groovy miniskirts and hipster pedal pushers below which were tiny, specially-ordered plastic sling backs. Using an old skill, making fabric rigid with sugar, she then made crocheted circles shaped over a thimble to produce trendy floppy hats. A shoulder bag, made in much the same way, completed the outfit. At this point demand for the dolls was so great that it was outstripping supply. Dot would line them all up on the velvet sofa in the parlour awaiting delivery.

Until 1963 that is. That year no more orders were taken by Cyril. Dot stopped taking delivery of the naked girls. Maureen no longer climbed the steps to the factory. Bert hung up his saw. It was all over.

"Sindy was my downfall," sighed Dot. "I might've been able to make the clothes, but the car – that was just a bridge too far."

The Golden Wedding party was a great success. The front room looked a treat with gold ribbons and balloons and masses of food. Friends and family came from far and wide to be greeted by the ecstatic duo and be offered a glass of sweet sherry from a tray held by Maureen. Sadly Florrie stayed behind at the Victory. Cyril, not trusting his staff to cope on their own, only came for a short while. Thankfully he'd got Wally to drop off a couple of barrels of IPA and plenty of port and lemon. Bert and his brothers' and sisters' musical renditions surpassed any of those heard in Tin Pan Alley and Ethel had brought her Dansette to fill in the gaps when the band was taking refreshments. Ken Dodd warbling *Tears for Souvenirs* seemed the most popular, having been in the charts for half of the year. (For her part, Maureen was mightily relieved when the Rolling Stones finally took over the number One spot with *Get off my cloud*.)

At one point the furniture was pushed right back to

allow a turning circle wide enough for a circuit of the Lambeth Walk and the Gay Gordons. Then when everyone needed a rest, Charlie was allowed to perform his show stopping party piece in the parlour. There hadn't been so much heat and light in there for years. Cyril was on high alert, filling buckets in the scullery, but luckily only the antimacassars got a slight scorching. There wasn't a dry eye in the house when Bert tenderly pushed a new wedding ring on Dot's finger. "The old one must be wearing out by now," he choked. Maureen took advantage of the moment to present a framed photo of the celebrating pair standing in the Victory yard with the mural's waterfall scenery as a backdrop. It was a pity that the Ladies toilet sign crept in, but no one seemed to notice. Throughout it all, Ethel and Fred's new Super-8 cine camera whirled and twirled as they filmed the event for posterity. Unfortunately, no-one seemed able to behave normally when they spotted the contraption being pointed at them, so there were quite a few stilted moments as guests would freeze, strike a pose, or stop tripping the light fantastic mid-step. Still, it was all very exciting and Maureen looked forward to seeing herself on the big screen. No one seemed to be in a hurry to go home and eventually all left with a chunk of cake wrapped in a serviette.

When it came to watching the cine film, Maureen went on the bus with Bert and Dot to Ethel's prefab. After a glass of eggnog, the lights were turned off and the film started to roll. It was immediately apparent that some essential focus adjustments were needed, and then there they all were, in glorious technicolour.

"Oo.. ah, I don't remember Betsy's frock being that colour..."

"Great Aunt Ada's lookin' old..."

Seconds later the projector jammed and the film

unravelled in a heap on the floor.

Bugger… I don't believe it... Lights!"

Ethel put the kettle on while Fred laboriously wound the film back.

"Right, that's done it, we're back in business. Lights off, Effel."

Watching the party highlights took longer than the party itself and everyone took a turn at sitting near the light switch.

Seven

Slosh Wash

Dot was throwing away the last of the wilted bouquets as Maureen came down the dark side alley towards the back door. Two weeks had passed since the party but the cards were all still standing on the mantelpiece along with a few slices of left-over cake.

"'Ello luv, fought we'd 'ave an early dinna cos of the regatta. Got pease pudden an' faggots wiv tapioca fer afters." Dot was in her Sunday best despite it being Saturday. "Can yer call yer Grandad, 'e's down the end of next door's garden looking fer our Tommy. 'Ere take this lettis it might 'elp wiv the search".

Maureen headed off, lettuce leaves in hand. Tommy the tortoise was well known for having a penchant for the weedy wilderness next door. He was adept at digging under the wire fence and so was frequently on the run. Bert was nowhere to be seen, but he must have heard her footsteps from the undergrowth.

"Mornin' Mo, it's like the black 'ole of Calcutta under all this ivy. Well I'll be blowed, 'ere 'e is, wiv 'is mates." Climbing cautiously over the wire to avoid getting his trousers caught, he emerged with an indignant Tommy in tow, juicy bits of weed hanging out of the sides of the tortoise's mouth. "Reckon I'll 'ave to get the paint out again," he continued, carefully placing Tommy back in his pen. "There's at least anuvver six escapees from Colditz in there".

Nearly all the neighbours owned a tortoise and it was nigh on impossible to recognise one from another. Consequently most had something painted on their shell. In Tommy's case it was *Tug Skipper*.

After their meal and the washing up, Bert, Dot and Maureen strolled down the prom to watch the Regatta. Cyril met them there and whilst he and his father got thoroughly engrossed in the event, Dot and Maureen slipped away to a quiet corner by the deserted band stand. They sat on a bench admiring the vivid purple of the late-flowering asters and mulled over the high spots of the previous weeks.

It wasn't long before the warmth of the autumn sun had lulled Dot to sleep, her navy straw hat, with its hand-decorated, giant plastic daisy heads around the brim, tipping forward over her eyes. The sight left Maureen contemplating her Nanna's amazing hat collection. Millinery had been her great love since she was a girl. She had more than a dozen, all personally decorated with feathers, flowers or ribbons and she would never have been seen out without gloves and a 'titfa', not even to the shops. The term *mad as a hatter,* she told her entranced granddaughter one day, came about because the poisonous chemicals used by hatters to cure the feathers of humming birds, caused the convulsions associated with St Vitus' dance. Not that such a thing put *her* off wearing feathers. She still had the wide-brimmed, brown felt masterpiece with peacock feathers that she'd worn the day she'd first met Bert at the Prom.

"He'd just started work at Tilbury," she said. "I was strolling along wiv some friends when 'e come over an' asked if I'd like a cuppa tea at the Riverside Caffee. I admired 'is cheek and 'e was so good looking, I couldn't say no."

Dot had had a stable childhood compared to Bert. She had loving parents and two sisters, the first of which didn't arrive until she was twelve. Her Dad worked in the docks and they'd always lived in Nile

Street close to the river. They weren't well off, but Dot did well at school and managed to get a job in David Greig's grocer's shop rather than going into service like lots of other girls of her age. She often told Maureen how she would weigh out butter on a marble slab and pat it into shape, and then put the takings in a little metal egg which would travel around the shop ceiling heading for the office. Of course, as was the tradition in those days, Dot gave up work the week before she got married.

On their wedding day, her two younger sisters were bridesmaids. Bert called them Thursday and Friday. It stuck, even Maureen coming to know them as Aunt Thursday and Aunty Friday. She never thought of them having *real* names.

It turned out to be the last time Maureen had a day out with both her Grandparents. Bert started to go downhill shortly after. He no longer felt able to walk down the Prom on a Sunday afternoon, nor go for a lunchtime drink at his local. As time went on he started to lose weight as he had no appetite and therefore little energy. It was as much as he could do to get down the stairs in the morning and sit in his chair next to the range in the kitchen. Dot would keep adding coal to keep him warm, prodding the grate with the poker which lived in the WW1 shell case next to the range. When Maureen was little, he loved to bang the poker on the grate and then rattle it against the sides of the shell case to make as much noise as possible - just to annoy Dot. He'd encourage Maureen to sit on his lap and then open his legs, letting her fall between them. She knew it would happen of course - and that he'd always save her - but that just made it more fun. Now Bert could barely keep his eyes open.

It took about six months before he asked to go into

hospital. By then his skin was sallow and falling off his bones. He no longer got out of bed. On her visits, Maureen read to him about the Kon-tiki raft that sailed across the Pacific to Polynesia. Cyril told her not to get too close to him for fear of catching something. Finally, an ambulance came and two men carried him out, sitting upright, on a stretcher. "See ya then me ol' China," he said as Dot bent over to kiss him. He waved to a few neighbours who'd come out into the street and gave Maureen the thumbs up sign. That was the last time she saw him. He was only in hospital about a week, with Dot and Ethel by his side. Cyril went a couple of times, but it wasn't deemed a suitable place for Maureen. Likewise at the funeral. Despite her protestations, she was told to stay behind with Aunt Lil and keep the kettle boiling for the funeral party's return.

Dot was determined to stay put in Gordon Street. Ethel was all for her moving into a flat, but she'd have none of it. Maureen was a bit worried as she'd often watched her grandmother struggling down the stairs in the morning.

"I'll be alright Mo," she'd say. "Just be at the bottom wiv me *do do* pills." Then she'd start the descent, coming down on her backside half a dozen stairs at a time. By the last one she couldn't speak, was totally out of breath and her chest was heaving. A *do do Chest-Eze* tablet and a sit down for half an hour did the trick. Dot was a large lady, around fifteen stones. She still wore stays, made with whale bones. These went over her underwear as she dressed in the kitchen.

"'Elp me do 'em up, luv," was Maureen's cue to struggle with the hooks and eyes.

"Why are you still wearing them Nanna?"

"'Ad 'em on every day for sixty years. Don't reckon

I could stand up straight wivout 'em!" she would laugh. "'Ard to believe I only 'ad a nineteen inch waist when I married yer Grandad, eh."

Ethel organised a home help for her Mum and brought electric bar heaters to stop her from carrying coal. She and Maureen popped in as often as they could, but it was clear Dot was finding modern-day life increasingly difficult. One morning she arrived unexpectedly at the Victory, clearly flustered.

"That's it. I'm not gunna use the Slosh Wash any more. I ain't 'avin' *my* washin' goin' in a machine after *they've* all used it, an' I ain't goin' back to usin' the old copper and mangle... not now Bert's gone. Can't lift like I used to."

The 'Slosh Wash' was Dot's name for the launderette round the corner, in Victoria Road - its recent changes in clientele clearly not suiting her.

"Sit down Mum. 'Ere 'ave a port and lemon," Florrie intervened quickly, deliberately loading the port to calm poor Dot's frayed nerves.

"I know 'ow ya feel Mum, the town's not our own anymore, but it's gunna be alright. Cyril's just said I can 'ave a washing machine. Gotta 'ave summink to look forwards to now that Harold Wilson's got in again."

Dot looked baffled.

Cyril's latest diatribe about Labour had obviously hit home with Florrie. The reasoning might have got a bit confused, but the message was clear. The country was going to the dogs, so why not splash out before they were all drained dry?

"Cyril says Drink Drive law's gunna stop people going to the pub cos they can only 'ave two drinks before they're over the limit... and it's all the fault of that *bitch* Barbara Castle. He says she's got 'er fingers in every pie, what wiv speed limits and seat belts, not to

93

mention the trains. Thank Gawd there'll never be a woman Prime Minister I say, we'd never live it down. Anyway 'e's worked out it'll fit in the bathroom."

"What will?" asked Dot, by now having completely lost the plot.

"Washing machine. Maureen can ferry yer stuff to and fro on 'er visits."

Dot looked round at Maureen, a look of quiet desperation in her eyes, as Florrie flicked the top off a bottle of Guinness. Despite it being only eleven o'clock in the morning it seemed a good time for her to be celebrating the great event with daughter and Mum-in-Law.

How funny, Maureen thought. She could remember sitting on the warm wooden-slatted draining board in her Grandparents' scullery having her face, hands and knees scrubbed when there was hot water left over in the copper. 'Sadie', the Sadia water heater, gave you hot water in the upstairs bathroom, but, downstairs, apart from boiling a kettle, the copper was the only plentiful source of the stuff. Heated by coal, it stood surrounded by various buckets containing washing left to soak in *Rinso,* all waiting their turn in the steaming cauldron. Bert's collars needed a good going over on the washboard in the sink before entering a bucket. When the water was deemed hot enough Dot would use long-handled tongs to drop in the clothes and then a *dolly stick* was used to agitate them. Maureen was banished from the scullery while this bit was going on.

The mangle, which was very heavy, had huge wooden rollers and handle and was used to extract most of the soapy water from the washing. It received quite a bit of verbal abuse when Bert's shirt buttons broke in the process. When it came to the cold water rinsing, a mysterious little bag called *Reckitts Blue* was added to one of the buckets for keeping whites whiter than white, while starch was added for stiffening the cotton. A few more turns of the mangle handle and the washing was finally ready to be pegged out to dry. It was exhausting just to watch. Bert would then use the residue of soapy water to wash down the scullery floor, whilst Dot had a lie down.

Then, as if by a miracle, this new launderette opened up not far from Gordon Street. Dot, reluctant at first, found that she could shove her smalls in on the way to the shops and pick them up on the way back. It was marvellous. Bert bought her a shopping trolley on wheels especially for the purpose. And when it was raining, she found she could transfer the finished washing to a drier and sit and chat for a bit whilst it all hurtled around in a huge drum. Heaven.

Florrie hadn't worried too much about a washing machine until this point. The new drip-dry fabrics were less work, and brushed nylon sheets (which seemed designed to trap your toe nails and make you suffer night sweats) were much lighter to lift when wet. It was only the linen tea towels, essential for putting a gleam on the pub glasses, which were getting a bit much. They would slop around in the bath until being transferred to a clothes horse in front of Cyril's mural on a sunny afternoon. Thankfully bath day was only on a Sunday.

"Not sure it's a good idea 'aving a washing machine plugged in next to a bath," Kev Curtis, local plumber and occasional Public Bar visitor, informed Cyril. He was lying on the bathroom floor sorting out the waste pipe. "But it's up to you of course."

"Naaa, can't see a problem," replied Cyril assuredly, not that it mattered to him as he rarely used it himself. "Pint's waitin' for ya downstairs."

Kev tightened the last nut and shot downstairs with

his tool bag, leaving Florrie to admire her new Hoover Keymatic 3226 with Boiling Pulsar Action. It was state of the art, came with a variety of programming key cards and cost a staggering 105 Guineas. Having waited this long, she was determined to have the best. In went two dozen soggy tea towels with yellow *Babycham* bambis prancing across them, for their inaugural spin. Dot was soon champing at the bit to try out the machine as her Slosh Wash now had an Indian manageress, which was the last straw.

"Which one of these'll boil me bloomers, Mo?" she asked, shuffling the key cards.

Bert and Dot had rented their Victorian house in the 1930's. It had been a solid upper-working-class area, five minutes from the train station, shops and river. But from the late 1950's Sikh migrants started to arrive to work in the cement and paper mills, where there was good pay with little need for English language skills. At that time they still regarded the Punjab as home, intending to return as soon as they had made sufficient money.

This changed when the Government introduced a work voucher scheme. The opportunity for migration, previously unrestricted, became limited to those who could obtain work vouchers. For many it became a race to migrate before the introduction of the Commonwealth Immigrants Act. Thousands of families arrived in an attempt to beat the deadline. This caused a dramatic change in the make-up of the Sikh community in Gravesend, many of them now living in close proximity to Dot.

Maureen had tried to make friends with one little girl she'd seen hanging around in Sudan Street in those early years. Despite not speaking one another's language, they had managed to learn and say each other's name. Unfortunately Dot wouldn't let Maureen go into her house, nor Sarabjeet come into theirs. Skipping and hopscotch lost their appeal after a while so, with the onset of cold weather, the friendship dwindled.

'Integration' wasn't a word that most people understood, let alone tolerated. The 'Darkies' were taking over and that was that. It didn't matter where they were from, they were all the same. And they weren't welcome.

"I know you've got that bloke *Darkie* who comes in the Public," Dot said innocently to Cyril one day, "but 'e's different. Bin 'ere all 'is life, well anyroad, since 'e was fostered by the Flyns. "

"Yeh, but Darkie ain't on 'is own now is 'e, Mum," Cyril responded sarcastically. "Race Relations Act's in force now. I 'ave to let 'em all in, and what's more there can't be an *unreasonable* delay in servin' 'em. Bit of a problem for Joyce, she's not one fer gettin' a move on. Might 'ave to get the old stopwatch out again."

"There's dozens of 'em livin' in one room," Dot continued unphased by her son's joke. "Can see 'em all piling out when the door opens... men wiv bandages round their 'eads and little boys wiv jam pots covering their tied-back long 'air... the women in saris - they must be cold - jostlin' in the market, not speaking a word of English, and don't get me started on the smell of all that foreign cooking... good job Bert's not still 'ere to smell it. I swear it's seeping frough me walls. They've got nearly all the 'ouses in our street now cos as one lot moves in, the 'ouse next door goes up for sale and all they can sell it to is more of 'em. It's a vicious cycle or whatever ya call it."

At moments like these Maureen was grateful that Dot had to stop to catch her breath. What could she say?

97

The fact is that, like many women of her generation, Dot had never been further than Brighton. She was starting to feel isolated and was genuinely afraid of the unknown. She'd been brought up in Victorian Britain, a land still basking in the glory of Empire and Imperial power, where one knew one's class and calling and viewed foreigners as 'beneath you.' And there was one rhyme Maureen had been taught which seemed to sum that era up:

When God made little black children,
He did it in the night,
He was in such a hurry,
He forgot to paint them white.

Mostly Maureen didn't know where to look, but just occasionally there were gems in amongst the ignorance. Recently Florrie had been to see *Goldfinger* at the Majestic. She didn't have a clue what it was all about, but rather fancied Sean Connery. The theme tune, sung by Shirley Bassey, really got to her and she couldn't stop singing it. So much so, that to Maureen's astonishment, she went to Woolworths and bought the single and a couple of LPs which she hoped to slip onto the turntable and give Russ Conway a break. Cyril was having none of it however.

"What d'ya wanna go wastin' yer money on that brassy tart fer. 'Er frocks barely cover 'er bits and what wiv flaying 'er arms all over the place, she only brings attention to 'erself. Oughta know better seeing as 'ow she comes from where she does."

"What, Wales?" a mystified Florrie responded.

"Yeh, *right*," Cyril said sarcastically. "If she comes from Wales, she must 'ave spent too much time down a coal mine."

"She does Cyril. She was born in Tiger Bay."

"I rest me case then," he said, storming off.

More washing meant more wet items to get dry. The bathroom was cold and damp, so the clothes horse was constantly in front of the fire. Ricky would have to get off his cosy chair and lie below the vests, ignoring the drips to feel any warmth. "This is askin' for trouble," Cyril said after he'd attempted to throw a lit match into the flames which had landed in Dot's bloomers. It must have set something off in his mind because, quick as a flash, he was up and sketching an ingenious plan on the back of the *Licensed Victuallers Times*.

Curly Campbell was asked if he could use his contacts at the docks to obtain a flagpole, which was manhandled through the Saloon and out into the yard - no questions asked - but with much swearing. Never to be beaten, Cyril was soon at it with sledgehammer, ready mix concrete and his green paint.

Suddenly, there it was. A gleaming flagpole, standing erect at the back of the Ladies toilet and directly in line with the bathroom window. Luckily the Manager of the Super had an extendable ladder for changing the neon *Now Showing* sign outside the cinema, so Cyril was able to easily attach pulleys from the window frame to the pole. For a few days an old pillowcase with *Guilty* painted in green fluttered in the wind – such was the clamour surrounding the conviction of the Moors Murderers, Ian Brady and Myra Hindley, who had been found guilty of killing three children. But Florrie was soon leaning out of the window, pegging on a couple of tea towels, pulling on the cable, adding more tea towels, pegging, pulling and so forth until there was a full line of washing dangling twenty feet above the ground. The real trick of it though was that customers heading for the toilet below would be blissfully unaware of their Landlord and

Landlady's smalls unless they happened to check for rain.

Unfortunately there was plenty of rain that summer. The tea towels didn't stand much chance of getting dry, and for those coming to watch the World Cup Final on television, the flagpole had been well and truly noticed. Cyril and the regulars trawled up and down the stairs as every round passed. The excitement reached fever pitch as England and Germany were warming up for the final. "Blimey, Cyril," someone said looking out of the window on their way up, "better get that lot in, rain's pelting down."

"Storm. It'll pass," Cyril spluttered through the cigarette smoke in the living room which was already making Maureen's eyes sting. She wasn't looking forward to the match. It was scheduled to last much longer than a boxing match and she doubted she'd still be breathing by the end of it.

"Where's Wink?" asked Ken. "Can't believe he's missing this."

Suddenly the buzzer blared out four, five, and then six times.

"Wot's up wiv Florrie?" Curly yelled, cupping his ear with one hand while pointing at the buzzer with the other.

"Better go down and see, Cyril, you might be in trouble," jeered the lads.

"Go and check luv," Cyril motioned to Maureen, so down Maureen went to check what was happening.

"No barmaids 'ave turned up," Florrie told her with a shrug. "Not that it matters, I'm 'ardly rushed off me feet. Bryn's just been in, says there's floods everywhere. Wind ain't done his wobbly 'air no favours neither. I've tried phoning Sylvia, but the phone's dead."

At that point their conversation was cut short by two

dozen pairs of feet stampeding down the stairs. Men scattered out of all the doors, disappearing left and right in the pouring rain. Cyril was last, delaying grabbing his coat and trilby to deliver the bad news.

"Soddin' TV's gone bust - off to the Nelson." And with that he, too, disappeared into the murk.

"Gotta be the weather," Florrie mused as the door slammed in the wind.

Next day they found out that the storm had caused havoc with communications, creating floods and preventing at least 4,000 local residents from watching England win the World Cup.

"Some bloody consolation," was Cyril's verdict on the matter.

It later turned out that Curly did some quick thinking that night. Clocking that Bryn was in the bar and hearing that Sylvia was trapped at home with no phone, Sir Galahad forgot the football and rushed to her rescue. England wasn't the only home team that scored that night. Bryn never walked Sylvia home again.

Eight

Avez-vous a bucket?

"Righto, Mo, we're gunna celebrate your comin' toppa the form wiv an outin' - no, a day out… yep, that's it, a day out… in France!"

Cyril blew confident smoke rings through pursed lips and watched them dissipate in the breeze. Maureen was stunned into silence.

"Course, we'll be takin' a couple of me mates along for the ride. Curly and Ken, Bryn, maybe Wink, and wot about Gerry? 'E's taken to talkin' a lot to ya. It'll be great. Now yer doing yer matriculation exams in French, you can order us up a couple of light ales no trouble. 'ow d' ya say which way to the Gents?"

"They're called 'O' levels now Dad and I haven't covered asking for beer yet"

"Good job I can say *parley voo English*? then."

'Oh God', Maureen thought, more embarrassment. A mini pub outing to France… with Gerry. Her heart sank. She waited until her Dad went down the cellar steps, clipboard in hand to do his fortnightly ordering, and then, shutting the door at the bottom, phoned Lorraine.

"What, ya mean that little bloke that's started to come into the Saloon?"

Lorraine was a mistress of understatement.

"He's a bit more than little Lor, he's a midget."

"Well he looks normal size when 'e's sitting at the bar," she offered in his defence.

"Yeh, but the other day I didn't even know he was there until he suddenly scrambled up onto the stool while I was stocking up. Frightened the living daylights out of me!"

"I reckon 'e fancies you, 'e's always chattin' you up."

"That's what my Dad said. Just my luck, the first bloke to take an interest in me only comes up to my waist. He's ancient too, well over twenty. I hope he doesn't come, it's bad enough with Wink, everyone'll be looking at us. So much for *my* day out."

"Serves you right for being a smart arse, see ya tomorrow," concluded Lorraine.

Maureen would never have described herself as a smart arse. When she took the Eleven Plus she had no idea what was going on. "Just a little quiz" was how it was described by her teacher. No pressure then, she thought.

"If only you'd gone a bit faster..." Mrs Wood said when she collected the papers. On the day the results came out all the Mums were assembled outside the Head's office.

"Come in Mrs Cooke," he said, "do sit down." Maureen stood in the corner, Florrie sat by his desk. He picked up a piece of paper, waved it aloft and said "Congratulations, my dear, let me shake you by the hand, your daughter has been selected for a secondary modern."

Well, thought Maureen, I must have passed. He said *congratulations.* Florrie remained stony faced as they exited. Once outside, she turned to her daughter and said: "Well that's it then, it's Woolwoofs for you, my girl."

Maureen trailed along behind her mother all the way back to the bus stop. There was nothing more to say. She was going to the secondary modern, not the grammar school, and that obviously wasn't acceptable.

Actually, as it turned out, it wasn't so bad after all.

For a start, there were boys there as well as girls and she soon found herself with a nice group of friends. By the end of the first year she was in the 'A' form and somewhere in the top ten. Florrie seemed reasonably pleased with her report. Lessons came and went with a fair amount going over her head. Art was her particular *bete noir*. But there was help at hand. On one occasion when she was instructed to draw a chair for her homework, Cyril ensured that half the Saloon Bar was issued with a pad and pencil to help out.

"Pass up Mrs James's chair from the snug, Wally. We'll stick it on the counter and see who comes up with the best one."

In the bath one Sunday evening, Maureen remembered, all too late, that she needed to sketch some autumn leaves for a still life. Poor Spud was given his bus fare and dispatched off to Woodlands Park to find a suitable tree. Being more used to laying his hands on things that fell off the backs of lorries rather than trees, this posed a challenge. But he persevered, with the result that Maureen not only came 1st that year, but, thanks to all concerned at the Victory, the next one too. She missed Bert and Dot clapping enthusiastically at the prize givings, like they used to. Cyril and Florrie said they were chuffed, but, as usual, were too busy to attend. Cyril did mark her achievements in his own special way however.

"Will ya do summink for me luv?" he enquired one day. "I need a darts trophy for this year's winners. Only I 'aven't got time to choose one meself. Can you go in the shoe shop next door; 'e keeps some for me in a glass cabinet at the back. Choose one an' I'll tell 'im what to put on it later... Oh, by the way, don't pick one wiv a dartboard on it, get one *you* like."

The bizarre request noted, Maureen dashed out the door, rushed into the shop and leaping over discarded stilettoes and winkle pickers, made her way to the back. Pointing at the first dartboard-free statue on a base visible through the grubby glass, she was lucky enough to get back to watching *Thank Your Lucky Stars*, just in time to hear Janice on the teenage jury say "Oi'll give it foive" in her thick Black Country accent.

As they say; no good deed goes unpunished. For years the trophy sat at the back of her mantelpiece, partially obscured by the largest bambi. And indeed it *was* years before Maureen discovered that it was actually a replica of the Greek sculpture *Discobolus*. The inscription on it read: *To Maureen, congratulations on coming top of the form. Dad and Mum*

"Come on Mo, Mrs Baker's expectin' you. You'll 'ave to do a few sums. But it won't be 'ard, it's only Woolwoofs after all."

Florrie was calling up the stairs. As prophesised, Maureen, aged fifteen, now had a Saturday job at Woolworths. Florrie had organised it knowing Mrs Baker, the manageress, who was the sister of Miss Knight from the snug at The Victory.

Heading off down Hamilton Road, Maureen mulled over the various bits of information she'd been given by all and sundry, not much of it complimentary.

"Don't take no notice, keep an open mind," Dot had said wisely. "Yer only Woolwoof material yerself, don't ferget. Only Grammar girls get inta British 'ome Stores."

Entering via a side door, as instructed, she followed all the women stubbing out their cigarettes in a bucket of sand, and then climbed a flight of stone stairs to the cloakroom where she lined up with other new recruits awaiting their issue of differently coloured overalls. Yellow was evidently worn when serving on the food counters, green for anything else. Please let me be green, she thought. Somebody had told her the worst counter was the delicatessen; something called salami, sold by the slice, got under your fingernails and smelt for days.

Breathing a sigh of relief on being handed a green overall, she was sent to the back of the shop - to the paint and polish counter. Scared to death at first, she soon discovered that she enjoyed it. It was hard and heavy work, dragging tins of paint, tiles and even pet food from the stockroom to the shop floor, but she learned all there was to know about gloss and emulsion and excelled in calculating how much of the shiny, bizarrely-patterned 'contact' was needed to cover your average kitchen shelves. Occasionally she would glance over at haberdashery and note with envy the two women there whose weightiest task was lifting needles, cotton reels and balls of knitting wool.

There was a whole new buzzer system to learn too, which made her feel quite at home. Tea breaks, lunch, dodgy characters and shoplifters were all announced by means of the buzzer. But apart from a few exploding cat food tins pierced by rats in the service lift, the first month or so passed without incident until…

"Look, look! There's Mrs Baker clinging on to 'im in the leather trousers. Blimey, it's a long way up. She's got 'er 'ands round 'is neck. They're on the ladder now. Look, there's clothes and stuff being flung out the windows… They won't be able to charge full price for that lot now, that's fer sure."

Florrie was giving Maureen a running commentary on the extraordinary event unravelling in front of their eyes. Smoke was billowing out of the upper windows of Woolworths and about a dozen women were leaning out, clearly trapped.

"Well I'll be blowed," she continued excitedly, "that's our window cleaner! What's 'e doing? They'll be dirty again in a minute with all that smoke."

"No, Mum, he's helping the women to get out. That's a policeman in the leather trousers. Motorbike rider. He's got the window cleaners to put their ladders up. Looks like there's three of them."

One by one, the women climbed out and perched precariously on the ledge, then, helped by the young window cleaners, descended to safety, many visibly shaken by the disaster.

"If I was one of *them* women I'd tuck me skirt in me knickers... Where's the fire coming from Mo?"

"Looks like the canteen. It's lunchtime, so it's busy," Maureen replied, greatly relieved that it wasn't a Saturday. By this time dense clouds of smoke were issuing from the building. She counted at least twenty fire engines and masses of firemen, some with breathing apparatus.

"Ooo look, here's an ambulance. Someone must have passed out. Ooo-a, Barclays' is being evacuated now." Florrie was almost hoarse with excitement.

Rumours were already travelling up and down Hamilton Road as to the cause of the fire. A shop assistant was reported as saying she heard a loud bang coming from the electric cables in the storeroom next to the canteen.

Soon the police started moving people along to let the firemen get on with their job. They were trying to lay hose lines to pump water directly from the Thames. It seemed the right moment for mother and daughter to head back to the Victory. Suddenly Florrie was in a rush. Ricky, who'd been patiently sitting on the edge of the pavement sniffing the smoky air and blinking as tiny flecks of ash circled his face, assumed it was time for 'walkies' and was straining on his leash to get to his favourite alley.

"No time for that," Florrie snapped, as if he

understood English. "Gotta get back and spread the word. There's gunna be a lot of salvage sold off cheap, you mark my words."

As they fought their way through the crowd of onlookers jamming the adjacent streets, the traffic at a complete standstill, they noticed that Dorothy Perkins had also been evacuated, water now pouring from both floors. Dripping shop assistants were huddled together and there was talk that the walls were cracking open in the heat.

"Don't reckon you'll be going to work for a bit, Mo," Florrie commented absent-mindedly, unaware she was stating the obvious.

After closing, Cyril and Maureen went for a stroll. Cyril wanted to see for himself what all the fuss was about. The fire was only just under control twelve hours after it started. The first and second floors were completely blackened, with part of the roof caved in.

"We've had twenty nine fire engines from eighteen stations all over Kent," a weary fireman told them. "A hundred and twenty men all told. Worst fire I've seen. Two of our blokes from Medway are in hospital. They're saying it'll amount to over half a million in damages."

Water was now being pumped *out* of the store, turning Hamilton Road into a river. It was lapping over the kerb, so they couldn't get too close.

"What the 'ell's that? Look…" Cyril was pointing. Maureen squinted in the dark, struggling to believe what she could see in the dim street light.

"I think it's a toy pedal car. *Z Cars* by the look of it… and there's a set of plastic traffic lights following it."

"Shame I don't 'ave a dinghy," he said with a laugh.

Bobbing about and crisscrossing from Burtons to

Timothy Whites was an endless stream of flower bouquets, wicker baskets, picnic sets, gaily patterned melamine coffee sets, Rotaflex space age lampshades, tomato shaped ketchup containers and a giant pineapple ice bucket complete with tongs. Just about every modern-day lightweight item Woolworths sold was making a bid for freedom.

"This lot'll be gone by dawn," Cyril sniffed knowingly. "Don't tell ya Mum, or she'll have us back out 'ere dredging with the net curtains."

Anyway, coming top of the class in the fourth year was the reason for the outing to France. Maureen wasn't in shock just because of Gerry being invited; it was more that when Cyril suggested going anywhere, he usually had an ulterior motive. For example, on quiet mornings in the school holidays when she was younger, he would whisper "Let's go for a walk, Mo," tapping the side of his nose to indicate that the destination was to be their secret. They would head off down the town, only to find a pub that had somewhere inside for Maureen to stand, or if she was lucky, sit drinking a lemonade while she waited for her Dad to finish his drink, then move on to the next hostelry. Cyril couldn't have her standing outside like some commoner's child. He would use his reputation as a fellow landlord to gain her access to a staircase or yard. The Nelson was her favourite, at least their stairs had carpet.

"Right we're off then, you know what to do," Cyril said to Florrie as he completed his final checks. "I've left the truncheon at the bottom of the stairs, and Spud's shown Eddie how to fire the starting pistol" (part of the ask-no-questions job lot from the Tokyo Olympics).

"Okey dokey, don't worry, just 'ave a nice day," she responded, deftly removing her tightly-wound curlers without looking up, and clearly looking forward to a nice day's peace and quiet. Each strand of hair had been wrapped in a Rizla cigarette rolling paper to encourage the Toni home perm lotion to do its job overnight. Consequently, as they were undone, ammonia fumes filled the room.

"Bloody 'ell woman, I wondered what that pong was all night. Come on Mo, let's get outa 'ere, I can't breathe."

And so it was. The gang gathered up their gear ready for the off. Wink and Gerry had, thankfully, cried off at the last minute and Bryn was out of the running as he had accepted a transfer back to his home town of Cardiff. There'd been a bit of a do for him in the Saloon, Florrie presenting her own take on pigs in blankets by frying chipolatas and wrapping them in slices of Mothers Pride. Cyril made a short speech about being sorry to see him go, but it didn't sound particularly heartfelt and not helped by Sylvia choosing that exact moment to visit the Ladies. Anyway Bryn and his wig were no more.

So Cyril, Maureen, Curly and Ken walked to the station and started on their epic journey. Arriving at Dover, they collected their day passports and boarded a cross channel ferry, heading for Calais. Cyril had been keeping an eye on the shipping forecasts as a couple of previously suggested dates had already been aborted. Today was still a bit choppy.

"Won't be too bad; just do what I say," he advised, but Curly and Ken ignored him, heading straight for the bar to down double whiskies as a stomach-liner. They should have listened because Cyril was on home territory and knew better than to eat or drink on board. It was his tried and tested method of avoiding sea sickness.

As they left the security of the harbour walls the sea became increasingly rough. Cyril was pleased to see that his daughter seemed to have his sea legs and showed no sign of feeling sick. Curly and Ken, however, were nowhere to be seen. Maureen was wearing her new green dress she'd ordered from *Fabulous* magazine. It was called *Dollyrocker Baby Doll* and cost £4. 14s. 6d. Made of crinkled cotton crepe, it was tent-shaped, with a sweet little collar and cutaway armholes. She'd shortened it herself to four inches above the knee, which had raised eyebrows, but, thankfully, no comments.

Standing on the first deck, because Cyril said staying in the open air was best to avoid the vibrations of the engines and the smell of diesel, Maureen leant over the side to watch the waves slapping against the portholes below. Her Dad, who had momentarily taken his eyes off her whilst trying to light a cigarette in the wind, suddenly yelled at her. "Mo, don't lean over!"

Here we go, thought Maureen. He thinks I'm going to fall in. I'll pretend I haven't heard him.

Next thing, she was aware of a plopping sound on the rail and deck around her and the sensation that something had hit her clean on the top of the head from a great height. Then the smell hit her, followed by a dawning that someone had been sick over the side from the upper deck and scored a perfect hit. Her long hair was matted, her glasses smeared and the back of her collar dripping with the contents of someone's cross-channel breakfast.

"Jesus Christ," shouted Cyril against the wind, "that's what I was trying to warn you of. Come on let's go." At that exact moment Maureen would have happily jumped overboard if that's what he had meant, but he started to propel her across the deck as if she were a guided missile, in the direction of the nearest toilets. She remembered going inside and down a flight of stairs with passengers reeling at the sight, the smell, or in sheer amazement at how someone could be sick on their own head. Finally reaching a Ladies, Cyril shouted inside for an attendant. Not knowing if she was likely to be English or French he hedged his bets…"Scusez-moi, avez-vous a bucket. Some cowson's been sick on me daughters 'ead."

A woman appeared with a red metal fire bucket which she proceeded to fill with freezing cold water. It was as much as Maureen could do to lower her head into it, let alone keep it there without breathing, whilst attempting to remove the matted hair adornment. Several refills later, there was no sign of sick, but the smell was still there. "Lucky you were wearing green, dear," was her saviour's only pearl of wisdom.

The men walked ahead for the rest of the day. They found several cafés serving beer which Maureen was only too happy to stand outside. She couldn't wait to get home.

"Serves you right," said Lorraine on the phone later, "you shouldn't 'ave been 'orrid about Gerry."

Florrie put the dress straight in the dustbin with no argument from her bedraggled daughter.

"Gordon Bennet Mo. You unlucky or what? The last time you went out fer a day wiv yer Dad I 'ad t'get rid of yer jacket and 'at, remember?"

It all came rushing back. Another disastrous outing. About eight she'd been then. The crying had started from the moment she woke up that day. Florrie, deciding that her daughter's boring straight hair needed a few waves, had doused her in perming lotion and wound the strands tightly the night before. Maureen's painful sleepless night was nothing compared to the uncontrollable frizz that revealed itself the following morning.

There was an hour or so of blame and recrimination

before the whole mass was shoved under a brimmed straw hat. Consoled with the news that she would be allowed to wear her brand new, pillar box red, suede jacket and pleated white skirt, the crying subsided.

Meanwhile Cyril had been pacing the Saloon Bar floor looking at his watch and tutting, valuable drinking time evaporating. At last they were ready. Curly, Ken, Lionel (of the wandering hands) and Maureen finally set off by train for their day trip to London. They were supposed to be visiting the Tower, but seeing the queue, Cyril decided it would be too dingy and smelly. The pubs around Trafalgar Square not so, apparently. So there it was, Maureen spent several hours being minded by the quartet in relays. Not a great deal to do in Trafalgar Square once you've stared up at Nelson and admired the four bronze lions at its base, fed the pigeons and had your photo taken holding a tiny monkey dressed as a Harlequin in a lozenge-patterned outfit of red, green and blue diamonds topped with a pointy hat complete with bells.

Numerous bags of pigeon food were bought by the men and thrown up into the air, encouraging a huge flock of scavenging birds to swirl around Maureen's head. Indeed, Curly thought it clever to scatter a handful of seeds into the brim of her hat encouraging anything up to six birds to perch comfortably on her shoulders, pecking away while the monkey foraged for fleas in the escaping frizz.

Scraping off the pigeon poo on their return, Florrie swallowed Cyril's story that it was in fact a raven, not uncommon at the Tower, which had pecked jacket and hat to ribbons, though she remained sceptical about wild monkeys protecting the crown jewels. Finding the task overwhelming, she stuck the offending items of clothing in the bin.

113

Nine

Grub

When the Woolworth lunchtime bell rang, Maureen shoved her overall in her locker and made a run for Gordon Street. Ethel had been giving her brother a hard time on the phone about what little he was doing for their Mother, so Cyril came up with a plan: Maureen would go round Dot's for her dinner, so as to give Dot something to do, and keep an eye on her. There'd be just enough time for a quick chat and a plate of congealed egg and chips before rushing back to work.

After about three months on the paint and polish counter, Mrs Baker realised that Maureen was the kind of girl she could rely on. She was soon moved on to whichever was the busiest counter on the day - shifting bedding plants by the dozen, shoveling strawberries by the pound, dolloping tutti fruit ice cream into cornets, cautiously collecting box loads of fireworks from the stockroom, ending up with a long tiring spell on the toy counter. When things were quiet after Christmas she began instruction on the responsibilities of a floor supervisor. That meant wearing a *blue* overall and dealing with *customer relations.* Her most tricky assignment - one which required the utmost diplomacy - was when a customer objected to a shop assistant from frozen foods addressing her as "me duck." Apparently, Mrs Lennard had been saying "Can I 'elp ya, me duck?" for many a year, and when it came to the Inquiry, her defense in front of all was "No bugger's ever complained before."

Whatever Maureen said to calm the situation must

have impressed Mrs Baker, as the very next Saturday she was whisked aside by Mr Norman, the floor manager, and put on permanent transfer to the downstairs office. Wow, Maureen thought, as she closed the door with its bars across the window, *responsibility*. Not a job that you could be late for. However, this was going to present problems at lunchtime as Dot frequently lost track of time and the delivery of egg and chips was becoming unreliable. Luckily, as it turned out, Dot was only too relieved to give up the task.

Any dreams Maureen may have had of a relaxing lunch upstairs in the Woolworth's canteen went out the window as Cyril now saw an opportunity to legitimately pop out from the Victory for an hour or two and meet his daughter for lunch at a hostelry of his choice. In a bid to avert suspicion he'd nonchalantly stand by the office door jangling the coins in his pocket, waiting for an opportunity to squint through the bars and inform Maureen of their rendezvous location.

So, once again, as the clock struck one, she'd have to hurtle off at full speed, fight her way through an assortment of drinkers to find her father and the ham sandwich he'd ordered for her. Of course, he wasn't on his own; Ken would always be in tow for him to talk to. Not Cyril's natural choice for company - life at the Price Reduction Stores rarely providing much in the way of stimulating conversation - but then Curly and Wink weren't to be seen in a pub on Saturday lunchtime. "'Ave to take their missus's shoppin'," Cyril would sniff disdainfully. It was taken as read that the men would accompany their wives arm-in-arm around Chiesmans posh second floor and be seen *circulating*, before perching uncomfortably on revolving stools drinking frothy white coffee from an exotic Gaggia machine. Later, in the Saloon, they'd laugh about being fish out of water, but that was a small price to pay for being allowed out the rest of the week.

Life in the downstairs office was very different from the shop floor. The first job was to get leather bags full of change from the upstairs office, load them into a basket on wheels and push the whole lot down in the lift. The bags of cash were kept in a huge black safe ready to be exchanged for notes passed through the bars in the door by the floor supervisors. Next would be paying the daily fresh food delivery men with notes from the safe, some of the bills amounting to hundreds of pounds. The shop switchboard was in this office too. Maureen had to learn all the extension numbers and do her best to answer questions from the public. But most exciting of all, she was in charge of ringing the bells. This involved a highly complicated language that all staff knew and relied upon. Recognising their tea breaks, lunch breaks and countdown to closing were key to a smooth operation. One long, continuous ring to the count of nine elephants meant 'medical emergency, ambulance on way' - as was required when a poor lady turned blue by men's toiletries. Another, to the count of ten elephants meant 'I need the store manager quick, shoplifter spotted'. In such situations Mr Norman had the power to apprehend anyone he caught. These generally turned out to be either older women or young teenagers. They would be left with Maureen, behind the bars, until Mr Frost the senior store manager arrived. He would then proceed to shout and threaten them with the Police, nodding to Maureen who would pretend to dial the local constabulary. Acknowledging their contrition, he would then escort them off the premises with a warning never to return. Just occasionally, a habitual offender would actually get nicked. A woman with a carpet bag that she regularly filled with frozen chickens comes to mind.

All this responsibility for one pound a day - well actually 19/9d after you take off thruppence for stoppages, Maureen mused - and yet I'm still not allowed to go to Lorraine's for a barbeque! Cyril's latest niggle was still fresh in her mind. Right from their first day together at secondary school Maureen had been in awe of Lorraine's ability to travel unaccompanied, catching two buses from the wilds of the countryside to get in to lessons. She, on the other hand, had to contend with Florrie guiding her across the road and waiting at the bus stop with her, surrounded by sniggering teenagers. Often it meant sheltering in a shop doorway until the last minute to avoid the jibes. Once, Florrie had tried to leave before the bus came, but on seeing Cyril gesticulating wildly at the living room window, thought better of it.

"Why can't I go to Lorraine's then?" an exasperated Maureen had demanded of her father.

"Too dangerous, you won't be able to control a campfire - it's a whole new ball game," Cyril replied, shaking his head.

"But it's a barbeque and we've got sausages to cook. Please let me …"

"What's more, you don't know what yer doin' wiv cookin'. It'll be game over if any sparks land on that PVC mac you wear. Wrong time of year for a fire, it's too cold, besides you'll get food poisinin'. Look, I've left me tea in the kitchen, go and get it fer me."

Fuming, Maureen went next door, grabbed the tea and headed back to continue her argument. On her return the room seemed eerily silent. She was sure that Radio City had been on just as she left.

"What's happened to the radio, then?"

"Dunno," Cyril replied unconvincingly. "Weather must be *that* bad, station's gone off the air."

With a weary sigh she turned the signal dial back to

117

the wavelength it had been on and gave her father a filthy look. Nothing more was said on either subject. She was just going to have to wait until she could ring Lorraine later to find out how it had gone. With that she'd turned the volume up and resigned herself to getting on with her homework. It was nothing new.

"So, did everyone turn up?" she asked Lorraine. By this time the Victory was full, so there was no danger of being overheard.

"Yep, it was groovy. The boys took over the barbie. Couldn't see much through the smoke but I'm sure Clive snogged Jacosia. Sausages could've done with a bit longer, but the burgers were fine."

"Shut up about the burgers and tell me more about Clive and the other boys. Anybody else get kissed?"

"Probably, I dunno. I went off to get the ketchup. You should've been there yerself and then yer wouldn't 'ave t' ask me."

"Couldn't get there, tornado blew the bus over."

"What?"

"Never mind, see you tomorrow, bye."

"GRUB," bellowed Cyril, leaping to his feet and kicking the dinner plate he'd just put down for Ricky.

'Now what?' Maureen thought, turning round to look. Florrie, who had been asleep in the chair, jerked upwards, eyes spinning. It didn't do these days to disturb her slumber as normal sleep at the weekends was becoming a problem for all concerned. Ethel had proclaimed that her Mother could no longer be left on her own all week and as *she* lived in a small prefab it was down to Cyril to come up with the goods. Dot was now stopping upstairs at the Victory on the weekends. Ethel had clearly got the wrong end of the stick as to the accommodation on offer. Dot and Maureen had to share Cyril and Florrie's double bed while they took it in turns to sleep in her single. One or other would have a disturbed night napping on the sofa. Dot had never been a pub-goer and so, staying upstairs, experienced the same loneliness as Maureen. She was used to regular meals with everyone taking part and to be able to breathe fresh air by opening windows. Consequently Dot didn't really enjoy her stays and spent a lot of time sitting on the bottom stair talking to Ethel on the telephone.

"GRUB - that's the answer," Cyril bawled again.

"Bloody 'ell Cyril, wossamatta wiv you this time? I fought the Boston Strangler 'ad broken in!" Florrie was only too used to being rudely awakened by Cyril's outbursts. They were usually sparked off by the TV news or someone failing the yes/no interlude in *Take your Pick,* but realising that the TV wasn't on, she took slightly more notice than usual, fearing that the commotion might have something to do with her. Ricky meantime was licking up the gravy that had spilt on to the carpet.

"It's no good, can't fight it anymore. If that's what they want - that's what they'll get!"

"Want what? Who?" Florrie yelled back, confused.

"Been against it right from the start, but it's no good…" Cyril sat down, took a deep breath, then shot up again and started waving his arms at Florrie.

"Where's the pub catalogue?" he demanded. "Need it quick."

"I dunno, do I? You 'ad it last," she groaned.

"You'd betta not 'ave sent it up Brookies. No, there it is. Bloody 'ell woman, you're sittin' on it. Geddup!" Grabbing it from under her, Cyril rifled through the pages. "Equipment…equipment, where's the bleedin' equipment section in this fing…?"

By now Maureen and Florrie were beginning to get

119

worried. Neither of them knew what he was on about, but if it had implications for their tiny kitchen, then it was serious. Florrie had visions of having to cook food for the pub in a space barely big enough to swing a cat. Maureen saw herself wearing an apron and having to juggle 'pub grub' up and down the stairs whilst hurdling over the cigarettes. The last time Ricky had heard raised voices like this, he'd watched Cyril's dinner - and therefore his - slide down the wall. Florrie, driven beyond the limits of tolerance on account of her husband's venomous tongue, had hurled his dinner at him one evening. He'd ducked in time, but the wallpaper wasn't so lucky. The telltale smear was still there.

"'Ere it is. HOT FOOD," he exclaimed. "Page twenny nine."

Maureen was perplexed. Her father wasn't keen on grub. In fact he didn't like eating. He was fussy beyond belief and rarely came to the table until his dinner resembled burnt dog food, which is why Ricky never had to eat stuff out of a tin. *That* was banned outright. Florrie only had to get the tin opener out before Cyril was retching with the smell. A classic example was when he'd found Maureen's old hoola hoop propped up against the dartboard trough and thought he'd teach Ricky a few tricks. He reckoned he could get the dog to jump through the hoop, raising the height each time, but Ricky had other ideas. When Florrie came up with the idea of tempting him with tasty titbits - scrapings of who know's what from Sid the butcher's floor which she fried up in a pan - the smell caused Cyril to decamp to the cellar for the night.

"Look, the Sun, the Bell, the Stoke Oven, even the Clean Pot 'ouse does it now. Got no choice, 'ave to go down that road." Cyril was greedily absorbing information.

Finally, Florrie could contain herself no longer. "What, ya mean you want me to cook chips and stuff?"

She remembered Mrs Jenkins raving about chicken in a basket, whatever that might be, with a plan to try something scary called scampi next time. Also Gerry had been bragging about his dinner date at the Berni in Bexley with the barmaid from the Bell. Went on about it for several days afterwards - melon boat with a cherry on a stick, T-bone steak (from the Argentine apparently), half a grilled tomato and chips and black forest gateaux (extra cream) all washed down with a schooner of sweet sherry. They'd had to queue for a table, he'd paid for both meals (12/6 each) and her bus fare home, but he won't be seeing her again... How someone so small could put away so much food was beyond Florrie, especially with an afters before and another afters after, but anyway that was beside the point. How on earth was *she* going to cope with providing such queer cuisine?

It was all a bit beyond Maureen. She'd never even been to a restaurant - a milkshake or a knickerbocker glory at the Riverside Café on the Prom being about the nearest she'd got to it - nor could she remember her parents ever going out together anywhere, let alone for a meal, during the sixteen years she'd been on the planet.

"Bloody 'ell ya daft woman, no... smell of fat would finish me off. No, *this* is what I'm on about." Cyril thrust page thirty eight in his wife's face.

She looked at it for a moment and displayed a mild sense of relief on not seeing a deep fat fryer anywhere on the page. Instead there was a range of warming cabinets.

"I'll make room on the counter for one." Cyril had made up his mind now. "Hot pork pies and sausage rolls. That'll keep 'em 'appy."

"Maybe Cornish pasties?" added Florrie hopefully.

"Never!" Cyril screwed up his nose, reinforcing his distaste by tapping the end of it. Any dish that had a place name too far from the Thames was on dodgy ground. "No foreign muck."

Maureen wrestled with how a pork pie - even with *English* mustard – could possibly tempt the hoards away from the Peking Palace which, according to Theresa was serving up strange dishes like 'birds nest soup'. But she knew better than to voice an opinion. Besides she could see the look of relief on Florrie's face.

Cyril and food were a constant nightmare. He didn't like eating, took no part in daily cooking, yet he had a passion for making - of all things - horseradish sauce and toffee apples. How he could complain about the smell of food after the aroma he created when horseradish root was ripe for mincing, was beyond belief.

Bert and Dot grew horseradish plants at the end of their garden. Up to five foot tall, they hid a crumbling brick wall. Bert had been to Smokey's and bought a second-hand mincer. Cyril seemed to get some kind of masochistic pleasure from the unbearable assault on his sinuses that forcing the white-tapered root into the mincing machine created. One time there was an almighty crisis. After adding vinegar to the minced root and leaving it to mature, he wiped his already irritated eyes with the stuff. It took three bottles of Optrex to sort that out. Anyway, the idea was that the horseradish would now be ready to dab on roast beef - if anyone was brave enough. As usual, Cyril made a huge mess and left Dot to clear up the peelings and leaves, plus the mincer which she left until the last minute on account of the pain.

By contrast, the toffee apple fest took place in Florrie's kitchen. Equally devastating in terms of debris, Cyril would exit after many hours and much swearing, proudly carrying a box of gooey, syrupy Cox's orange pippins for all to enjoy, or endure. The toffee spelt danger. Overcooked it had a bitter, burnt taste and carried a real possibility of breaking a tooth or welding dentures together. Undercooked it would get in your fillings and slowly rot the cavities from the inside out. Ricky liked to lick this confection until the fur round his mouth became rigid and clumped into stalactites.

"Are ya ready then? What do I look like?" Cyril was wearing his new knitted waistcoat in a slightly darker shade of beige than usual. His shirt sleeves, which were used to being rolled up to the elbow, looked uncomfortable, pinned down at the wrists with barrel shaped cufflinks.

"Nice," Florrie replied, puffing on her cigarette. She was getting nervous and needed two fags in quick succession.

"You still gunna wear that old black dress? Does nuffink for ya, ya know."

"Gordon Bennett thanks! I've put a necklace on, so shuddup."

Maureen glanced at her Mum. It was true she no longer looked as if she cared much about her appearance. She was always wearing the same shapeless knitted dresses with their shiny marks from over-hasty ironing without checking the temperature. Not that long ago she'd looked quite pretty with her bright blue eyes and tightly curled dyed auburn hair. She even looked quite feminine in her Crimplene.

"Must be 'er age or summink," was Cyril's sensitive judgement on the matter. "'Air's nearly all grey now."

123

"Yer not gunna go on about the EEC or nationalisation all night I 'ope," Florrie warned as she rummaged in her drawer for a brooch and some earrings.

Not much chance of that, Maureen thought, given that the supertanker, *Torrey Canyon*, had just run aground off Lands End and was being bombed by the RAF to burn off the pollution. Cyril was going to have a field day with that.

And so here they were, ready to go, slightly apprehensive as they made their way downstairs to meet Mr and Mrs Jenkins. The bar staff was already on high alert having attended a compulsory debrief on survival without their employer, everyone remaining on their best behaviour until the Landlord and Landlady left the building.

The Jenkins' had recommended that before ordering the heated cabinet, Cyril and Florrie should sample a pub meal, just in case they were making a hasty decision. Cyril had no intention of changing his mind; however both he and Florrie were flattered to be asked to accompany the great Mr and Mrs J to a meal at the Nelson. Dot and Maureen were looking forward to fish and chips with sixpenneth worth of crackling which Maureen was going down Hamilton Road to get when the coast was clear. Full to bursting, Dot went to bed early, but Maureen, being somewhat concerned for her parents since she couldn't imagine what they would do with a menu, waited up for their return.

Ricky barked as the main door was slammed and the ritual of sorting keys for the three different locks began. It was only just after closing time, so Maureen crept downstairs as she could sense tension in the air.

"Bloody 'ell Florrie, I can't believe you said it. D'ya know nuffink about wot goes on when yer out eatin'?"

Florrie was helping herself to a much-needed Guinness. "That's better," she said licking her lips. "Gotta have something to get rid of the taste of that *Liebfraumilk* wine - like sucking lemons it was. Anyway, you're a fine one to talk. Going on about what a rip off buying a colour telly is. You might 'ave guessed the Jenkins 'ad already got one."

"More fool them," Cyril sneered, helping himself to the whisky optic. "Two 'undred and fifty quid - just to watch the *Virginian* in glorious Techno colour for only four hours a week. More money than sense. Anyway that's got nuffink to do wiv the price of fish; I'm talkin' about yer drink order when we first got there."

"Don't know what all the fuss is about. We got it, didn't we?" She sounded indignant at the criticism.

"Well that's as may be, but did you see Mrs Jenkins' face? She looked 'orrified. I didn't know where to put meself."

"'Orrified or not, she was quick enough to ask for a slice of lemon on the side – not that I've gotta clue why," Florrie retorted. "Anyway, I'm off to bed."

Later, sitting at the bar, Cyril took pleasure in enlightening Maureen on her Mother's social *faux pas*. Apparently, the waitress in the upstairs restaurant at the Nelson had asked the party of four if they would care for an *aperitif* before their meal. Three of them pondered for a second or two. Not so Florrie. Quick as a flash she jumped in on all of their behalfs. "We'll 'ave a pot of tea for two – 'ot and strong - and two light ales, please."

The warming cabinet duly arrived and was ceremonially switched on, whereupon it sat with its culinary delicacies from the Price Reduction Stores hissing away gently all day and all evening. Occasionally the lid would be opened for a hungry, non-discerning customer, but mostly it was Cyril who would eat them, instead of his dinner, after closing time.

Maybe it was the smell of hot pastry, but a few weeks later a group of male students from the Technical College up the road started to come in looking for a quick snack at lunchtime. Maureen's trek across the saloon bar took on an unexpected frisson of excitement. She imagined them watching her as she tried to appear nonchalant. 'Maybe it's the school uniform that's putting them off', she wondered, when they ignored her walks past. 'I'll wear some lipstick and keep my coat on'.

But it was all to no avail. Back in the living room, Cyril announced that the "lads weren't keen on the pies" and that they'd rather have a cheese roll.

"Reckon if you go down the Price Reduction Stores first fing every morning and pick up crusty ones, that'll keep 'em comin' in," he instructed Florrie.

Cyril had no idea how much extra work this would mean for Florrie and he never stopped reminding her of "'ow you do nuffink compared to me, wiv all me responsibilities." So Maureen would catch the bus to school while Florrie headed for the shop, returning to butter and fill four dozen rolls. These would then be crammed into a roll-top plastic case specially ordered from page forty of the Pub Catalogue, and lay there waiting to be eaten.

"They're goin' down a storm," Cyril said after a few weeks, "but we ain't gunna retire on the proceeds."

Ten

Up the Creek

Maureen was in her bedroom sellotaping Melody Maker magazine's double-spread photo of Peter Frampton to the wall. Cyril had finally admitted the wallpaper had *'ad it*, and was allowing pictures to completely cover it. Her decision to fill the gap with groups other than the Beatles had not been taken lightly. Enough was enough. A whole year of enduring the entire Public Bar breaking spontaneously into *We all live in a yellow submarine*, in earsplitting disharmony, had tested Maureen's devotion to the Fab Four to the limit. The final blow came at the annual outing when the crowd began to chant *I am a Walrus* as they boarded the 'chara' heading off on their own Magical Mystery Tour. Wink wheezing *goo googa choo* was the last straw.

Suddenly the door banged open to reveal Florrie standing there with a curious smile on her face. "Fought you an' me could 'ave a weekend away. Been offered a *shallee* on Canvey. Belongs to Arson Stan."

She seemed dead chuffed with herself, not only for securing the hire of it, but also for having convinced Wally the bus driver to take them in his Vauxhall Viva.

"Stan won't be using it for a bit, not now 'es at 'Er Majesty's Pleasure on the Isle of Wight. Sylvia's stayed there wiv 'er girls, so I reckon it'll be alright. We'll pick a time when yer Nan's going off on one of 'er club's Blossom Outings so's not to upset 'er apple cart. What d'ya reckon?"

Clearly excited by the idea, it was Florrie's first

opportunity to have a few days away since they'd taken on the Victory. Bit of a mixed blessing though, as it had only come about because Cyril could cope quite easily now that trade had slackened off.

Maureen was reserved in her response. Arson Stan had lived up to his name one too many times, and been put away. As a result, she wasn't quite sure what state the chalet might be in. Mind you, Sylvia had been there, so it couldn't be that bad, could it? And hadn't Tina, Sylvia's daughter, enthused about convoys of bikers? Maureen wished she'd paid more attention during their brief chat at the paint and polish counter, but since the *hand in knicker* incident they only met in secret due to Cyril's warning about keeping her distance.

"Can Lorraine come as well?" Maureen replied, slowly warming to the idea.

"Oh, I fancied it being just us and Ricky," Florrie responded, disappointed. "There's lots of amusements; Bingo, caffees, shops, oh and pitch and putt."

The idea of hitting a small ball around in the pouring rain wasn't high on Maureen's agenda, unlike the thought of dressing up and sampling the evening entertainment. The situation called for diplomacy.

"So you reckon you and me'll be good at golf then?"

That did the trick. As Florrie's dream of lounging in a deck chair with a copy of *True Romance* magazine began to dissolve before her eyes, she relented.

"OK then, I s'pose Lorraine'll keep ya company."

Her sigh said it all.

"So d'ya think we're going where it's *happening*. What are ya gunna wear then?" asked Lorraine excitedly on the phone that evening.

"Well I've got my new orange dress with its kipper

tie I got from the market. White zig zag tights and white patent shoes. What about you?"

Lorraine had a similar list involving the latest style-set by Twiggy - the face of the Swinging Sixties. Neither girl was built like this sixteen year old androgynous supermodel with her waif-like figure and boyish haircut, but they weren't going to let that deter them. Cyril had more or less given up complaining about skirt lengths and had turned his attention to eye makeup. 'Panda eyes,' according to him, made you look like a tart. Dusty Springfield, in particular, fell into this category.

On the night before, the girls excitedly packed and repacked the hard plastic cherry red suitcase, newly purchased at a substantial discount-from Strongie's stall at the market. Cyril had said that there was limited space in the boot of the Viva, so they were sharing the one. Florrie was making do with an old carpet bag of Dot's. Ricky was most dismayed to see his lead and bowl disappear inside.

As they travelled in Wally's car through the new Dartford Tunnel and round the Essex coastline to Canvey Island, Florrie was already tiring of the giggling. The dog spent much of the journey pinned to the parcel shelf. He'd been panting and shivering, never having been in a car before. Eventually the girls fell silent as they passed through acres of green marshes empty except for grazing horses. Then as they finally emerged from the reedbeds and crossed the *Welcome to Canvey* border, all Maureen could see were huge petrochemical facilities. It didn't look too appealing. Across the creek, on the Kent side, were the burning flare stacks of the Shell Haven oil refinery.

"Don't fancy a dip in that," sniffed Lorraine, nodding at the greyish-brown water of the Thames Estuary.

Having settled themselves in at the Hole Haven chalet park and ascertained that the all-important washroom and toilet block was a five minute walk away, the girls left Florrie heading for Liptons while they battled against the wind along a pathway leading up to the giant concrete sea wall. It was incredibly muddy, their shoes inadequate, and to top it all, huge birds were dive-bombing them from overhead. Ricky was staggering about, pulling on his lead, totally disorientated. He hadn't recovered from being tossed around on his shelf, let alone having sea spray in his face, birds squawking, unfamiliar smells and waves crashing close by. And where was his alley? Poor dog, his eyes were virtually popping out of his head.

Struggling on, the girls found themselves being drawn by the sound of motorbikes revving up on the ramshackle wooden jetties just ahead.

"There are lots of blokes here," whispered Maureen. "Let's get a cup of coffee."

"Don't like coffee," replied Lorraine, missing the point.

"Neither do I. What's that got to do with it?" She pushed her friend through the door of the local fleshpot - Irene's café. "This weekend's definitely improving. Glad I brought me false eyelashes."

Finding a couple of empty seats they stuffed Ricky under the table and checked the place out. It was horribly stuffy and the windows were all steamed up. The smell of the deep fat fryer mingled uncomfortably with cigarette smoke and tomato ketchup. They stayed just long enough to study the overflowing talent during two very milky coffees in brown transparent glass cups and saucers.

"Got anything leather with ya?" whispered Lorraine as they shut the door behind them. "Don't reckon we stand a chance without it."

"I'm more of a mod than a rocker," shouted Maureen, trying to be heard above the howling wind on their return to the chalet. "Looks like *this* event's tonight. Better leave it to me to ask my Mum." She was reading the remaining strips of a weather-beaten poster stuck on the public conveniences sign. Getting out on their own was going to require tact.

"Hang on, which one is ours?" They both stared at a sea of identical dwellings. Luckily Ricky had recovered his senses sufficiently by this time and could sniff out a lit Players Weight even behind a closed door, so they were home and dry.

Using up a whole 2/11d pot of face shiner, extra thick eyelashes with tiny diamonds on each end, white lipstick and white nail varnish, they decided they were ready to head to the chip shop for their tea. Maureen, however, had an unexpected problem. As she'd replaced her glasses, her lashes became wedged, making blinking difficult. Picking the moment carefully, she finally blurted out the question she'd been rehearsing.

"Mum, there's a talent contest later at the Casino Ballroom. Anyone of any age can enter so it might be fun for all of us. Can we go?"

Already missing her constitutional Guinness, Florrie thought about it. She'd rather fancied the look of the white weather-boarded Lobster Smack pub, which had something to do with Charles Dickens, but as the girls might not have been allowed in, realised it was the best way of keeping everyone happy. "If yer like," she said.

As hoped, the *main drag* was heaving with shiny black motorbikes and matching riders. Rock salmon and chips in hand the girls surveyed the scene. The amusement park, drab and deserted earlier was now brightly lit and thrillingly noisy. Thankfully the wind

131

had dropped so a huge big dipper called the *Wild Mouse* had sprung into action, hurtling over its metal tracks. Whether screeching up the inclines, rattling round corners or thundering down the slopes, its participants were squealing in delight, or terror. The tamer rides were busy too, along with a dazzling slot machine arcade with bustling change kiosks. In one corner, middle aged ladies were sitting in a circle, pens in hand as a bingo caller, surrounded by saucepan sets, towels and fluffy toys for the winners, yelled numbers. Outside again, between the dodgems and a speedway track, a jukebox was blaring out Procol Harum's *A Whiter Shade of Pale*. A large crowd of local teenagers were gathering, some couples dancing. A lot of the motorbike riders were sitting on the steps of the dodgems eating hotdogs and smoking fags.

Maureen and Lorraine stood and watched in wonder for quite some time until Florrie arrived and moved them on quickly. She was outnumbered though. There were boys busking opposite the Monico Hotel, boys performing on stage at the Casino Ballroom and loads of boys in the audience. *Talent* was literally all around them, and yet, apart from a couple of wolf whistles, no matter how many times Maureen and Lorraine paraded up and down, no boy actually spoke to them. But there was always a *chance* and it was exciting just listening to the throbbing psychedelic rock music and roaring motorbikes on their way out. Heaven knows what Florrie made of it. She was certainly tight lipped all the way back to the chalet and only melted when a relieved Ricky swamped her in an overwhelming welcome - clearly having thought he'd been abandoned forever in this strange place.

By the next afternoon, Florrie had found the Bingo quite addictive and left the girls to their own devices. They walked Ricky along the shoreline to Labworth

Beach and ate ice cream in the glass-and-concrete café on the front. "Ugly building," Lorraine commented. "Tutti-frutti's not bad though."

"Says here, it's a 'modernist building made of reinforced concrete'", Maureen started reading from the postcard she'd picked up. "S'posed to look like the bridge of the Queen Mary. I know what my Dad would say. "Tow it out to sea and sink it". C'mon, let's go get some doughnuts from the machine outside the Casino."

As it was Saturday, local bands were playing at the Ballroom, but the three hundred tickets had already been sold. Ricky licked the sugar from the discarded doughnut bag as the girls retreated dejectedly from the box office. It didn't seem worth getting dressed up, so Maureen left off the false eyelashes and Lorraine her ribbed sleeveless jumper, saving her from shaving under her arms for the second night in a row. Florrie had no intention of cooking on her holiday, so the three of them finished up eating chicken and chips at Irene's before wandering down into the slot machine arcade below the Ballroom and going their own way again. If it wasn't bad enough already, when they looked up they could actually see the ceiling flexing up and down due to all the action on the sprung floor. A little later, the Tunnel of Love turned out to be cold and damp and the Ghost Train distinctly unghostly. Hanging on to the chain holding them in, the girls saw Florrie strolling along with a giant smurf under her arm.

"I won full 'ouse," she said waving the blue creature with a white pointy hat in their direction. "Either of ya got a clue what the devil this is?"

The four of them made their way back to the chalet park, the sound of the beat from the Casino Ballroom disappearing with each footstep. Then, as they went through the gate the music seemed to be getting louder again. The games room, a wooden hut containing a darts board and skittles - previously dismissed by the girls - was now a beacon of light resonating to the sound of thumping drums. With a spring in her step Lorraine flung open the door to reveal a packed holiday crowd watching a live band of young boys. Sensing an opportunity for an unexpected extra nightcap, Florrie made her way to the bar while Maureen and Lorraine worked their way to the front of the stage. There was a good hour left of ear splitting rock and roll before Maureen left clutching her autographed photo of Pat Turner and the Panthers, a local band thankfully not quite good enough to play that night at the Casino.

The last few hours of their weekend was spent sitting on the sea wall watching the tankers going in and out of the refineries and listening to the announcement coming over the deserted dodgems' loudspeaker: *Press the pedal and turn the steering wheel. One way round and no deliberate bumping.* All the bikers had headed off across Benfleet Creek in the direction of Southend. The abandoned dodgem cars were sparking but still. All in all it had been a memorable weekend, not quite the 'Summer of Love' they'd hoped for, but at least they'd got two photos as a reminder: one of the girls sitting on a couple of slot machine horses flanking the grand entrance to the Casino and one of Florrie celebrating with her smurf. They'd even made a flimsy vinyl record, in a kiosk not unlike a telephone box. You pressed a button to start, then sang *All you need is love, love lalala love*, over and over again until the three minutes was up, except, right at the end, Florrie opened the door too early with the result that her immortal words, "Silly idea this is... waste of half a crown," were captured for posterity.

"She perked up alright when she saw all those rocker

blokes."

Maureen could hear she was being talked about in the kitchen. Florrie's voice was full of disgust. "Dunno what would 'ave 'appened if one of 'em 'ad spoke to 'er. Menacing they were. She's got no sense, would 'ave got on the back of one of 'em motorbikes and been gone."

"It's the way she looks now... you should stop 'er... too much on show," Cyril said.

"That's right, blame me. What can *I* do about it?" Now Florrie was sounding indignant. "It's that Lorraine *I* blame - bit of a Lolita, if ya ask me."

Maureen was stunned to hear Lorraine being spoken about in that tone. She had got used to hearing herself described like this, but why pick on her friend?

"You know what *your* daughter asked me a few weeks ago? What *Tampax* was."

The unmistakable sound of Cyril frantically stirring his tea spelled the end of that conversation. Maureen had indeed asked about *Tampax*. She knew what they were for, of course, but was hoping that Florrie might help her move into the modern age. Instead Florrie leapt up in embarrassment and scurried out saying:

"They're not fer you, just fer married women."

Sitting on her bed mulling over this latest gem, Maureen was aware of her Mum lingering behind the door. "You'd better listen to me," she said, poking her head round.

Maureen braced herself.

"I wasn't even allowed to pull me stockings up in front of me brothers." With that, her head retreated and she was gone.

Mystified, Maureen wondered if that was her Mum's version of a sex education lesson. Should she file it away with the previous gem about not sitting directly on the seat in a public toilet? It was obvious that Florrie was clearly out of her depth and had no idea how to communicate with her daughter. Their relationship was hard going to say the least. Lorraine said *her* Mum was her best friend. They shared secrets and had lovely jokey chats. Florrie, on the other hand, was always somewhat distant, certainly never up for a chat; any conversation usually beginning and ending with "I just don't understand you?"

The more she thought about it, the more she wondered what it had been like for Florrie growing up, and what kind of relationship she had had with her own Mother. She occasionally came out with sayings gleaned from 'her old Mum', quoted with obvious fondness, but Maureen couldn't remember her, having being very young when she died. With so little history on offer, there wasn't much to go on.

Then there was the way she'd changed during her years with Cyril. Had he finally worn her down? She used to stand up to him, their arguments loud and vicious, sometimes resulting in silences that lasted for weeks. "Must be a full moon," Cyril would sneer. Florrie would remain steadfast – uttering as few words as possible, even to Maureen. These days, though, she was more likely to give in and withdraw. Cyril's tongue could lash out unchallenged. So why had they stayed together? Why did they have her? They never had any more kids, so was she one too many?

It may come as no surprise that Cyril met Florrie in a pub. It was during the War when he was home on leave. The *Lime Hoy* hostelry in the town became his mainstay. Florrie was working there as a barmaid in the evenings, while by day she had a job in the local submarine telegraph cable factory which had been turned into a munitions factory in support of the war effort. They made Bofors guns there and had already been bombed twice. Next door was the Red Lion Wharf where the Mulberry harbours, built from local concrete, were being prepared for the D-Day landings. Florrie still had the cigarette lighter made from a V2 rocket which had dropped nearby. Its aluminium shrapnel had scattered all over the factory yard and a blacksmith had melted it all down to make the lighters. At least, that's what Cyril said.

Florrie's Father had worked all his life as a labourer in Bevan's cement factory on the Northfleet riverside. Indeed, all the components that made up Florrie's family worked here and lived alongside one another in a row of forty tiny four-roomed cottages and three pubs called the *Crick* by locals, right at the river's edge. Florrie's dad had been one of fifteen children born at number 40 (seven not reaching adulthood). It was hard to imagine their living conditions. There was a flight of shallow concrete steps at the end of the Crick, permanently covered in white cement dust, which led straight into the factory. The grinding process was deafening and dusty and Bevan's had a greater capacity than any other cement works in Europe. At the foot of the steps was the cooperage and staveyard, where about 50 coopers and hoopers, including Florrie's Grandfather, used the staves - narrow strips of wood - to make barrels which were each filled with 3cwt of cement.

Florrie's other Grandfather, Samuel, spent all his childhood in the Stanway workhouse outside Colchester. With his Mother dying very young, his Father hadn't been able to make a living on the land, so he too entered the workhouse, staying there until his death as an old man. Samuel came to the cement works to make a new life for himself. Florrie appeared to know nothing about him, not even his name, and his guilty past would have remained a closed book were it not for an unsettling event which occurred in the

Victory some years back. Out of the blue, a frail, unassuming elderly lady appeared in the Saloon Bar asking for Florrie. After a few pertinent words, an ashen-faced landlady used her prerogative and politely asked the ladies in the snug to vacate for a short while. Enough to alert all to a possible scandal, ears were now wagging, including Cyril's, who circled close to pick up snippets himself. He wasn't disappointed and never tired of rubbing Florrie's nose in the revelations that were to follow - always behind closed doors of course - so as not to affect the takings. For her part, Florrie never talked about it again.

It transpired that Samuel had had two 'wives' living in adjacent parishes. One was certainly genuine, as the other was still married to another man, a petty criminal, living in Ipswich. Anyway there were two lots of children as well. Sadly, when 'wife' No. 1 eventually went back to her real husband in Ipswich, the three surviving daughters were clearly not wanted and were put in the local workhouse. The lady in the pub turned out to be the youngest of these, looking for details of her Father. The truth was he'd been busy producing fourteen more children with wife No. 2 at 34 The Crick. With nothing more to be said on either side, Florrie's newly found 'aunt' went out the door never to be heard of again.

After her parents met (somewhere between cottages 34 and 40) and married, the family were elevated to a nearby street privately owned by the cement company. Opposite the front of the houses, a wall of concrete panels had to be built as protection from the steep drop into the former chalk pit.

Despite having quite a lot of relations, Florrie was only close to her younger sisters Mavis and Maud and to one aunt. Sadly another had been killed outright when a bomb dropped on their Anderson shelter in

Factory Road during a Second World War air raid. Mavis and Maud would come round to the pub most Saturday evenings with their husbands and, leaving them in the bar, make their way upstairs to join Florrie in the kitchen. All three could be found huddled together, elbows resting on the sink, puffing away on their cigarettes and gossiping about their men - and probably Maureen as well. The tap would be running to wash away the ash and to cover up their chitchat. Cyril referred to them as Hubble Bubble, Toil and Trouble. "Better watch the witches when that full moon's out," he would say to Maureen. When they got peckish they'd snack on cockles, whelks, brown shrimps, saveloys and celery. Several ounces of salt to the ready, Florrie would issue the needles necessary to prize the cockles from their shells.

"Keep an eye on 'em Sook. Let me know when they start sticking those needles in that little Cyril doll they're 'iding under the tablecloth," her Dad would joke.

Maureen couldn't think of anything else she knew about her Mum. By contrast Cyril talked all the time about his childhood. His parents obviously doted on him and his sister, but his broken arm and the months he'd spent isolated in the sanatorium miles away from home, recovering from diphtheria and scarlet fever, with Bert and Dot staring at him from behind a glass partition, weighed heavily on his mind. He'd taken Maureen to see the house he was born in and the Hall where he'd celebrated his 21st. "I got a fousand fags that day," he'd say every time they walked past.

He taught Maureen to recognise the tugs on the Thames, where he'd spent his working life prior to taking over the Victory. In no time she could recite the history of every vessel and what part they played in his life.

Cyril had started out, aged sixteen, as a cook on the *Ocean Cock* tug. Work on the river was already sparse and the unions were flexing their industrial muscle. Not progressing fast enough, he moved to the Erith and Dartford Lighterage Company in 1936, as an unlicensed 'boy' at £1.10 shillings a week. Apprenticed as a Waterman and Lighterman on the Thames, his money quickly rose to £4.5.0. Maureen knew these precise details because her Dad kept a diary until the end of the War. It talked of 'finding a new enterprise whilst young,' which probably explains his brief foray into the catering business when he and another 'cook' from the tugs took over a working man's caff on the riverside.

He was greatly affected when the *Ocean Cock* was sunk in the Thames in 1938 with the loss of four of his friends. A year later, he gained his freedom of the River - just in time for the outbreak of war. Originally called up for the Navy, someone among the 'Powers That Be' decided that his was a reserved occupation, so by late 1940 he was still on the Thames, although no longer lightering as supplies weren't getting through. By then he was Second Mate on the *River Thames*. On December 21st he had a close call. He'd just left the tug for two days shore leave when a couple of hours later it hit an acoustic mine, blowing her bottom out. The skipper was the only survivor.

After a month on survivor's leave, Cyril joined the *Sun X* as deckhand and spent the rest of 1941 towing invasion barges around the South Coast. Maureen had been brought up knowing what an important part the London tugs had played in the War. Indeed the *Sun X* had taken part in the Dunkirk evacuation, bringing back two hundred and eleven men.

From her bedroom window she could see their

distinctive black and orange funnels churning out thick smoke whilst maneuvering up and down the river. It always made her feel safe to see them, knowing that several of her uncles and cousins were aboard them at any time, although by the mid-Sixties such activity was on the wane due to the steady decrease in river trade.

In August 1942, the *Sun X* was requisitioned by the Ministry of War Transport to work on the Clyde. It took a month to get there as they first had to tow two barges to Falmouth and a submarine target to Tenby on the way. So Cyril's war was spent making long trips all around the coasts of Scotland, England, Wales and Northern Ireland. Three years and seven months to be exact, in all weathers, with only a week's leave every six months or so. His entrepreneurial streak clearly hadn't left him though, as he also recorded being part-owner of a greasy spoon caff in Souchiehall Street, Glasgow. There must have been relief on all fronts when VE day arrived and the caff returned to the safekeeping of Glaswegians, and the *Sun X* to its owners on the Thames.

So Cyril went back to lightering, spending his free time in the *Lime Hoy* getting to know Florrie. Love blossomed and eventually they got married. Soon the two became three, Cyril, Florrie and *The Victory*. To be landlord of his own pub had always been Cyril's dream. Some less charitable members of his family said that as he spent so much time in one, he might just as well live in one.

Eleven

No More Monkeying Around

"Bloody cow! Infringement of personal liberties, that's what it is. We're gunna 'ave a Publicans protest against impendin' bankruptcy."

Cyril had just returned from an emergency Licensed Victuallers meeting at the Conservative Club and was breathing fire. Barbara Castle, the Transport Minister, had done the unforgivable - she'd introduced the *Breathalyser*. If anything was designed to whip Cyril into frenzy, it was the Labour Government's interference in ordinary people's lives. The Public Bar crowd was sympathetic enough, but then none of them came to the pub by car, so Cyril crossed over to the Saloon to continue his diatribe.

"Coppers can stop ya by the roadside and make ya breathe into a tube on the spot. If it goes green or summink, yer done. Two pints'll be yer lot. Barely enough ta wet yer whistle"

Unfortunately, no one in the Saloon drove to get their pint either, but they did their best to show solidarity for their incensed Landlord.

"Tippa the iceberg," said Wally. "I'll 'ave to think twice before I take the wife out in the Viva. Next thing, they'll try an' stop us smokin' in pubs too. Take away all our little pleasures."

"Thank God, that'll never 'appen," snorted Cyril. Cigarettes were passed round and lit in defiance.

"It was bad enough last year when those three little 'itlers started work in the town," he continued, dragging on his Rothmans. "*Traffic Wardens* they're called, dishin' out bitsa paper fer parkin' too long. Two quid fine apparently. Pity they ain't got nuffink better to do. Curly better not leave 'is bike on the railin's no more. That's bound to be at least ten bob. Dunno wot the world's comin' to."

That night, after closing, the lock-in lasted into the early hours and the whisky bottle got well and truly drained.

"Mo... Mo!"

Maureen was enjoying her Saturday morning lie-in when she heard her father yelling from his bedroom.

"Yer Mum's gone down the Price Reduction Stores. So run down and open up will ya. Me 'ead's as big as a bushel basket. There'll only be Warbling Wilf for a pint on 'is way 'ome from the night shift."

Maureen dragged herself out of bed, threw on some clothes and went down to the Bar where she encountered Gert the cleaner frantically scrubbing the coconut matting on the floor below the pumps.

"Sticky stuff this," she said over her shoulder. "Alright dear?"

Maureen nodded, not knowing whether she was enquiring after her well-being, or seeking approval for the job in hand. How Gert was still in the job, seeing as she regularly drank the profits, despite Florrie's attempts to put a stop to it, was a mystery. Anyway, as Maureen removed the tea towels from the pumps, Gert shoved her bucket into the Gents, tied on her headscarf and grabbing her coat, was off.

Minutes later, a familiar knock on the window heralded Wilf's arrival. Maureen stuck a pint glass under the Mild pump and let him in. Wilf was a porter in the hospital mortuary and was deaf and dumb. He'd been the butt of many a joke over his job, but he was always smiling and everyone liked him. He'd nod

143

violently if he saw his drink order was right and lay out the exact money on the counter. Cyril had a stack of Toby beer mats especially for him to scribble on the blank side if he had something extra to say, but today he hadn't - no doubt grateful for not having to lip-read Mein Host in full flow, Maureen thought. By the time she'd mulled over last night's rant, Warbling Wilf had downed his pint, waved and was gone.

"Thanks Sook," her father said, finally making his appearance, the Epsom salts having done the trick. He was waving a copy of the Daily Mirror at her. "Look at this load of old rubbish. Some bloke called Desmond Morris says we're just 'Naked Apes'. Speak for 'imself. What's 'e on about?"

Thankfully, not really being interested in Maureen's opinion, he chucked the paper on the floor to soak up the frothy overflow from the first pint of the day and changed the subject.

"Listen, you up for a walk down the prom later? I think 'e's due about four. Not every day you get to see someone important floating past ya."

Francis Chichester, in *Gypsy Moth 4*, was due to sail up the Thames on his way into London to mark the end of his epic nine-months-and-a-day single-handed voyage around the World.

"Absobloodylutely amazing for 65," Cyril continued. "Yacht's not bad eiver. 'E only stopped once in Sydney and done it faster than the Clipper ships in their 'eyday."

"Would you like to have had a go then, Dad?"

"Not on yer nelly, boats are fer getting from A t' B as far as I'm concerned."

Allowing themselves plenty of time to bag their usual spot above Bawley Bay, they set off in the direction of the river. As the crowds gathered, you could hear the sound of hooters and sirens in the distance. Then, on the horizon, a flotilla of boats of all sizes started to come into view. There were tugs and ferries and PLA dredgers, and right in the middle, this little yacht, with the local pilot cutter alongside, it's crew waving flags furiously.

"It looks so small," ventured Maureen. "Can't believe he's gone all the way round the world in *that*."

"Well it ain't the new QE2 that's fer sure. Fit into one of its cabins I reckon. Still, at least they won't need to swop over Pilots 'ere," he said with a laugh.

Maureen, who'd been taught the rules of the river by her father, knew that a sea pilot brings a ship into the estuary as far upstream as Gravesend. Here the river pilot takes over, and it is his job to pilot the vessel upstream.

"Dad would 'ave loved to see this," Cyril said wistfully as the flotilla moved past the power station, fort and docks on the far side of the Thames, before disappearing into the distance. "Let's go and call in on Nanna, see 'ow she's doin'."

"Good idea," Maureen responded, noting that it took a maritime hero like Francis Chichester to make Cyril feel sentimental.

Taking a short cut through the Churchyard, they circled round the bronze statue of *Pocahontas*. "Wonder if they'll ever find where she's buried," said Maureen. "They say she might be under the church."

"Funny old business if ya ask me," Cyril replied dismissively. Stories of 'Red Indians' in Gravesend were a bit too exotic for his tastes. He'd never totally trusted Tonto's motives, with all that Ke-mo sah-bee stuff, in the *Lone Ranger*.

Pocahontas was a young Native American Princess who had been married to an English tobacco planter, John Rolfe, back in the early seventeenth century. Their marriage supposedly helped stop disputes between the tribes and the colonists. Rolfe brought her back to England where she soon found herself the centre of attention, even being presented to King James 1st in 1617. Sadly, just as she was leaving on the return journey, she became gravely ill and died off Gravesend.

Heading up Victoria Street, they passed several of Cyril's old pub haunts, before reaching 42 Gordon Road, where he'd been brought up. Bert had once drawn Maureen a picture to show her how beautiful the front railings had been before they were taken away to be melted down for the war effort and never replaced.

The scullery door was reached via the passage down the side of the house and they both noticed a sickly-sweet aroma wafting down it from somewhere inside. Quick as a flash Cyril was in there tackling the rhubarb stewing on the stove which, by this time, had lost its liquid, the syrupy remains blackening the sides of the saucepan. Turning off the gas he threw the hissing saucepan into the huge Belfast sink. Dot was nowhere to be seen.

"I knew she wouldn't be able to stay 'ere long on 'er own," he muttered. "Too dangerous."

Maureen didn't like to tell her Dad that this had happened a lot over the years. Dot was easily distracted. Bert used to say stewed fruit wasn't properly cooked unless it was brown and chewy.

Dot strolled back into the room "Oh, 'ave I dunnit again?" she said with a laugh. "'Ello you two, nice to see ya." Surveying the damage to her pan, she left it to soak in the hope of saving it from the dustbin. "Glad you've come, I've got summink to tell ya. Not sure where I stand, really. Miss Payne next door 'as died. In 'er sleep, so no notice. 'Er nephew come round 'ere yesterday. They're gunna sell her 'ouse, and mine too - wiv me still in it!"

Maureen didn't know a great deal about Miss Payne except that all and sundry thought the name suited her. She owned both halves of the semi, lived in one and had rented the other to Bert and Dot for nearly thirty years. Maureen only saw her when she came to collect the rent, or over the fence when she rounded up tennis balls that had flattened her gladioli. The balls never came back of course.

"She must 'ave been bloody old, now I come to think of it," mused Cyril. "Always looked the same, even when I was a lad."

"Anyway," said Dot, getting back to the point, "Effel says now's the time I should move to that flat near 'er."

"Might 'ave guessed she'd be in on the act," her son snapped back.

Cyril and his sister had hardly spoken since Maureen was born. Whatever had caused the friction must have been more than a row over a fish tank, which was what Maureen had always been told. Both sides never had a good word to say about each other and sometimes Maureen got caught up in the middle. Once, when she jokingly called her Nanna a nitwit for forgetting something like the burnt rhubarb, Ethel who'd been hoovering at the time (but in earshot) took offence and that evening rang Cyril to ask what *he* was going to do about *his* daughter calling *her* Mother a rude name. The tremors were felt for weeks.

Consequently, Ethel and Fred made a point of steering clear of the Victory. It was a pity really, because not only was Cyril a favourite uncle to their sons during the War (they called him Uncle B, as in Uncle-be-home-soon), but he then missed their growing up, despite living round the corner. Whether by choice or not, the relations sided with Ethel, so although Maureen was well used to being chatted to when she was out shopping with Dot, if she was with Cyril they'd all cross the road and avoid eye contact. Uncles would dive into the bookies or the barbers if Maureen saw them first and shouted hello.

"This place is definitely too big for me, even wiv the 'ome 'elp," sighed Dot. "I'll miss me garden though."

"Sounds like you've already made up your mind, Nanna," Maureen whispered.

"Made up *for* me, more like," she whispered back.

The family all pulled together to clear the house, although not necessarily at the same time. The walnut dining table and six chairs in the front room were not going to the new flat. Nor was the matching chaise longue whose cold green cracked leather Maureen ran her fingers across one last time. The only person who'd sat on it recently, besides herself, was the insurance man from the Pru. She imagined it must have looked very grand in its original setting. Bert had bought the whole set from a decommissioned liner at Tilbury dock. Unfortunately he'd made a bit of a mess of it when he sawed off the ball feet and castors, causing Smokey Fishman to take a sharp intake of breath when asked what he'd give for it: "Pheeww, dodgy, Dot... what I give, I might not get back. Tell you what though, I'll take it off yer 'ands fer a pony, cos I know yer need shot of the lot."

"Twenny five quid! That all?" Dot replied with feigned indignance. "Come from *The Queen Mary* that did Smokey. I was expectin' a monkey."

Then there was Uncle Joe's porcelain collection on the mantelpiece which had been brought back from Shanghai, plus Bert's collection of musical instruments from which Cyril bagged the ukulele and mandolin, along with a huge bundle of sheet music from *The*

148

Black and White Minstrels shows - Bert's favourite television programme. Not being able to read music, Bert had picked up the tunes by ear, but liked to have the words to sing along to the Dixie melodies when trying to recreate them on his piano.

"Might come in 'andy if *Talent Night* makes a comeback," Cyril said as he wrapped it all up in brown paper and string to make it easier to carry. Maureen suddenly had a vision of Curly, Ken, Spud, Wink and Sid the butcher blacked-up and crooning to *Way down upon the Swannee River* – all white teeth and gloves. Shuddering at the thought, she turned her attention to the wind-up 'His Masters Voice' record player she'd been given. It came with a variety of 78's - including *Doing the Lambeth Walk, Ginger get yer 'air cut, When Father papered the parlour,* and *Down at the old Bull and Bush.* They must have been played hundreds of times because they crackled like fingernails on sandpaper.

Maureen also knew where to look for the collection of home-made tricks and jokes. Famous at parties, she lovingly tried them all out, one by one. There was the book called *More stories to read aLOUD* which triggered an explosive cap on opening (though it was too damp to work this time), the kaleidoscope containing soot on its rim; the box of matches that was somehow full one end, but not the other; the pen concealing a spring device which would jump in your hand, and the bits of thin metal in a spectacle case which sounded like smashing glass when dropped.

"Don't reckon I'll be wearing this again, eh Mo?"

Dot was now in the parlour. Round her neck was a somewhat-worse-for-wear fox head stole and she was modelling it, laughing as she did so, its paws dangling over her shoulder, bushy tail hanging down her back and ever-so-slightly bared teeth giving it a grotesque expression.

"D'ya remember what you used to do wiv it?" They both giggled at the memory of the poor thing, a dog lead tied around its neck, being dragged around the house in place of a pet.

Together they assembled the family sepia photos, all taken in an East End studio, consequently all with the same background, then the paintings and pictures that Bert hadn't been able to resist on his weekly visits to Smokey.

"Not sorry to get rid of these," she said. "Can't believe Smokey wants 'em back though," adding them to the *Not Taking* pile.

In the kitchen, where everyone had spent most of their time, the huge pendulum clock came down, along with the air raid black-out blinds and the large Bush valve radio which Maureen and Ethel were struggling to lift.

"Won't be listening to Lord Haw Haw on that thing again, thank the Lord," said Dot.

William Joyce, nicknamed Lord Haw Haw, was a Nazi propagandist broadcasting from Germany to Britain during the War. Bert and Dot couldn't resist listening to him whilst pouring scorn on his outbursts. The funny thing was, they actually knew him slightly. Joyce had briefly owned a radio and electrical shop in Whitstable where they had holidayed in the 1930s. Bert promptly stopped browsing the latest range of Morphy Richards electrical appliances when handed a leaflet promoting Oswald Mosley's *British Union of Fascists*, with his receipt.

Something tucked inside the art deco style wooden surround of the bakelite radio set became dislodged and floated to the floor. It wasn't the receipt, but Maureen recognised it and handed it to her grandmother. Dot smiled, a tear forming in the corner of her eye.

"Ah", she said. "Yer Grandad's sweetheart." It was a black and white studio photo of silent movie star, Bebe Daniels, in a bathing costume, which used to be propped up on the front of the radio. Bebe gained Bert's admiration on her radio show *Hi Gang* which continued transmitting during the Blitz. Then later, Maureen would join in too, listening to *Life with the Lyons*, featuring Bebe and her whole family. Remembering it now, conjured up the smell of cabbage boiling dry as Dot would inevitably get involved in the antics and forget the dinner.

Maureen took the photo and added it to her collection. The radio was always on at Bert and Dot's: *Listen with Mother, Two Way Family Favourites, The Clitheroe Kid* - more often than not preventing anyone from being heard. But that was the joy of the place. It was full of life, all the time.

After numerous telephone arguments between Cyril and Ethel about who was going to get what, the door to 42 Gordon Road was finally closed and Dot moved into her new flat. It was a sad moment for both Dot and Maureen.

"Was Gerry in then? Did 'e talk t'ya? What about any of them boys from the college? Surely they must 'ave noticed yer by now." Lorraine was on the phone for a post-mortem conversation on the events in the bar the previous Saturday night.

"Yes, no and no, in that order. Nothing much to report I'm afraid. Dad said to keep out of the Saloon for a bit if I'm fed up with Gerry paying me too much attention. It's my fault because of the way I dress. I'm *asking for it* apparently."

"Bloody 'ell, we'll be left on the shelf if we're not careful. 'The new young woman needs to *act nonchalant and rise above the attention*,' that's what

Cathy and Claire say."

"Who?"

"Cathy and Claire. You know the Agony Aunts in my Jackie magazine. That's their advice this week. What's *nonchalant* mean?"

"I think it means pretend we're not interested."

"Wot's the point of that? The blokes'll be off wiv someone else before we get a look in. Pity about those college boys, do ya reckon they'll come back? Fought we might be in wiv a chance there"

"They've never once said a word to me. Not even when I wore my sling backs. Don't reckon we'll see them again, not now the Bell does beefburgers and chips."

"Wish yer Dad would get wiv it. Anyway, what was he goin' on about after closin' this time?"

"The Common Market and how France doesn't want us in."

"But I thought he didn't want to be in it?"

"He doesn't. Totally against it, in fact"

"'E should be pleased then."

"You'd think so, but he hates the French for voting against us even more."

"Sorry I asked. Oooo, nearly forgot, what's the latest on Sylvia and Curly?"

"Well, I heard Mum talking to Mrs Jenkins. She's given him an ultimatum. Got to make a choice, apparently. Not prepared to be his *bit on the side* anymore. Threatening to spill the beans."

"Gawd, that sounds serious."

"Yeah, might have to get another barmaid."

"Blimey. Tell her to write to Jackie's problem page. Hey, did ya see the *Monkees* episode last night? They've got a new LP out. Just been reading about it on the music page. Can't wait to get it. Says they're gunna last much longer than the Beatles, especially now that

Brian Epstein's dead. I'll lend it to you when yer get bored with that *Sgt. Pepper's Lonely Hearts Club Band* rubbish."

"Righto Lorraine," Maureen replied, mildly irritated. The Monkees were entertaining enough, but everyone knew they didn't play their own instruments and the running joke was about them being referred to as the Pre-Fab Four. But this wasn't the moment for such things. Lorraine sounded disillusioned enough for one day.

"Last thing. It says on page twenty four that we should embrace the sexual revolution and hold a love-in. What d'ya reckon?"

"I'll start on the invites. Bye."

Twelve

Rivers of Blood

It was an omen of things to come. At least that's how Cyril described the demolition of St. Mary's Parish Church, opposite the Victory.

"Can't believe it, never fought it possible. Fancy knocking a *church* down... country's goin' to the dogs."

Ricky, Maureen and her father were looking out of the living room window watching the last congregation filing out into the churchyard.

"'Ere they all come," he continued, "must 'ave been packed to the gunnels in there. Fink I'll just open up a few minutes early, in case any of 'em's in need of a bit more 'oly water before they make their way 'ome."

With that, he pinched out the last half inch of his cigarette and, flicking it expertly into the fire, rushed downstairs. Ricky gave out a token bark at the sudden burst of activity, jumped off the back of the settee and rushed after him in the vain hope it might mean *walkies*. Maureen continued to watch the stragglers dispersing until the church doors finally closed. It was hard to imagine that St Mary's would be gone soon - to be replaced by an office block of all things. Maybe Dad's right, she thought, perhaps it is an omen. Perhaps it's time to move on.

She'd overheard her parents talking about giving up the Pub a lot lately. "No pleasure in it anymore, customers always wanting something else, takings barely covering costs, *Harold Wilson*" - you name it, there were loads of reasons to chuck it all in. But while her mother seemed overjoyed at the thought of retirement, her Father was full of resentment.

Ironically, now she was older, Maureen was enjoying being behind the Bar - a fact that had not gone unnoticed by Florrie.

"She's a bit too flirty for my liking. Bad enough 'aving too much to say to the likes of Curly and Ken, but some of 'em didicoys in the Public don't need no encouragement." Quite often, Maureen would be standing only two feet away when she was being talked about. The royal 'She', used as a sentence starter, apparently made her invisible.

"She went up on the train last week - shopping. Oxford Street's not good enough anymore, no, somewhere called Carnaby Street. Come back full of that *Swinging London* stuff, whatever that means. Bought some short trousers – *queuelots* she called 'em – neiver one fing or anuvver if you ask me. Reckons she's gunna use body paint now as a peace sign. Bet she won't put it nowhere discreet neiver".

"Piece of what?"

"Oh m'gawd Cyril, *Peace* - as in *ban the bomb*."

Cyril shook his head; it was all bad news these days.

"Mouffy too now, she is. Keeps saying I don't *dig it* – whatever that's s'posed to mean. I'd like to know who's been putting ideas in 'er 'ead. That Mary Quant needs shootin'."

The fact is that Maureen had no intention of painting signs on any part of her body, but it was a good way to wind her mother up. As far as having 'ideas put in her head', it was simply the case that she was beginning to take an interest in the world outside the Victory. Ok, she may have been full of hasty opinions, but at least she was starting to question what she was told. That didn't go down well with her father. They had their first serious disagreement over the

Vietnam War and Cyril's one-time hero Muhammad Ali. Maureen supported Ali's decision to declare himself a conscientious objector, thereby avoiding the Draft. That was red rag to a bull as far as Cyril was concerned. Defending a *conchie* within his earshot was nigh on treasonable.

"I agree wiv the Yanks," he yelled. "Should 'ave been thrown in jail, never mind losin' 'is title. It's unpatriotic."

In the summer of 1967 Ali had been sentenced to five years in prison for draft evasion, but his conviction was later overturned on appeal. However he was stripped of his heavyweight title and banned from professional boxing for over three years.

It was strange to hear Cyril supporting America, because he disagreed with everything else American that year. The social phenomenon called the 'Summer of Love' sounded sordid to him. Hippies, Flower Power and Psychedelia were part of a new and dangerous vocabulary, corrupting the young and leading them astray. Drop outs practicing free love would definitely not be welcome in the Victory. Even the trustworthy BBC news was suddenly full of John, Paul, George and even Ringo heading off to the Himalayas to study transcendental meditation with a *guru* called the Maharishi Yogi. "Wot's that all about then," he said, genuinely baffled.

It all got a bit close to home when, one Saturday lunchtime, a Hare Krishna procession pitched up outside Chiesmans department store and proceeded to chant their mantra, bells jangling aloft, their burnt orange robes and bald heads visible all the way up Hamilton Road. Curly and Wink were standing on the bench peering over the top of the bevelled glass windows while Cyril and Eddie stood outside the Saloon Bar door in case there was any danger 'that lot' might stray in.

"Look at the state of 'em", Cyril said waving his hands about, "They look brainwashed. Why else would blokes wear sandals and tablecloffs, wiv paint all over their faces... and wot are they yellin' about? Same bleedin' fing over an' over again."

It was only after the tribe disappeared up the Overcliffe that everyone felt safe enough to open the doors and resume drinking.

Maureen, who had earned enough money in Woolworths by working Friday evenings and school holidays to buy a small Dansette of her own, could often be heard in her bedroom singing along to *If you're going to San Francisco, be sure to wear some flowers in your hair*. She even talked about wanting to *go* there. What Cyril must have made of *The Doors* urging her to *Come on baby light my fire*, is nobody's business. Florrie, for her part, became increasingly tight-lipped. Reports of teenagers losing their inhibitions and becoming promiscuous on *The Pill* were filling the pages of Woman's Realm. It was only a matter of time...

Having recently been promoted to the giddy heights of the 'Upstairs Office', Maureen was now responsible for Woolworth's forty or so tills; emptying, taking roll readings, tallying-up the takings, balancing the books and packing the money into the safe. Evenings were turning into late nights. She would walk around the shop floor carrying large amounts of notes and change in an old leather bag hanging over one shoulder, wondering what she would do if challenged. Mrs Baker had suggested making it a permanent job, but something was holding Maureen back from agreeing. Maybe it was waiting to see how she'd do in her 'O' levels. One thing was for sure though, she wasn't going to tell her parents about the job offer, knowing they would be all for it.

"Ya won't need 'O' levels to work in Woolwoofs," Florrie had said scornfully. "Still, look on the bright side, if ya get one, s'pose we could try Marks's or Boots's."

1968 started badly for Cyril. His pet hate, Harold Wilson, endorsed the '*I'm Backing Britain*' campaign, suggesting that everyone should work an additional half hour each day without pay. That nearly led to a riot in the Public Bar.

Student demonstrations broke out in Paris, quickly spreading around the globe. There were rumblings of revolution everywhere. A freedom movement briefly flowered behind the Iron Curtain challenging Moscow's communist stranglehold over Eastern Europe, while, in America, the Vietnam War provided the catalyst for protest amongst the young. Just the word 'student' was enough to enrage Cyril. They were constantly on the television causing havoc and mayhem and he had no time for them. He used terms like long-haired louts and lefty cowards for anyone who was the slightest bit anti-establishment. The problem for many of his generation was that young people were suddenly defining themselves as being *different* and free to hold alternative beliefs and values to those of their parents

"Should never 'ave got rid of National Service," he would growl, "ain't enough discipline in the World."

Maureen was forming views very different to those of her Father. It was hardly surprising. Vietnam was the first war to be beamed directly into peoples' living rooms, where you'd witness events in the raw and experience the stunningly disproportionate level of violence meted out against the Viet Cong and civilians alike. The carpet bombing, the napalm, the sheer scale of American power *shocked* - spawning an anti-war movement that united people of all social classes and backgrounds.

There were heated exchanges over 'The Battle of Grosvenor Square', when, in March, an anti-war demonstration culminated in bloody rioting outside the American Embassy in London. They watched in horror as protestors threw ball bearings under the hooves of police horses, cars being overturned and windows smashed, but also the police riding into the crowd and dragging people through hedges wielding their batons. It was brutal, and it brought home to a growing television audience the realisation that ordinary people weren't prepared to sit back any more.

But it was the 'race' issue that was to cement the rift between father and daughter. They often clashed horns over the situation in Rhodesia. Cyril argued forcefully that it was only right that Prime Minister Ian Smith headed the majority party in a parliament where 50 of the 66 seats were reserved for the white minority. Then in April, the US Civil Rights leader Martin Luther King was gunned down in Memphis, provoking nationwide rioting and the mobilisation of the National Guard to maintain order. This was a man who had been awarded the Nobel Peace Prize and who advocated the use of non-violent protest in support of equal rights for black people in America. Within a week of his death President Johnson had signed an important amendment to the Civil Rights Act prohibiting discrimination in the sale and rental of houses to non-whites.

That didn't go down well with Cyril. He had no time for Civil Rights and as far as he was concerned what happened in America would happen in Britain and woe betide anyone who couldn't read the writing on the wall. That was when Enoch came to his rescue.

It was still only April when the Conservative

politician Enoch Powell made a controversial speech in Birmingham in which he warned against the consequences of continued immigration to Britain from the Commonwealth. Wilson's Labour Government had introduced a Race Relations Bill which prohibited discrimination on the grounds of race in all areas of British life. Powell described it as offensive, saying that it was likely to result in 'rivers of blood' just as it had in America since the days of slavery. Well, that's the way it was reported in the papers. What he actually said was "As I look ahead, I am filled with foreboding. Like the Roman, I seem to see the River Tiber foaming with much blood."

"At least 'e's 'ad the guts to say what we all fink," was Cyril's take on it as he read out bits aloud from the Evening Standard to a packed Public Bar. "Listen to this: *'In this country in fifteen or twenty years' time the black man will have the whip hand over the white man'.* Says it right 'ere. Rivers of blood, that's what it's gunna be unless we send 'em all back!"

The more he ranted, the more he showered ash all over the counter. Maureen, who had witnessed Cyril's venom privately upstairs, now reeled in shock as she realised everyone was nodding in agreement.

"It's like watching a nation busily engaged in 'eaping up its own funeral pyre.' He says we're insane to let 'em in so as they can breed at our expense. An' 'e's right... bloody immigrants'll soon outnumber us!"

The redder his face got, the more the veins on his neck bulged out. By now, even the more reserved members of the Saloon were leaning on the counter. Most seemed enthralled by Cyril's performance, but Maureen saw the door open and a few couples quietly leaving. At that moment Florrie appeared from upstairs and stood next to her daughter. They both knew better than to speak, and although Maureen was aware that

160

her Mother shared the majority view, she sensed her discomfort. "Never discuss religion or politics from behind the Bar," she whispered sagely.

"Evening, Mr, Mrs Jenkins; still warm out?" She was speaking more loudly than usual in the vain hope that Cyril would take note. Whatever Mr and Mrs Jenkins thought, they looked ill at ease.

"We won't be able to get an 'ospital bed soon, or get our kids into schools," continued the ranter. "There'll be no jobs for us. All by bleedin' Act of Parliament! Gotta send 'em back, no uvver way. Enoch's right."

Maureen had stopped counting the number of times Cyril said "'Ave that one on me," to anyone who had something to add to the cause, and Florrie was getting concerned about their disappearing profits.

"Only one word the piccaninnies seem to know in English is *Racialist*...." Says it 'ere in black 'n white. What does that tell yer, eh?"

A hush descended over the bar. Florrie winced. Sylvia's voluptuous chest heaved. Mrs Jenkins choked on her gin and tonic. That was the final straw for Maureen. Alf Garnett was tame compared to this, she thought, fleeing upstairs in disgust and embarrassment.

Edward Heath sacked Powell from the Shadow Cabinet the day after the speech. Three days later, as the Bill was being debated in the House, a thousand dockers marched on Westminster protesting against his victimisation. They were joined by meat packers from Smithfields. Within a few days the strike had expanded to include four and a half thousand dockers. Cyril's protest consisted of a few banners made out of an old roll of lining paper and some unwanted Toby Ales pub umbrellas, using the left-over green paint from the yard. They read: *DON'T KNOCK ENOCH* and *BACK BRITAIN, NOT BLACK BRITAIN*. He gave them to Curly and his brothers Arthur and Reg, who were on

161

strike, to stick in the grass by the dock entrance. Cyril, of course, couldn't go himself. Too much to do in the pub.

"Looks like we might be moving, Nanna." Maureen was half way through her lemon meringue pie, without the meringue. (Dot couldn't be bothered with whipping egg whites anymore.)

"Really," she replied, clearly surprised. "I knew yer Mum fancied a bungalow, but never bargained on yer Dad agreeing to it. You sure?"

"Well no-one's said much to me, needless to say, but I've overheard lots of conversations. The pub isn't paying its way anymore because Dad won't move with the times. So, what's Mum been saying about bungalows then?" Maureen was intrigued, if not a little worried. The thought of *where* they would move to hadn't occurred to her.

"Yer Mum's often said 'ow loverly bungalows are. Besides, the Jenkins live in one, I've passed it on the bus. Big it is, got a bit of an upstairs - 'chalet bungalow' it's called... like in that film *Sound of Music,* you know, the one with the Nun singing on a mountain top. Maybe she's got 'er eye on one of 'em?"

Struggling to connect Julie Andrews to Gravesend, Maureen imagined what it would be like to be neighbours to the Jenkins. Joey would have to be replaced by a cockatoo for a start. And what about Ricky? He'd have to bath once in a while. It was more of a keeping-up-with-the-Jones's sort of area than the middle of town and she couldn't see how they'd be able to manage the social class act. Still, as long as it wasn't too far away she could catch the same bus to school.

Dot came up with a theory. "S'pose takin's 'ave taken a dive due to Curly moving away. That was a turn-up werenit. Is that barmaid moping, or 'as she already got 'er claws in someone new?"

Whilst negotiating terms for ending the dock strike, Curly said the redundancy package he'd been offered was too good to refuse and after talking it over with Sandra, had decided to move to a cottage near the sea at Dungeness. It came as a shock for the Public Bar crowd and especially for Sylvia who didn't get the hoped-for answer to her ultimatum.

"Pub's a lot quieter without Curly, that's for sure," answered Maureen. "Think everyone's missing him, especially Dad. Wink isn't champing at the bit at six o'clock anymore and Reenie doesn't come in on a Saturday now that Sandra's gone. As for Sylvia, well she's putting on a brave face under the circumstances."

"Doubt she'll be a shrinking violet for long", came the voice of experience.

"We've got some news, ain't we Cyril?"

Maureen looked up from her homework at her Mother's beaming face. "Been looking at bungalows. Found a nice one, ain't we?" Florrie was clearly hoping her husband would reinforce her enthusiasm.

"Well," he hesitated, "we're *lookin'*, but I ain't sure about livin' too far out."

"Oh Cyril, there's pubs everywhere," Florrie reacted angrily. Maureen could sense this was already a contentious issue. "You an' me'll go and 'ave a look tomorrow, on the bus, see what ya think Maureen."

Florrie lit a celebratory Players Weight.

"Anywhere near the Jenkins?" was all Maureen could think to ask. Florrie shook her head.

"Well, Mo, what d' ya think? Loverly ain't it?"

Florrie and Maureen were standing outside their potential new home.

"Posh area eh!" she whispered, thankfully not

waiting for a reply. "Mrs Jenkins says it's number two on the top ten most desirable locations, after Khartoum Crescent - *her* road of course. Miss Jones - you know, from the Doctors - and that bloke Jarvis, our local Conservative councillor, live just down there on Crimea Circle. Remind me to tell yer Dad that when we get back. Might cheer 'im up. Four an' 'alf fousand it costs. Take all our savings, but ya can't go wrong buying somewhere round 'ere."

Florrie was on a roll, and a determined one by the sound of it.

"How will I get to school?" Maureen asked, finally managing to get a word in edgeways.

"You'll just 'ave to walk, it's only 'alf a mile, Mrs Jenkins says. Course, *I* can get the bus to the shops, every 'alf 'our."

Maureen had stopped listening. She stared at the 1930's double-fronted bungalow and quietly hated Mrs Jenkins. It looked harmless enough, but what would it be like once the three of them were stuck inside it alone? A dull sense of dread came over her. She could hear her mother talking, but the words seemed hollow and distant. It wasn't until the bus dropped them back outside the smoky, smelly, weird and wonderfully noisy place she called home that her senses returned. She'd never thought it would be such a relief to get back to the Victory.

The next few weeks seemed to go very quickly. Cyril was permanently walking around with a clipboard under his arm and a pencil behind his ear. "Brewery'll want a complete inventory of all the improvements I've made. No uvver pub's got a bottle shunter, let alone the buzzer system."

"When ya gunna tell the customers?" Florrie asked more than once.

"Can't 'ave 'em jumpin' ship when they know. Not till we're gone anyway". He moved her out of the way of the tankards being counted.

Maureen suspected the real reason was more to do with putting off the inevitable. Eventually when he could put it off no longer, Cyril broke the news to the assembled crowd of customers and staff.

"Are ya moving on somewhere else then Cyril? Just tell us where and we'll all be there," said a loyal Ken.

"Semi-retirement," confirmed the soon-to-be ex-Landlord. "Got a few irons in the fire somewhere, but it's under wraps at the mo'." His voice had dropped to a whisper.

Maureen had no idea what her Father's bravado was all about and suspected he hadn't a clue either.

"Well, *I'm* looking forward to putting me feet up!" Florrie said emphatically.

No one asked Maureen, which was probably just as well.

At the farewell party all the regulars signed a scroll with *Best wishes on your retirement* engraved on the top. A collection had been made and Mr Jenkins made a speech about how things would never be the same, whilst handing over a wall clock in the shape of a star. Eddie took some photos with his box brownie when Cyril played the piano, to rapturous applause, thrilling the audience for the last time with his own renditions of Russ Conway and Mrs Mills, wanky finger and all. Maureen danced with Gerry (who held on a little too tightly) Wink, Sid, Ken and Spud whilst there was generally much talk of get togethers, reunions and parties to come. Cyril promised to pass on his varied expertise to anyone interested (just to keep his hand in you understand). Florrie warmed up some sausage rolls for old times' sake and used up the last of the pickled onions, eggs and gherkins. Ricky sat on his flap wearing his hat, basking in the adoration of his fans unaware that this was for the last time too. Maureen rang the bells and yelled *Time Ladies and Gents!* at Cyril's request, to a loud cheer from both bars. Overcome, Florrie shed a tear and Mrs Jenkins took her out to the Ladies to help powder her nose.

When Eddie was ready to walk Sylvia home, Cyril filled three glasses with Johnnie Walker whisky and fumbled his way through a genuine speech about appreciating their loyalty. Eddie flung his arms around his embarrassed employer. He said he didn't fancy working for anyone new and had decided it was time to retire. He wouldn't be coming back.

Cyril, Florrie and Maureen cleaned up in silence, the noise of the packed pub still ringing in their ears. Florrie eventually headed upstairs with the takings while Cyril and Maureen went for a walk down Hamilton Road. The air was crisp, but dry.

"Well Mo, just the official 'andover in the morning and that's it."

Even in the dark, Maureen could tell from his shaky voice that her Father was devastated. He'd been talking about 'throwing in the towel' for so long that it had gained its own unstoppable momentum. They stood by the old Town Pier looking at the lights bouncing off the water. The cast iron creaked as the waves lapped at the pillars. There was nothing more to say. Cyril lit up and flicked the match into the river. Maureen doubted they'd ever do this again.

Someone from the brewery came and checked Cyril's lists as he boxed up a few selected mementos of life in the Victory. With the papers signed the new landlord stepped up to the plate.

"Seems mighty strange sittin' 'ere," Cyril said, his

voice suddenly sounding small and insignificant. "Fancy a final Guinness Flo?"

"Go on then," nodded Florrie, much more at ease than he was. But Maureen certainly felt strange. All three were sitting at the round table by the window in the Saloon. It was lunchtime. Joyce was behind the bar as usual, looking to all intents and purposes as if nothing had changed. But changed it had, and quite dramatically. Maureen wondered fleetingly if she would get on with her new employers. Sylvia too. Not Theresa though. She'd left some months ago when Cyril told her that he couldn't keep both evening barmaids. Luckily she'd walked straight into a job at The Nelson. Maureen had bumped into her in Dolcis and heard how classy the customers were there.

Cyril returned from the bar with the drinks and sat fidgeting, checking his change. Maureen was dimly aware that her mother was talking about wallpaper and carpets. Looking up at the door every time it opened she willed Mr and Mrs Jenkins to turn up to ease the tension.

When they did eventually arrive, Mr and Mrs J politely declined a drink from Cyril, suggesting instead that they all got off as quickly as possible. They didn't want the removal men to be kept waiting. Florrie picked up Ricky and balanced him on her hip; Maureen carried a screeching Joey in a small cage borrowed from Mrs J. Cyril picked up the pub sign he'd taken down from above the door at the very last minute: *Cyril Albert Cooke licensed to sell wines, spirits, beers and tobacco* and tucked it under his arm. He waved to the few morning customers and shouted "It's all yours" to the new Landlord and his wife. Sid the butcher was standing in his doorway. He'd wiped the blood off his hands especially to shake Cyril's.

The menagerie bundled into Mr Jenkins' pride and

joy – a green Morris Minor Traveller with its distinctive wooden trim. "Last one for the *Skylark*," he joked. "Fares please." But it fell flat. Just drive, Maureen thought, fighting back the tears.

It only took ten minutes to get to Disraeli Drive.

A world away.

Thirteen

Bungalow Blues

"It looks smaller than I remember," Florrie said, tying Ricky's lead to the kitchen door.

"Optical illusion, Cyril replied matter-of-factly. "Rooms always look bigger when they're empty."

"But that's just it, they're *not* empty. Never realised we 'ad such big stuff. Where's it all gunna go?"

Florrie was getting flustered. Mr and Mrs Jenkins had bid a hasty retreat after dropping them off, full of excuses for not coming in. From here on in, it seemed, they were on their own. The removal men, having filled up the rooms, were now concentrating their efforts on the circular hallway.

"Did ya 'ave to bring the cellar thermometer? It's no wonder the men don't know which room to put it in… and what's the point of the keg bung mallet?"

"Paid good money for 'em, not 'aving any other buggers take advantage," Cyril snapped back.

Maureen entered with some trepidation and with a sick feeling in her stomach. This was the first time she'd seen the inside of her new home. Joey was squawking loudly after his car journey and throwing himself against the bars of the small cage, so she put him down in what she guessed was the dining room. Not that the term had ever been used by anyone in her family before. Probably just be called the 'back room' from now on, she thought. Spotting the bird's normal cage and stand she busied herself rearranging his own furniture and filling the feeder with a fresh helping of Trill. Relieved to be back in familiar territory he flew from side to side before straightening his feathers in his mirror and settling down to appreciate the space. Glad someone's happy, Maureen pondered, miserably.

Back in the hall, Florrie was still in shock over what was continuing to fill the bungalow. Cyril, having given up trying to hide various items, was now re-directing the removal men up the side of the bungalow to the garage at the top of the garden. Well, it said *garage* on the estate agent's description, but, in truth, it was a converted Anderson shelter left over from World War Two. Thankfully, Cyril had never learned to drive; 'not interested,' being his formal declaration on the subject. 'Too chicken more like,' in Ethel's eyes. Just as well, as there was barely enough room for a bubble car, let alone anything else, and even then you'd have trouble getting in and out.

Maureen strolled out of the French doors and headed up the garden path to be greeted by a removal man carrying a dartboard-sized tub of water which was sloshing about and overflowing onto his shoes.

"What the dickins is this?" he said, confused. "More to the point, does it go in the garage, or out?"

"I'd stick it inside as quickly as possible if I were you," Maureen told him, raising her eyebrows and looking back to see if her mother was watching.

"Get ya drift… right. Just that giant mural to unwedge from the van. Reckon we deserve a cuppa after that. Make mine two sugars, luv."

As she wandered back down the garden she could hear her mother yelling "Cyril, Cyril!" Tensions were clearly rising and it didn't sound like things were going to plan.

"Oh there you are, Maureen. 'Ave yer seen yer Dad? 'e's scarpered."

This was one of those situations that required diplomacy. Whatever you say, make it sound good, even if you don't mean it.

"Well he can't have gone that far, can he?"

"That's it. I might've guessed you'd take 'is side. This is *my* time now. Been waiting years to get 'ere an' I'm not 'aving you spoil me moment."

Maureen shrank back at the force of her Mother's anger.

"Go an' find 'im, an' when ya do, ask 'im what the bleeding 'ell he intends to do wiv the THIS WAY TO THE GENTS sign. Tell 'im I'll stick his bloody arrow somewhere he won't like it."

Cyril by this time was happily re-arranging the 'garridge' into a smaller version of the Victory. Having found somewhere to hang the bell, a few of the darts trophies were now perched on a shelf above. He had made sure the legs of his bar stool found their usual groove in the coconut mat on the cement floor and was sitting down admiring his work. As Maureen entered he lit a Rothmans and flicked the first flecks of ash into his favourite Toby Ales ashtray. "Pass us a Pale Ale, Sook," he said, nodding towards a pile of sacks cleverly disguising a crate. Taking a bottle opener out of his waistcoat pocket, he carefully prized off the top. "Cheers," the ex-landlord said, raising his glass to an unseen pub audience. Wiping the froth from his mouth, his shoulders began to shake and he started to laugh. That set Maureen off. Soon the laughter became unstoppable. Cyril nearly fell off his stool and Maureen had to hold on to her sides as they were hurting so much. At that point the fridge mirror fell over, cracking the glass. "Whoops," cried Cyril, "another omen." With that they dissolved into hysterics.

"S'pose we'd better be getting back," Maureen spluttered. "Mum won't be happy."

"Time Ladies and Gentlemen, *please*! 'aven't ya got *new* 'omes to go to?" Cyril announced, ringing his bell as he stood up. He closed the door of the New Victory and wandered off down the garden. "Time to face the music," Maureen heard him mumble under his breath.

Florrie was busy moving bits of furniture around, too engrossed to chastise anyone. The removal men had gone and the silence was deafening. Ricky had been let off his lead and was rushing from room to room, no doubt looking for the stairs. Maureen sympathised with him, wishing they could both escape upstairs to make their exile tolerable. As it was, there was nowhere to hide; the rooms were small - her own bedroom being the smallest. Something else disturbed her - every door, with the fortunate exception of the bathroom, was glass. Teak frames with thick vertical panels of reeded glass to be precise. It was actually possible to stand in the hall and locate everyone, even if they looked fuzzy.

"Blimey," Cyril said, "won't do to 'ave too many pints… makes yer eyes go funny."

Florrie soon worked out that by pressing your nose right up against the glass, the image on the other side became quite clear.

"Come on Mo." Cyril's distorted shape loomed into view through the kitchen door. "Let's go out an' sample our new local."

Maureen was only too pleased to get out. After all, it had been eight hours since they'd last been in a pub. Florrie was too busy looking for eiderdowns and ashtrays to take any interest, so father and daughter strolled alone to the nearest pub, the Lord Tennyson. It was good to be in the open air, but what pleased Cyril most was that it only took ten minutes to reach the *Lounge* door. "Ooo," he chortled, "that's posh." But they didn't stay long. Realising that everyone inside was a total stranger made them suddenly feel self-conscious and uncomfortable. It was all too modern with matching wicker chairs and a carpet, nothing like what they were used to.

The first few days went quite quickly, sorting out stuff and deciding what could be squeezed into small spaces. The front room had polystyrene ceiling tiles, a fluorescent tube light, a deep red carpet and a gas fire which Cyril had serious doubts about as there seemed to be a permanent layer of condensation between the secondary double-glazing panes. By the time the sideboard, settee and armchair were in, the room was chock-a-block.

"Maybe we should 'ave waited till we checked the size of the room before we got the furniture from Smokey," Florrie said in retrospect. "Smells a bit too," she added, stuffing Izal toilet freshener blocks between the cushions.

In the back room the table was pushed against the wall, with a chair at each end. No need for a third, Cyril said, since he had no intention of eating his 'grub' in company. Joey lived in one corner, the telly in another with the remaining armchair in the prime viewing position. Maureen's desk, blocking the French doors, completed the picture.

"What do we need 'em opened for?" was Cyril's inevitable comment. "We got a back door to go out of. Besides, they're a security risk."

So there it was; an unfriendly front room and an overcrowded back.

Maureen's bedroom, which had been described as 'a cosy 8' x 6' nursery' on the estate agent's details, was confirmed by its *Thunderbirds* wallpaper. Despite valiant efforts on everyone's part, no way could be found to get the wardrobe and dressing table to fit. They had to be 'temporarily' housed in the hall, meaning that Maureen had to collect her clothes with her parents' criss-crossing in front of her.

"First job, Mo," Cyril said, cheerily brandishing his mallet, "I'm gunna dismantle 'em and make a built-in wardrobe with all the bits. Won't be enough room for a door on it, but I reckon it'll look real trendy wiv a pull-out rail. Might 'ave to stand on yer bed to get yer outfits out, but heh-ho, there 'as to be sacrifices in the name of fashion."

Lying on her bed surrounded by images of Tracy Island and Parker in the Rolls, Maureen privately wished he'd think of replacing the wallpaper as his first job. She pictured the shade of varnish he would use to enhance his carpentry. Why can't it just be white, she thought? No, not a hope. Cyril was a mariner and mariners prefer boat varnish.

By the end of the week Ricky still hadn't calmed down. Missing his usual audience, he compensated by barking loudly. Also, totally unused to using grass or empty flower beds as the site of his early morning constitutional, he was becoming constipated. Florrie took him to the vet, who gave him a tablet to calm him down. It occurred to Maureen that Cyril could do with one too given that he was constantly circling the hall wondering why no one from the Victory had been in touch.

"Early days, Cyril," Florrie suggested, "s'pect they're leaving it till we've settled in."

Cyril remained unconvinced. "Think I'll just 'ave a wash and a shave and get the bus into town. Might pop in an' 'ave a lunchtime 'alf. Ken'll be starved of company by now."

After the third lunchtime visit in a row, he returned surprisingly early on the ten past two, in high dudgeon.

"Can't take a bit of criticism. All I said was the beer looked cloudy and tasted a bit flat. There was no need to fly off the 'andle. I even said I'd be 'appy to pop down the cellar and give it the once over... check they'd added enough finings to the barrel, or not got it on the level, or summink."

"Oh Cyril," said Florrie with a sigh. "Why can't you just keep yer mouff shut?"

"Well, 'e needs to be told 'ow to do things proper. That cellar's been running like a well-oiled engine room fer sixteen years."

"Not yer problem anymore. Gotta let 'im get on wiv it. Did ya see any of our regulars?"

Florrie offered her husband a consolatory cigarette to ease the pain, but Cyril wasn't going to be put down by someone telling him to keep his opinions to himself.

"Yeh, most of 'em, all suckin' up they were. Ken was lappin' up every word. Even Joyce was moving a bit quicker. But I did 'ave a quiet word wiv Mr J in the Gents. He said the evenin's ain't so great. Anyway I shan't be going in there again, not even if 'e begs me... An' wot's more 'e's lost the chance of callin' on me exspiteese. 'E'll be sorry, you wait."

"Did Mr Jenkins say anything about 'is wife?" enquired Florrie picking out the only snippet that interested her.

"Conversation's a bit limited at the urinal, but 'e did say that they'd come round to see the 'ouse soon. So you'd betta get that smell out of the settee."

Venturing out less, Cyril got on with his carpentry projects. The wardrobe, of sorts, was duly built and miraculously turned out to be white thanks to Florrie putting her foot down. Unfortunately, there were screws and bolts sticking out all over the place which had a habit of ruining Maureen's tights whilst she was trying to look at herself in the mirror. Florrie took it upon herself to choose her daughter's new wallpaper and went for a purple psychedelic look.

As an added surprise, she spent the days while Maureen was at school making a patchwork bedspread.

Ingeniously, having decided that her old Crimplene dresses were no longer *Mod,* she used a triangular wooden template, shaped by Cyril, to cut round and then randomly match the pieces - some still bearing their telltale cigarette burn holes. The effect was overpowering, particularly first thing in the morning when trying to focus without her glasses - not made any easier by the difficulty of locating the exit amid the swimming scenery caused by the reeded glass.

Meanwhile, impressed with his handiwork, and determined to put his light oak varnish to good use somewhere, Cyril fashioned three wooden flying ducks for the chimney breast in the front room, while the back room got his free-standing fish. A few days later Florrie discovered him standing in the garden holding his old beer order clipboard.

"Smokey's got in a job lot of perspex sheets," he told her innocently. "Perfick fer a lean-to. Gunna stick one on the back and grow tomatoes. He's deliverin' 'em tomorra. Just drawin' up some plans."

"'Ope yer looking in the paper for jobs," sniffed Florrie. "Need to start thinking about it soon. It was only me that was s'posed to be retired now, remember?"

"Leave me be, woman. All in good time" he snapped back. "I've still got me irons in the fire, don't forget"

"Mmmm…," Florrie murmured, unconvinced. Cyril's 'irons' were reliant on leads promised by the Victory regulars and there was still no word from any of them.

"So, wotsit like then. Must be a bit strange not being in the middle of town. Is yer bedroom bigger?"

Lorraine was trying out the new phone number.

"There's nowhere to be on my own and my

176

bedroom's barely got enough room for a bed. There's glass doors everywhere and I've hardly had any sleep due to my Dad grinding his teeth all night long. There's no room for my Nan and we haven't seen a soul from the pub since we've been here."

"Must be a bit of a shock. S'pose that's why 'is teeth are all worn away. Was probably doing it in the pub, but you couldn't 'ear it over the traffic. Anyway I thought about you when I checked out Marjorie Proops' agony page in the Mirror this morning - some girl lookin' fer advice on 'ow to meet more people."

"Yeh, was the answer any use?"

"She recommended joining the Women's Royal Army Corps."

"Blimey, bit drastic. Gotta go, Mum's waving at me through the door. Making too much noise... bye."

The smoke was thick in the back room. Florrie and her two sisters were watching Richard Chamberlain save yet another life in a repeat of *Dr. Kildare*. Never having had much time to watch television before, Florrie had become obsessed with the gritty details of every plot. There was no way she'd miss *Peyton Place* or *The Forsyte Saga* and Cyril would have to wait until the coast was clear before he had any chance of watching *'Z' Cars*, *The Saint*, a new series called *Dad's Army*, and the smalmy Hughie Green in *Opportunity Knocks*. Come to think of it, it was thanks to that other new programme *Gardener's World* that Cyril's lean-to construction came to house his famed giant tomatoes.

Maureen, on the other hand, tried to keep out of the back room. There weren't enough seats for a start and the cigarette smoke seemed to accumulate in the polystyrene tiles, pervading the space with a sickly, pungent smell. The two programmes she'd been used to watching on her own at the Pub, *The Prisoner* and *The Man from Uncle* had been declared unfathomable and were no longer on the viewing schedule. Her new bedroom was too small to house her Dansette, so she'd managed to wangle the right to play music in the front room. You'd hardly call it 'her space', but at least it gave her somewhere to escape.

Cyril was driven mad by the fabulous guitar intro to *Voodoo Child,* Jimi Hendrix representing just about everything he hated about the younger generation. Jack Bruce, Eric Clapton and Ginger Baker (aka *Cream*) didn't fare any better and there were regular rants about hippies and druggies the moment Maureen stuck up pictures of the Beatles, or anyone else for that matter that skipped off to India to commune with the Maharishi Yogi. He even ripped one poster off the new wardrobe claiming "blasphemy on me white paint." Another time, when Maureen returned from Maidstone Market exhilarated over having bought a bright green Afghan coat, his verdict was "You look like a bleedin' Christmas tree." Hurt, she defiantly wore it until the smell and weight, when wet, finally got the better of her and her crushed velvet trousers.

"Go on, ask 'em. What have you got to lose?" Lorraine said, elbowing Maureen during assembly.

"You don't know what it's like. I can picture their faces now. They won't talk to me for weeks if it all goes wrong."

"What can go wrong? It's only a bit of a party. Be brave, besides I've already invited the boys."

"Bloody hell, Lorr, you might have waited."

Suddenly the weight of the world was resting on Maureen's shoulders. She practiced her speech all the way home.

"Mum, can I have a few friends round to listen to music… you know, a bit of a bungalow warming?" She deliberately avoided the word *party.*

"How many exactly?"

At least that's not a 'no', Maureen registered.

"There'll be six of us altogether, in the front room… so we don't disturb you."

"S'pose you'll be wanting sausage rolls?"

"Lovely."

Lorraine came early. She brought her brother's lava lamp to help create the right atmosphere. "The constantly moving, heated wax floating in oil will give a mesmerising, hypnotic effect," she said, reading from the box as she plugged it in. They both stared as the vivid blue rocket-shaped device warmed up and blobbed its first blob. "Think we might need a bit more than that to do the trick," Maureen said with a laugh.

They arranged the furniture so there was room for the Dansette on the coffee table. Meanwhile Florrie seemed quite happy warming up the oven. "Just like old times," she said heading back to the kitchen. The girls giggled away trying on different outfits - single file in the bedroom due to the lack of space. Maureen settled on a gold spandex top and a black suede maxi skirt with fringing. Lorraine went for a hippie look in flowery kaftan and beads. Throwing caution to the wind, they even lit joss sticks in the fireplace.

"Bloody 'ell, what's that 'orrible smell?" Cyril complained after returning from planting his *Big Boy* tomato seeds in the half finished lean-to. "Fink I'll go down the Tennyson fer a pint, I'm feelin' a bit sick."

Rob was the first to arrive, long players under his arm, closely followed by Mike and Sally. Chris came last with a carrier bag bulging with what looked suspiciously like beer. Maureen rushed to the front door and herded them into the front room, but she wasn't quick enough. Florrie made a bee-line for the carrier. "I'll take that," she said, "I've already got some shandy."

Turning to Maureen with a petrified glare she added, "You never said there'd be *boys*! Good job yer Dad's gone out now."

Rob pushed the door shut with his foot and, fully intent on his mission, started sorting his record collection. "Thought we'd start where it all began," he announced. "First two singles are *Arnold Layne* and *See Emily play*."

They all listened politely before Lorraine broke the ice with "Can't really dance to it, can yer?"

"Moving right on," Rob responded, mildly put out. "Here's *Piper at the gates of dawn*, with Syd, just before Dave joined; then *Saucerful of secrets* which I've just got. John Peel says it's like a religious experience. They're bound to do this in Hyde Park. Can't wait. Get the lights, Chris. We'll appreciate it better in the dark. "

Whether or not anyone besides Rob was appreciating Pink Floyd in all their glory Maureen couldn't tell, but from the shadowy movements of Sally and Mike, it was obvious their thoughts were elsewhere. When the glare of a torch started flashing to and fro through the glass door panels, Maureen became concerned. When it settled against the glass and an eerie bodyless face in fuzzy silhouette appeared above it, Chris nearly had a fit. "What the hell is that?" he yelled.

Suddenly the door burst open and a body fell inside, dropping its cigarette onto the carpet. Everyone stunned into silence.

"Turn that 'orrible noise off!" a demented Florrie screamed whilst picking herself up, "or you'll all get pregnant."

Chris sensibly did the gentlemanly thing and stamped out the burning cigarette before the hole in the carpet got any bigger.

"Dave Gilmour must know something we don't," Rob said tapping the side of his nose after she'd gone to get the sausage rolls.

"Better watch the *vibes* next week," said Mike slurping on his shandy. "I'm too young to get pregnant."

Lorraine had to leave the lava lamp to cool down that night.

"Think it went well," she said unconvincingly, tucking the empty box under her arm.

"Mmm. Don't imagine they'll want to come here again though." Maureen was picking out pastry crumbs from the record player's nooks and crannies. "It's hardly the 'den of iniquity' Mr Jones calls our fifth year common room."

"Yeh, well I s'pose it's hard to compete with all that smoking, gambling and loud music. See ya tomorrow. Bye. "

"Well I'll be blowed, that's a turn up for the books," said an excited Florrie putting down the receiver. "Cyril, Cyril, wake up!" She was shaking her husband who was sleeping in the chair, grinding his teeth. "Blind o' Reilly, I'm gunna make an appointment fer ya to get those teeth taken out. Drivin' me mad. False ones fer you now, especially if yer gunna get a job. You need to look *respectable*, not like a tramp."

"Bloody 'ell woman, leave me alone. I'm doin' all this work on the 'ouse fer you. Who was on the blower then?"

"Someone from the Victory. 'ave a guess who?"

"See I knew they'd be in touch sooner or later." Cyril leapt up, tripping over the pouffe. "When do they want me to be ready? Better 'ave a wash and shave. Can yer lay out me waistcoat while I'm in the barfroom. Is Wink coming as well as Ken?"

"Stop, Cyril. It wasn't them. It was a woman"

"Mrs J then. I knew the Jenkins would be itchin' to come round to see me improvements. When they comin'? We could take 'em to the Tennyson for a drink."

"Nope, not them either."

Cyril sat back down, kicking the pouffe out of the way in disgust.

"Actually, it was Sylvia. Ringing to talk to me. Wants an 'eart to 'eart. She's coming on the bus tomorrow."

Cyril's face was a picture.

It turned out that Sylvia was finding it hard to get over Curly moving away. There hadn't even been a postcard. With Eddie gone too, there was no one to walk her home and, to top it all, the new landlady was very forward with the male customers, which put Sylvia's nose out of joint. Florrie was strangely sympathetic and so an unlikely alliance was formed.

From then on Sylvia started to visit regularly – the only one of the Victory's old crew that ever did.

Fourteen

The Night I Went Blind

As the weeks wore on, the isolation felt by Cyril and Florrie seemed to grow in intensity. They were like fish out of water. Florrie was used to a punishing routine with no time to herself. Cyril missed the company and the feeling of self-importance. *He'd* been filling the time painting over all the inoffensive wallpaper. Deemed too bland, the embossed magnolia swirls in the hall were now a sizzling orange, clashing nicely with the red carpet. *She'd* discovered a surprising interest in tennis. Two weeks watching Billie Jean King win at *Wimpleton* - in glasses not dissimilar to Maureen's - had kept her enthralled. For Maureen, the myopic Billie Jean's rise to fame and fortune in the face of such adversity offered a glimmer of hope for the future.

Unexpectedly, the pair seemed to be getting on a bit better away from *The Victory*, Cyril's relaxed approach to finding a job being the only flashpoint. Sadly, for Joey the Budgie, persistent company had taken its toll. The first casualty of claustrophobia, he was found dead on the floor of his cage early one morning. Cyril buried him under the lean-to to prevent Ricky from digging him up.

"Don't think we'll get another one," said Florrie mournfully. "Too much of an imposition."

Hanging up her coat on her return from school, Maureen overheard Cyril asking Florrie something in the kitchen.

"What d'ya reckon on Bournemouth, then?"

There didn't seem to be any response from Florrie, not that that stopped Cyril.

"Now we've got a bit more time wiv our little girl, I fought it might be nice to go as a family, togevver like."

Still no response.

"Always a first time fer everyfink. We can all muck in togevver, to keep cost down. There's summink called a 'sofabed' in the kitchen. We can be self-caterin' so we don't 'ave to eat the dodgy grub. Loads of fings to do – bars for me to sample, Bingo - yer favourite, and top notch shows for Mo. Can't go wrong."

Maureen stood silently watching her father wandering back and forth brandishing a brochure with *Bournemouth Bournanza* on the front. Her mother was standing with her back to him at the sink, putting out her cigarette under the running tap. Neither seemed aware of their daughter's presence.

"Cyril, we 'aven't got any spare cash for an 'oliday. All our money's in 'ere." She waggled her finger at the ceiling. "And what's more, now we own our own 'ouse, we're not entitled to any benefits. We're not old enough to get old age pension and besides you're s'posed to be getting a job, aren't ya?"

If anything was designed to rile Cyril it was being told what he was supposed to be doing. Even worse was talk of benefits and pensions because that brought the Labour Government into the conversation and would set him off on a rant. When Florrie next managed to get a word in, it was all about how she'd never had anything new. How the furniture had come from Smokey, most with its wartime *Utility* mark still on it. Except for the sideboard of course, that had come from Dot. Too big for her flat, Ethel had seen fit to charge her own brother five quid for it.

184

"Don't talk to me about that sideboard" Cyril spat. "Ripped off by me own sister, so they can 'ave all new stuff in their bloody council 'ouse."

Finally noticing Maureen, Florrie saw her opportunity to escape and motioned to her to retreat into the back room. She looked worried. By the time Cyril had calmed down she had smoked two more cigarettes in quick succession. Maureen was bewildered. All her childhood she'd daydreamed about going on holiday with both her parents, but now aged seventeen it was more like a nightmare.

At that point, Cyril's head appeared round the door. "Been thinkin' about the job business, as a matter a fact," he said. "There's a pub I've got me eye on in Whistable. Would be completely different being Landlord by the seaside. Might be able to catch up wiv old Curly. I'll 'ave to look at a map. See 'ow far away 'e is."

Florrie went very pale and gripped the edge of the chair. She looked straight ahead. But there was worse to come.

"I know you don't want to be involved so much Flo, so my idea is that I run the Pub with Mo. You can stick to the cheese rolls. I'll do all the front of house stuff and she can do the ordering and keep the books straight. She's gunna leave school in a few weeks anyway and this is much better than Woolwoofs."

Florrie didn't say a word. Maureen stifled a gasp.

"Gotta move fast on this one I reckon. It's near the front."

Realising he was getting nowhere with his wife, Cyril now turned his attention to his daughter.

"I remember going there on 'oliday wiv me Mum and Dad. Let's get the train on Saturday, Sook, see what we think."

Maureen was dumbfounded. The prospect of a

185

holiday was bad enough, but this was unimaginable. Just because she might not have made any plans yet, didn't mean that running a pub with her Dad was on the agenda.

There was no point in arguing once Cyril had the bit between his teeth, but it was plain to see that her Mother was devastated. The bungalow had been her dream for years and it was inconceivable that it was going to be lost after only a few months.

To keep Cyril happy, Maureen agreed to go. Florrie went into the doldrums. Walking from the bus to the station, Cyril had quite a spring in his step despite battling with an umbrella determined to blow inside out. By the time they'd crossed the bridge and got on the train, rain was pounding on the windows, but at least the carriage was pleasingly warm. Cyril talked incessantly throughout the Medway towns and on to the coast. Maureen stared at the bleak scenery, occasionally catching uninspiring glimpses of the murky sea.

"S'pose it's best to see it on a day like this then, without the rose tinted specs, eh," Cyril quipped. Maureen wished she didn't have to get off at the next station. As it was, walking against the wind through the town risked losing the map. It took a while to find anyone to ask for directions, but finally they fell upon *The Fisherman's Tavern* with its rattling FOR SALE board.

'Oh my God,' she thought as they entered the dark, smoky, empty bar. 'This is even worse than the Victory'.

The existing landlord grabbed Cyril's hand and shook it violently, his desperation all too evident. He took them on a whirlwind tour of the bars, kitchen, cellar and accommodation upstairs. Greasy floors, choking ashtrays and overflowing drip trays. Congealed jellied eels, welded chips, warm, sickly cellar and unmade beds. Whatever enthusiasm Cyril started out with had waned by lunchtime. A look at the books was the final straw.

"Pub's a dump," he confirmed on their return. "Wouldn't touch it wiv a bargepole. It's losing money 'and over fist, that's why the geezer wants shot of it. Be a mug takin' that on."

"Didn't go well, then?" said Florrie, unable to hide her relief.

"Nah. In fact Whitstable's a dump all round. No amusements or pier, or sand fer that matter. Even the Woolwoofs ain't a patch on ours. Can't see it's got much of a future. Never be a Ramsgate. To top it all, we couldn't get any decent grub, could we Maureen. No cockles or whelks, only raw oysters. No-one's gunna eat 'em, just the smell made me feel sick."

"Looks like you'll 'ave to get that job then," added Florrie with a wry smile.

"'Ave you got the foggiest idea what that was all about?" Lorraine was scratching her head as they emerged from the gloom of the Majestic. They'd just endured Stanley Kubrick's *2001: A Space Odyssey.*

"Nope," answered Maureen. "I was nearly dropping off, thanks to last night."

"We 'ad a laugh though. You likely to see that bloke again?"

"Dunno. Hope so. Not that I could see him all that well without my glasses. Supposed to be going out tomorrow."

"Let's go for a coffee. I wanna hear all the details."

"You don't like coffee…"

They pushed their way through the crowd hanging around outside the Ritz café and fumbled their way amid the cigarette smoke to an empty table.

"Go on then, spill the beans," Lorraine continued

187

eagerly. "Last I saw was you dancing with 'im, then you disappeared in the back room where it was all dark. So did you find out much between the snogs?"

"Give me a chance," Maureen replied, unwinding a thick scarf now too hot to wear inside.

"Bloody 'ell. Is that a love bite? 'E didn't waste no time then. Right, start from when we were sitting on the stairs and they all turned up in Harrington jackets. I'm all ears." Lorraine shuffled on her seat to get comfortable.

"Well... his name's Mike, he's nearly eighteen, goes to the Grammar and yes, before you ask, he's a good kisser."

"I can see. You're gunna 'ave to wear a polo neck for a few days to 'ide that. Anyway, go on…"

"We chatted on the stairs, he asked me to dance to *Sitting on the dock of the bay,* but I had a bit of trouble following him in the crowd. I hope I was dancing with the right bloke."

"Ha, ha very funny."

"You can laugh, but it's quite scary when you're as blind as me. Anyway, once we'd shuffled into the dark, he couldn't see either, so it was OK."

"So, where are you meeting him tomorrow?" By this time Lorraine was more excited than Maureen.

The girls had been going to discos and the odd party for a few months now, but with no success. Maureen decided it was her glasses that were holding her back. Her new plan of campaign was to familiarise herself with important landmarks in advance - toilets, the way out, fire exits etc and then pop her glasses into her handbag. The main drawback was having to drop her bag into the pile in the middle of the floor surrounded by dancing females. With the current fashion for bright green accessories, she'd have to wait for hers to be the last one left to positively identify it, and run the risk of being trampled in the process. Anyway it had worked out so far.

"He's coming to pick me up at the bungalow."

"Bloody 'ell Mo, yer mad. Yer Mum'll 'ave him for breakfast. That's assuming yer Dad don't bore him to death first."

"I know, I had to think fast. Shock got to me. Couldn't believe he wanted to see me again. If I'd said meet here, or in a pub, I wouldn't have known who he was cos I don't really know what he looks like. So I panicked. "

"See the problem. Gotta go Mo. Last bus. Good luck."

On that note Lorraine downed the last dregs of her hot chocolate and flew out the door.

Maureen walked to her bus stop opposite the Victory. She watched the lights of passing cars dancing across the pub's green tiles. How long had it been? Seemed like an eternity. Why not just walk inside the Saloon? After all she'd probably know everyone there. No doubt Mr and Mrs Jenkins would be sitting in their corner, by now firm friends with the new Landlord and Landlady. Or maybe the Public Bar, more reliable. Ken or Wink would buy her a drink. Molly might even be playing darts, or Sylvia would be there and they could chat about her daughters...

The last bus to Ottoman Square loomed into view. She stepped up into the warm, paid her fare and glanced back as her old home disappeared into the night.

Cyril was still up when she got in. He was watching the news, feet up on the coffee table, enjoying a pale ale. "This year just don't stop. Now Bobby Kennedy's gone 'n got shot, trying to be President like 'is brother. Wanna Golden Wonder?"

Maureen declined the crisps and headed for her glass door. Would the news of a boy interested in taking her out surpass the death of a Presidential candidate? Most definitely, she thought. Undressing in a tight corner between the wardrobe and bed (the only place completely out of view from the hall) she slid into bed. Sleep was slow to come. Thoughts of Hal the computer controlling her spaceship with a group of Grammar School boys leering through the porthole, floated around in her head. Bang...bang... suddenly Florrie appears from nowhere, spots the love bite and shoots at them. She misses, getting the President's brother instead…

It took exactly ten hours for her to pluck up courage to tell her Mother that a boy was going to be standing on the doorstop in less than sixty minutes. Florrie nearly choked on her cup of tea and grabbed for her cigarettes. "But it's Sunday," was all she could think of saying.

Maureen had wondered if it was going to be worth the pain and the effort anyway, as she wasn't sure Mike would hang around long after seeing her wearing glasses.

"Thank God yer Dad's gone to Dot's to fix 'er safety chains. Effel's on the warpath again, uvverwise we'd never live it down. Grammar, you say?"

They both circled the hall until the doorbell rang. Florrie pipped Maureen to the post; opening the door just enough to get a good initial look. She stood in front of her daughter. Oh my God, thought Maureen, that's it. No hope now.

"I wan' 'er back by eleven, right," was all she said.

So Maureen was off on her first date. Immensely relieved Mike hadn't made a bolt for it. They walked to his friend's house. She kept giving him sideways glances to see what he looked like with the benefit of

20/20 vision. Quite tall, slim, nice hair, buttoned down Ben Sherman shirt - not bad at all. Conversation seemed to be a tad stilted, but that's to be expected on a first date, she thought; unaware of the route they were taking.

"Here we are then," said Mike eventually, pushing open a massive gate. "Sorry if it's all a bit intense inside."

Maureen realised that she was close to the posh looking Golf Links she passed on her way to school and that she was not at all prepared for what the evening might have in store. Swallowing hard, she followed Mike to the large front door. Stuart, one of the group from the party, welcomed them in, handed out lit candles and led them to a dark room with a decidedly hippieish aroma. "Sit down," whispered their host, "we're about to start. Trevor's gone for the words."

The pungent joss sticks engulfed her airways and made her eyes smart. Mike pulled her down onto a large cushion on the floor. Counting the candles, there appeared to be several bodies on similar cushions around the room. Maureen imagined the headline in the Daily Mirror. *Religious cult carry out ritualistic killings near posh Golf Links.*

All feelings of apprehension were soon alleviated when Stuart revealed that this was a Simon and Garfunkel appreciation session. *Bookends* was played and someone opened a philosophical debate over its increasingly complex themes of old age and loss. Maureen felt out of her depth, if not a little bit bored. Maybe dating someone from the Grammar was going to be beyond her.

Florrie summed it up nicely: "Well then, I knew it. What could 'e possibly see in *you*?"

Maureen didn't hear from Mike again. Convinced it

191

was down to the glasses, she decided to try contact lenses. As she was working full time now, whilst waiting for her results, she'd finally saved up enough from her £8 a week salary to get them.

"They will hurt at first," the optician said as he prised her eyelids open. The pain was excruciating. "It'll take a little while to get used to them, but soon you'll hardly know they're there."

Maureen wasn't so sure. She emerged with a survival kit of solutions to keep her hard contact lenses clean and struggled to the bus stop. As bad as her eyes felt, it was nothing compared to how her parents made her feel.

"It ain't natural," was Cyril's initial comment. "Very dangerous when they go round the back of yer eye. Seen it on the telly. Yer'll go blind."

"Why're ya trying to make yerself summink you ain't?" was Florrie's take on the subject. "You're supposed to wear glasses; you shouldn't be trying to look like that."

"What like most other people you mean?" Maureen flashed back. She wasn't going to accept any more put-downs.

"Yer getting above yerself, you are," her mother countered dismissively, heading for the kitchen and the ashtray.

Days went by, but the eyes didn't really improve. The lenses still felt like bricks. Sunlight made them stream and the slightest bit of grit meant that the lenses had to be removed instantly for fear that her screams would alarm the neighbours.

"I can't look at yer no more, it's makin' me feel sick. Yer need to go back to the quack you got 'em from," sneered Cyril.

"You're over-reacting," the optician remarked. "Don't panic, blinking will help and your tears will get rid of the grit. You'll just have to wear sunglasses to stop the waterworks."

To take her mind off things Maureen chose a grey day and went to visit Dot.

"Blimey," her grandmother said. "You alright? Yer eyes look like roadmaps. Have yer broke yer glasses?"

Ethel, who stopped hoovering to come and have a look, was equally sympathetic. "Yer eyelids are all puffy, like mushrooms, and yer staring all the time. Yer gunna 'ave to make the best of what yer got wivout 'em. After all no one married Aunt Betsy cos of 'er gammy polio leg, but she still done alright. Bit lonely, but she come 'ere fer 'er 'olidays. Let 'em fall out on the carpet and I'll suck 'em up."

Maureen was speechless.

She persevered and the pain receded, just in time for Clive Mont's wedding. Clive had left school unexpectedly to become a plumber's apprentice after talk of a girlfriend's expanding waistband and a pram on order from the Co-op. Lorraine and Maureen had spent some time choosing their outfits from the Freeman's catalogue whilst lounging on the sofabed in the common room.

"We 'ave to be careful not to upstage the bride," Lorraine noted, pointing to the instructions on wedding etiquette.

"Alright then, I'll stick to page one nine four; *Clothes for not relations (close or distant), not close friends, just members of same school class*, look…"

They both giggled.

"No seriously we need to play it down."

In the end Maureen went for a beige, ribbed, clingy, knitted dress with a tie belt, topped off with a matching felt beret. Slinky gold tights and beige ankle-strapped shoes completed the look created by Faye Dunaway in

Bonnie and Clyde. She hoped it was suitably subdued.

The Church was next to a building site and the wind was blowing. Grit got into Maureen's eyes while the photos were being taken, but she blinked stoically and did her best to look like she was crying out of emotion. The ordeal continued throughout sandwiches at the pub and the disco that followed. By the time she got home her lenses felt like coarse sandpaper and the pain taking them out was indescribable. Sliding into bed, all she could think about was sleep and the joy of closing her eyes.

That was, until about two hours later, when she woke with the most unbearable pain and realised that her eyelids were so swollen that they could barely open. Even more alarming though, all she could see through the tiny slits was severe fuzz, very much worse than normal. Shit, she thought, I need help. Dismissing the temptation to stumble outside and flag down a passing car so as not to alert her parents, she realised there was nothing else for it than to grope her way across the hall to her Mother's bedside.

"Mum, I can't open my eyes."

Florrie shook Cyril. "Cyril, you were right, Maureen's gone blind."

Cyril shot up like he'd been fired from a cannon and headed for the bathroom. He was on automatic pilot having had several pints at the Lord Tennyson. The sound of the door slamming was nothing compared to the dull thud of his head hitting the side of the bath.

Florrie rushed to the door.

"Cyril, Cyril. Are you alright?"

Not surprisingly there was no reply. As her mother forced the bathroom door open, Maureen could just about make out a large blurred shape folded in half over the bath.

"Oh God, Cyril, Cyril..."

Apparently there was a trickle of blood circling the plug hole.

The sudden burst of adrenalin mixed with several pints of light and bitter must have caused him to pass out. Helping to straighten him up against the edge of the bath, Maureen could vaguely make out a gash over his left eye where he must have banged his head on the taps on the way down.

"This is going to need stitches," Maureen said, thinking her mother was still in the room. Realising she wasn't, she turned round to make out a shape circling the hall, cigarette in hand, wailing "I'm the only one left, I'm the only one left..."

To cut the story short, Maureen somehow managed to summon an ambulance and the three of them were delivered to Casualty - Maureen with huge patches over both eyes, Cyril with one over his right eye and Florrie, according to the ambulance men, in need of blinkers to stop her eyes rolling in their sockets.

They were all kept in for the rest of the night. Cyril had five stitches and Florrie was put on a course of tranquillisers. The nurse who washed out Maureen's eyes couldn't believe such mayhem could have been caused by such a small a piece of grit. Mr Patel, the taxi driver, needed quite a bit of convincing to take two people with three eye patches between them, and a mad woman who'd lost the capacity to walk, back home in his car. Maureen made up a new headline on the way...
Dawn debacle causes devastation in Disraeli Drive.

Cyril, of course, relived the story many, many times, showing off his scar at every opportunity. He called it *The night I went blind* and it went along the lines of how he temporarily lost his sight when he tripped and fell into the bath. The number of stitches averaged around a dozen depending on how many pale ales he'd had before his narration.

And Maureen's part in the event? Well, it was quietly forgotten.

Fifteen

Jobs for All

"Mo, you go down first and steady 'er from the front. I'll navigate and push from behind."

"Blimey Effel, you make me sound like a barge."

"Stop laughing Mum, I can't get a firm grip with you wobbling up and down like that."

It was all getting a bit hysterical. Maureen and Ethel were trying to get Dot down her stairs. It was her 80th birthday and Ethel was having a tea party for her at her house. Dot hadn't been out of her flat now for several months and this palaver confirmed that she wasn't likely to be staying there much longer. In retrospect it wasn't the most suitable flat. With a flight of stairs to mount from the front door and being too far from the shops, Dot had become dependent on Ethel. An unsatisfactory situation and something else to bend Cyril's ear about.

"I'm takin' a risk," whispered Ethel as she finally managed to prise Dot into Fred's car. "Gettin' 'er to go back up later's gunna be a challenge."

Having almost had her Grandmother fall on top of her on the way down, Maureen pondered over how they were going to get her back up the stairs without killing someone?

It was a nice afternoon. Dot loved being the centre of attention. Her great-grandchildren were there as well as her sisters and their families. Lots of photos were taken. Gone, it seemed, were the cine films along with the raucous parties. Maureen wondered if Ethel might still try to keep up the tradition, not that Maureen would be invited seeing as how Cyril and Ethel were constantly at each other's throats. She fleetingly wondered if she should ask, but thought better of it. That whole chunk of her childhood had disappeared along with her Grandad. Almost nothing of her life now bore any resemblance to the past.

As predicted, Dot was much more reluctant to help herself back up the stairs having consumed gallons of tea and Victoria Sandwich.

"Won't be long before we 'ave to put 'er in an 'ome," puffed Ethel. "It's all gettin' too much for me. Can ya warn yer Dad, 'e might 'ave to pull 'is finger out and 'elp sort it?"

Maureen had her own issues with her Father, so riling him with a message like this from his sister didn't seem like a good move, particularly since she'd just been invited to go on a holiday to Jersey with some school friends. Testing the water with Florrie hadn't gone well.

"Yer not going," she said. "But don't just take my word for it. Ask yer Father." Maureen's heart sank. The subject of holidays had become a seriously sore point in Disraeli Drive. The much debated Bournemouth Bournanza hadn't happened. Florrie had reviewed their dwindling finances and decided a holiday was out of the question. Indeed, it was so serious that she got herself a job at the Co-op checkout next to the Lord Tennyson.

"*My* retirement lasted a long time then," she'd hissed at Cyril whilst hanging her overall on the back of the kitchen door. "Didn't even make me a cuppa tea after me first day."

Her husband had been far too busy to take notice. Another batch of perspex had caught his eye at Smokey's. The clipboard was once again full of sketches. This time there was enough of the magic material to make an inner and an outer porch doubling the chance of a warmer winter. Cyril had escaped visiting the local Labour Exchange a little while longer.

Maureen braced herself and headed up the garden path following the unnerving sound of a blunt saw cutting through plastic.

"Yer won't like it," he snarled. "Won't stand a chance against those Jersey Gigolos - it's famous for 'em. Just 'old on to this while I tighten up the vice. I'm tellin' ya, they prey on girls like you." Before Maureen could argue, Florrie was behind her.

"See I told yer," she sniffed, pushing her way round in front. "Come on Cyril, leave that now and get ta bed. Yer got an early start tomorra."

Florrie was pleased with herself. It turned out that her brother had got Cyril a job in his factory. Maureen noted the look of despair on her Father's face. The job was as a floor sweeper.

"Can't be fussy," she'd argued, "after all, yer didn't last long at the Admiral Nelson."

That was another story. Theresa had been kind enough to phone when a job came up as a barman. She knew that Cyril wanted to keep his hand in. He'd gone off with a flourish wearing a new beige knitted waistcoat. Crestfallen on his return, he said "I never even got behind the bar. In the cellar all the bleedin' time I was, until everyone 'ad gone 'ome and then they wanted *me* to wash up. They obviously don't know who they're dealin' with. Need to put things straight. Even had to take me waistcoat off, place's run by a manager see, following some sort of brewery fashion code."

Not being able to set the record straight, Cyril walked out of the job after only a few weeks. It had been a blow to Maureen as she had been allowed to go with him at the weekends. Sitting up at the bar on a high stool, with a weak Dubonnet and lemonade in hand, seemed the very height of sophistication. By comparison with the Victory, the Nelson was classy. The carpet was completely burn-free, the furniture matched, and Dean Martin could be heard quietly crooning *Everybody loves somebody sometime* through ceiling-level speakers. People sat in alcoves eating meals ordered from menus, and almost all the ladies wore fur coats of some kind or another. It had been a short-lived exposure to a different world.

Maureen couldn't see how this new job would last any longer, but she admired him for accepting it. He dutifully set off for the bus the next morning with his sandwich wrapped in tin foil, a mere shadow of his former self.

It didn't go well.

"You 'aven't come 'ome on the bus like *that...*?" Florrie snarled, aghast at the state of him on his return. He was wearing a dirty boiler suit made for a much larger and taller man, a flat cap, and looked utterly crushed and bedraggled.

Lifting his head he barked back at her, "You made me go for this shit job. Thought you oughta see what shit looks like. I've left me broom and filfy bucket behind though."

Florrie headed for her sink and cigarettes, saying nothing.

Maureen hid in her room. Lying on her bed, mulling things over, it was clear that this was another turning point in her parents' relationship. Florrie seemed stronger in her silence, the happiest of the three of them in their new surroundings. She looked relieved to get away from Cyril during the day and having the evenings on her own to watch *Coronation Street* with her fags and a Guinness from the Co-op. There was no sign that she missed anything, or indeed anyone, from the past - not even Mrs Jenkins. Sylvia's visits had dried up lately too. Florrie had overheard gossip in the Price Reduction Stores concerning 'the new Landlord at the Victory walking home the blonde barmaid'. Sylvia knew that Florrie wouldn't approve of that boundary being overstepped.

Cyril, in complete contrast, was losing his sense of self-worth. All he wanted to do was turn the clock back. He was clearly lonely and deeply bitter that he hadn't heard from a single Victory customer and took his frustration out on the television, or when re-telling the goings on at the Lord Tennyson, swearing and complaining about everything. Like before, at the Victory, he seemed to think this Landlord needed the benefit of his 'experteese' too, only to catch sight of him disappearing down the cellar steps the moment the Cooke family entered. Maureen wasn't spared his venom either. Having been told she looked like a *tart* on many occasions, he now added *slut* and *whore* to his charm repertoire, with a permanent look of distaste on his face as she dressed up for a night out.

Of course, feelings were never aired or discussed, so getting upset gained her no sympathy from either parent. Maureen still had no idea how much, if at all, her parents cared about one another. The only evidence was that they were still together. She'd never seen them touch, and certainly not kiss, but then so many unhappy people were still married, weren't they. Divorce was still somewhat taboo; you just *got on with it*. So was theirs a home without love, or was love something hidden and not considered proper to talk of? Presumably they must have loved each other in the beginning? After all, she'd come along. But then, even from a small child she'd felt so different from them, often wondering if she'd been adopted. Without any signs of affection, how could she know that they loved her? It seemed as if she was always the cause of all their anguish. Did she love *them*? Well, that's what you're supposed to do isn't it? But trying to put into words what she really felt was really difficult. How do you know your own emotions when your memories of being loved are so few and far between? It had been so different with Bert and Dot, hadn't it... just about all of her happy memories involved them. The attention they gave her, the cuddles and kisses, the overwhelming feeling of warmth. Without doubt she felt loved by them and feelings of love overwhelmed her when she thought of them.

Shifting her position on the bed, Maureen turned her thoughts to the bizarre goings on of a couple of years previously. 1966 was the one and only time a five year census had been carried out in the UK to trial an alternative method of enumeration. Every household was given a short form, with a sample group being asked to fill in a longer form to collect additional information. Cyril grudgingly filled in one of these which he then asked Maureen to check. All seemed in order, so when the enumerator came to the door to collect the form, Cyril sent Maureen to deal with it.

"Can you explain these crossings out?" the enumerator asked. Maureen was confused as there hadn't been any when she checked it. Sure enough the answer to one question had been altered. As she read it aloud, she heard herself saying that her Mother had been married to another man for ten years before getting divorced and marrying Cyril. "Thank you for clearing that up," the woman said turning to leave. Maureen closed the door, her head spinning. It was all news to her. Naturally she didn't mention any of this to her parents as she rejoined them in front of the television. All she could think of at the time was whether she might, miraculously, have some half brothers and sisters somewhere.

She went back to considering the facts. Florrie got married the first time in 1940 and divorced in 1950 according to the census details. Soon after, she married Cyril. Interesting that Maureen had been told that her parents met during the War and indeed that the photos of the honeymoon, when Cyril took Florrie to Greenock Docks to relive what he'd endured during the War, had 1949 written on them. It really didn't matter to Maureen, but getting divorced once must have carried a stigma, so twice would have been out of the question. One thing was certain; she'd never get to the bottom of it.

After a row in the Victory, Florrie would take the dog for a walk or occasionally go to the cinema - never saying a word. Cyril, by contrast, would seek out Maureen and be quick to give his side of the story. Often he'd say "there's fings about your Mother you oughta know, I'll tell ya when you're older". Shocked at the time, Maureen now wondered if her Mother's previous marriage and divorce was what he was alluding to. Cyril certainly thought himself a cut above his wife, there was no doubt about that - her father working in a cement factory, the family living in a council house in Northfleet, the lady turning up in the pub implying that Florrie' grandfather was a bigamist… his snobbery was there for all to see. For the first time in her life Maureen felt sorry for her Mother. Maybe her behaviour towards her daughter was based on guilt. Maybe she was frightened that history would repeat itself again.

Turning her thoughts to the future, Maureen had no intention of becoming like either of her parents – not if she could help it. Sensing her emerging independence, she determined to make up her own mind about what path to follow and take every opportunity offered her. After all, she'd been offered a job, could possibly get an 'O' level or two soon and, contact lenses permitting, might even meet a boy. One thing she was sure about though was that if she ever got to care about anyone, she'd do her best to let them know.

Towards the end of the summer, Maureen was staggered to discover she had passed all her exams - eight 'O' levels.

"Fink we'll 'ave yer Nanna round fer tea to celebrate," said Florrie doing a little jig. "Effel keeps going on about 'ow we never 'ave 'er Muvver now. This'll be a good excuse. I'll pop to that new Bejams and get some of that frozen artic roll they've been advertising. What d'ya reckon Cyril?"

Cyril nodded absent-mindedly, then got up from the armchair for the umpteenth time and paced the route from the new front porch to the hall trying to open and shut the three doors without causing an air lock. If you dropped your keys whilst bringing in the shopping you could find yourself in all kinds of trouble.

It took quite some time to prize Dot out of the back of Fred's car and even longer squeezing her through Cyril's obstacle course. It was a test for the perspex's flexibility that's for sure. Cyril made a mental note to exit via the back on Fred's return. Dot, who was now totally dependent on Ethel, didn't want to stay very long but she was suitably enthusiastic about Maureen's 'low levels'.

When the news reached Woolworths, Mrs. Baker immediately offered her the opportunity to embark on a management training scheme where she was to start learning how to calculate the wage packets. But the idea of being isolated in an office, tucked away behind the coldmeat slicer sounded very lonely and smelly.

"Fink you might be above 'em now, anyway," Florrie announced triumphantly. "Let's show yer *susstificates* to Marks and Sparks like I said. See what they come up with."

Maureen wasn't too keen on that idea either. In fact she'd already taken the initiative and been in touch with Marshall and Snellgrove, in Oxford Street, and had an interview lined up with the Manageress.

"'Ere we go, getting ideas above yerself again," was Florrie's predictable response. "A job in a posh department store in *London*. You won't fit in… those bits of paper 'ave gone to yer 'ead."

"What you should be thinking of Sook," said Cyril trying a different tack, "is a nice little Council job, in the typing pool. Isn't that where the Jenkins' girl works? Florrie? By the clock tower."

"Think so, but we 'aven't 'eard a word from them since we moved in 'ere."

"Bet if I popped inta the Victory, I could get 'er to talk to ya about it."

"That's just another excuse to go in again, Cyril."

"Bloody 'ell woman, I'm tryin' to do some good 'ere. Give us some credit!"

Maureen went for her interview at Marshall and Snellgrove and was offered a job on the spot at £13 a week, which was £5 a week more than Woolworths. Trouble is, the weekly train fare wiped out the difference and you had to take the three hours travelling time into account. So she turned the job down and, instead, met Denise Jenkins for a chat.

"See, I told ya. Local council job, that's the answer." Cyril was chuffed with himself.

Denise had indeed convinced Maureen that a typing job was worth pursuing, but she had her own idea which council she would try. Going up to London for the shop interview had given her an unexpected buzz. She applied - and got - a job as a clerical typist with the Greater London Council, at County Hall on the South Bank, starting at £20 a week. At least that sweetened the travel costs, if not the time. Cyril, of course, was gob-smacked when he was told and frothed at the mouth.

"Gunna work in London - yer must be mad. Full of wierdos and dossers in cardboard boxes. I'm telling ya, yer'll be trampled underfoot in all the riots. Ken went to see that film *Alfie*. Blokes like that Michael Caine are just waiting fer gullible birds like you. They'll 'ave yer in that Soho sex scene before yer can say eggs is eggs. What's wrong wiv 'ere?"

Maureen wasn't going to have another row. The truth was that she was really looking forward to meeting all the wierdos. In fact, the more the merrier. After her own family, they'd probably seem quite tame.

Cyril wore himself out declaiming the Capital's debauchery which meant he lacked the strength to continue with his theory of corruption by Gigolos on a small island off the coast of France. Giving up the fight, he finally agreed to Maureen going on her first week's holiday. Indeed, melting slightly, he sent her one of his Big Boy tomatoes wrapped in tissue and packed in a small cardboard box. The attached note said 'grown in Gravesend from seed from Jersey. Show 'em how it's done Sook!'

Despite her best efforts, the Jersey Gigolos kept themselves to themselves, but she still had a lovely time with her friends, experiencing her first flight from Southend Airport, losing her inhibitions - and her contact lenses when she blacked out briefly in a disco queue suffering from sunstroke. But too soon it was over and her first day at work loomed.

Very early on the Monday morning she got the bus to the station and caught the 7.30 train to London, her stomach churning with a mixture of apprehension and excitement.

The day passed in a blur.

"So, 'owdya get on in the smoke then?" Cyril said with a smirk on her return, his feet soaking in Florrie's foot bath. "It's gunna be a long old day fer yer. Out the 'ouse before seven in the morning and not back till after seven in the evening. Bet yer 'ated the train, didn't yer?"

"It was fine," said Maureen, ignoring the jibe. "All of us new ones were taken to different departments." She held her breath: "I'm in the Intelligence Unit of the Director General's Department". That had needed to be practiced several times on the train, to be sure of getting it right. She knew there was no chance of needing to explain it, which was just as well.

"Ha ha very funny," chortled her Father. "Come an' look at me feet will ya. Wot d'ya reckon, does me skin look a funny colour to you?"

Cyril's feet did indeed have a grey tinge to them. The skin looked as if it was beginning to peel as well.

"It's all the bleedin' muck on the factory floor I 'ave to sweep up. Grease off the machinery. Reckon I'm getting allergic to it."

"Allergic to 'ard work, more like," Florrie chipped in, unable to resist the opportunity. Without stopping for breath, she turned her attention to her daughter. "No point in looking in the oven love, 'ad to chuck away yer dinner. Pan boiled dry. 'Ere's two bob, take the dog and get yerself some fish and chips."

As another full scale row about dirt and synthetic socks got underway, Maureen grabbed Ricky's lead and prodded him awake. The dog had almost given up all hope of getting a walk these days and couldn't believe his luck. In fact, he'd recently discovered a way through the hedge and joined a gang of waifs and strays patrolling Disraeli Drive. Maureen had found him once, very much the leader, his pedigree shining through and loving being the centre of attention once again. Unfortunately the exploit didn't go down well with Florrie. She flung him unceremoniously in the bath to get rid of the smell, leaving him sulking in the corner. Poor Ricky. At least Maureen now had somewhere to escape to.

It was good to be outside and to mull over the events of the day. A smell of autumn was in the air and the nights were starting to close in. So it was official, she worked in London. The South Bank and the Old Vic were on her doorstep, Oxford and Carnaby Street a tube ride away. Someone in her office had already shown her where to buy cheap clothes at a street market called The Cut and talked about somewhere trendy called the Kings Road. As for the *Intelligence Unit* - how grand! Whatever it was, it was the luck of the draw that got her into it. Had she been sitting on a different chair around the table, she might have finished up in Planning or Housing or Roads, or whatever. One thing was for sure though; she looked forward to fathoming out what went on there - providing she could find her room again in the rabbit warren that was County Hall.

Sixteen

Peace and Love

Maureen was rudely awakened by her Father's abrasive tongue: "That's it Florrie, get up and lock the door. Look at the bleedin' time... She can stay out all night now!"

"Shudup Cyril, go back to sleep. She's in bed. Been there over an hour."

Maureen groaned. She'd found getting to sleep hard enough in the first place. No chance now. Turning over, she re-lived the events of that evening's party at Rob's house, in minute detail - what she'd been wearing, the music, the dancing, the laughing, the fruit punch, the hairspray inconveniently clouding her contact lenses, but most importantly, who was there.

Rob was now at the local college which meant he'd made new friends and invited them to the party. The regular boys stood back in amazement as this new crowd arrived on the scene, preened and groomed and riding an array of Lambretta and Vespa scooters. They sat outside for a while summoning Dutch courage wiv cans of lager, fluffing up flattened hair in their mirrors. The net curtains twitched as the girls stole a peek at them - recoiling the moment they looked like being seen.

"I like the one wiv really short 'air, see... on the right. 'E's wearin' a fishtail parka," Lorraine whispered excitedly whilst hastily smearing on coral pink lipstick.

"Mmm... he's OK; prefer the one in the long coat."

"What! Wiv the really long 'air and sideburns? Trust you to be different, Mo. Do you think I've got

209

time to go to the loo?"

Maureen shook her head without taking her eyes off the window. "Oh my God, they're coming in. Quick, let's sit on the stairs, pretend we haven't seen them."

Maureen's heart was racing. With only seconds to flick back their hair, they tried looking nonchalant as the gladiators entered the ring, crash helmets under their arms. Stealing a quick sideways glance Maureen counted six altogether; three in knee-length green parkas with fur-lined hoods, followed by one in a corduroy battle jacket who clearly liked the sound of his own voice; an oddball with a pony tail in a bogus WW2 aviator's jacket made out of fake leather, and lastly, the tallest, with shoulder length hair and piercing blue eyes, in a Greatcoat, who swept the floor on entry. He was the one Maureen was interested in.

The boys made their way to the kitchen followed by the girls at a discreet distance, but after hanging around the drinks for a bit, seemingly getting nowhere, Maureen and Lorraine headed into the lounge. Suddenly the Greatcoat whooshed alongside and asked her to dance. *Money Money* (fast) rolled into *Hey Jude* (slow and long) which felt nice until *The Crazy World of Arthur Brown*'s rendition of *Fire!* broke the spell. Forced back into the kitchen and armed with yet another fruit punch she discovered that John was eighteen and was doing something or other with computers. He lived quite close, in Nightingale Avenue, and had brothers and sisters. Not bad for a start, she thought. More importantly he was very good looking, had nice teeth, unruly hair which Cyril would *love*, was good fun and seemed to like her. So much so in fact, that he'd asked for her phone number.

Of course, she hadn't given it to him - too much of a risk that her parents would answer. Swallowing some excuse about the line being down, his next suggestion was to meet at the Lord Tennyson. Another sticky moment as Maureen pictured Cyril boring the pants off everyone with his 'I was a most respected Landlord' speech. Thinking on her feet she startled John with, "I know, meet me off the train. It's only across the road from the college and we can decide which pub to go to then." It worked. John seemed happy and a date was set for the following Friday. Dead chuffed with herself, Maureen realised that she hadn't given a thought to Lorraine and hadn't seen her leave. Guess I'll be in the doghouse tomorrow, she mused as sleep finally took over.

The week dragged terribly. Every day the train seemed to go slower, the typing and photocopying never ending. Lorraine kept phoning for news, of which there was none.

"He hasn't got my phone number Lorr, so I just have to hope he doesn't change his mind"

"What'll ya tell yer Mum?"

"That I'm working late, of course. Then if he doesn't turn up, I can just get the bus back, no harm done. Hope he does though, I really like him."

"All right luvvergirl, don't rub it in. I still 'aven't forgiven you fer abandoning me."

Wednesday... Thursday... all Maureen could think about was the scooter and how she would break the news to John that, assuming things progressed, it would have to be parked at least a quarter of a mile away in case Cyril heard its engine running.

Friday finally arrived. Maureen got up an hour early to perfect her appearance. She still had long hair, but now it rested on her shoulders with the ends flicked up, thanks to foam rollers worn overnight. Dedication comes at a price though - like curler imprints on the face if laid on all night, or pillow whiplash if you turn too quickly. The flick had a habit of drooping by the

211

evening, so a top up by means of a new instrument of torture was available. You plugged in your *Carmen Rollers* and when they were hot enough, a little green dot went blue. The air would be that colour too if your hair got stuck in the rigid spikes and started singeing.

On hairwash nights, Cyril would be in his element. Maureen's giant rollers were bad enough, but Florrie had hers dried with what her husband called the brain sucker. This was a heavy duty plastic bonnet with a flexible pipe (not dissimilar to the one carrying waste water from the washing machine) running down her back to a dryer unit strapped round her waist, which was plugged into a socket and laughingly called 'portable'. When switched on, hot air would circulate around the bonnet causing it to inflate. It could be very uncomfortable, but it meant Florrie couldn't hear Cyril. Sometimes she would deliberately send him into an electrical fear-frenzy by soaking her feet in the plugged-in foot bath at the same time.

Maureen got off the train, her heart thumping as she scoured the ticket office, and the street outside, without success. There were loads of people surging through, with others milling around trying to keep out of the rain. Bugger, she thought, my *hair*... Suddenly, a figure loomed out of the shadows carrying an open umbrella.

"Better get under here," he said with a smile. It didn't matter that she remembered the Greatcoat more than what he looked like. Walking straight past the Victory, he guided her to the nearest *In-pub.* From then on, time seemed to stand still. They had a lovely evening with no awkward moments whilst Maureen sipped her gin with undiluted orange squash. She was surprised, but pleased, when he didn't smoke and even more delighted when escorted to the bus stop rather than the back seat of his Lambretta.

"Didn't think you'd fancy your first ride in the rain," he said.

"Is this it then? Are ya going out together?" Lorraine whispered down the phone, barely able to contain herself.

"Come on Lorr, it's only been one date, but I am seeing him again on Tuesday."

"Sounds like it. Ironic that you met 'im at a party after all that time you spent walking past 'em college boys in the Victory. So, don't s'pose you'll be wantin' to go out wiv me again, not now yer got a boyfriend."

"Lorr!"

"Anyway, good luck telling yer Mum and Dad."

In fact, Maureen waited until she'd been out with John quite a few more times before she broke the news. By then she was fairly certain that his seeing her in glasses hadn't put him off.

"At the college, you say?" Florrie said, showing slightly more interest than usual. "Them boys always appreciated me cheese rolls. Well you'd better bring 'im to tea on Sunday then."

Oh God, Maureen thought; not the infamous Sunday tinned tea. What on earth would John make of her parents? She'd already met his. They were young, full of life, ate normal teas and had made her feel very welcome.

"So, you're John then," sniffed Cyril. "What d'ya reckon about the Krays then? That Detective Nipper's arrested 'em fer stabbin' Jack the Hat. Never found 'is body yer know. Leave a bit of salmon in the tin fer me to 'ave later, Flo."

Maureen winced. John'll think we're an East End

213

gang family, she thought.

"Your parents seem very nice," he said unconvincingly as they headed out to walk off the tea with Ricky in tow. "Reckon they'd be lost without a tin opener though. Didn't know you could get cream in a tin, let alone potato salad."

"Sorry about the tomato."

John laughed. "I nearly choked when he said have one of my *Big Boys*. Could hardly look him in the eye."

"You'll come again then?"

"Looking forward to it already. Just one thing though, why don't they have their tea the same time as us?"

"Old habits die hard and, besides, we've only got two chairs." Maureen caught a glimpse of John's bemused face. My God you've got a lot learn she thought.

They reached John's pride and joy - his black and orange Lambretta. Ricky showed his appreciation by cocking his leg up against the back wheel. Maureen dragged him off as John thankfully, saw the funny side of it.

On her return, Maureen hesitated briefly at the kitchen door. She could hear Cyril summing him up. "'Air's a bit long. Not sure 'bout them purple trousers eiver, and 'e knows nuffink about the wartime Enigma machine, despite working wiv a computer."

"Don't worry," Florrie replied, "don't expect anyfing will come of it. 'E goes to the college. Wanna bit of Artic Roll? There's a bit left."

Thanks to John, Maureen's first Christmas in the bungalow turned out to be more bearable than she'd anticipated. She'd been a bit alarmed when Cyril turned his spare polystyrene tiles into giant stars and hung them on the Leylandii in the front garden. They'd never had a Christmas tree and Florrie couldn't see the point of starting now, so it seemed a good idea. Fairy lights were hung around the new porch and an inflatable reindeer stood amongst the geraniums filling up most of the space. Not that it mattered, hardly any people used the front entrance and no-one came back for a second visit. Florrie flatly refused to use it, arguing that the air lock made her ears pop and from now on she was using the back door. She wasn't alone in her protest either. The postman said it was too painful to enter and was leaving the letters under a brick on the steps. Cyril complained that the notification of his pools jackpot would get soggy when it rained, but the postman wouldn't be moved.

Perversely, the milkman started leaving the milk *inside* the porch which really got up Cyril's nose. "I've told 'im not to! It's too 'ot in there. Milk's off in a jiff. Don't understand the bloke; I stuck up a sign saying MILK 'ERE, with an arrow pointing round the side where I put the old Toby Ales crate for 'im, but he says he ain't got time to go following signs. Dunno what the world's comin' to."

So with the polystyrene stars, the twinkling fairy lights, the airlock and the stale milk, Christmas got underway. Dot turned down their invitation to Christmas Day dinner. She was staying with Ethel, so Fred would have to lay off the sherry to bring her. Besides, the family were all going to be there and they were having turkey.

"More lamb chops fer us then," said Cyril sarcastically. "They're my bloody family too, not that you'd know it".

If it hadn't been for John rescuing Maureen every few hours when tensions rose, it could have been a disaster. She spent a lot of time at his house, where life was chaotic, lively and fun. Florrie and Cyril, on the

215

other hand, spent most of their time at the Tennyson. No one, it seemed, wanted to be in the bungalow.

Florrie was well aware that Maureen was happier when she was in John's company and that they were spending more and more time together.

"What's 'e see in you then?" she asked, charmingly, one dinner time. "'Ope yer not throwing yerself at 'im. Remember wot I said about pulling up stockings in front of me brother... Blokes take wot they want an' leave yer in the gutta if yer stupid enough to let 'em."

1969 got off to a mind-blowing start. John took Maureen to the Shaftesbury Theatre in London to see *Hair*. Described as an American tribal love-rock musical, the whole experience was exhilarating and somewhat shocking when the whole cast emerged naked out of a huge white sheet while continuing to sing *Let the sunshine in*. A hasty decision was made on the train home not to leave the programme on the coffee table in Disraeli Drive.

The Beatles performed live for the last time on the top of the Apple building - until the neighbours complained - and Led Zeppelin released their first album. John and Maureen professed their new found love for progressive rock and Artic Roll... along with that for each other. There was rarely an evening that they weren't together having tea or trying to be alone to play their music.

Now, privacy was becoming an issue and although John's parents understood, there were just too many people in their house to make that possible. John came up with the idea of using Maureen's front room as no one else seemed to use it.

"They'll never leave us alone in there," Maureen said sceptically, remembering the last time she'd had guests in there. My Mum'll be pacing around with a torch again."

"They're reasonable people," John replied optimistically, clearly determined to give it a try. "I'll be round on Tuesday with the LP."

'My parents, *reasonable*?' Maureen thought as he left.

"See, told you it would be OK," he said, blowing the dust off the needle. "Couple of strange looks and a bit of sniffing, but we're in aren't we?"

Maureen sensed embarrassment looming. *Led Zeppelin 1* got underway. Mid-way through *Good times, bad times,* Florrie came in to see what they wanted for Sunday tea.

"Usual tins OK? Might 'ave SPAM this week."

During the chorus of *How many more times*, Cyril burst in, duster in hand. "Seen me rollocks anywhere?" he enquired.

John stifled a laugh.

"In the fireplace," Maureen pointed wearily. "*Row*locks, John, you know, boats and things."

John's mirth was barely containable as he closed the door behind Cyril and recklessly turned off the light. As expected, it wasn't long before Florrie's form was back at the door torch blazing. A bit later, as *Dazed and confused* reached its throbbing climax, she could contain herself no longer and the door burst open again.

"Need to get the dog a toffee," she said, squinting and pointing Ricky, who was tucked under her arm, at the sweet bowl on the sideboard as if expecting him to make a selection. An almond crunch was unwrapped and placed in his mouth. Maureen and John then watched in amazement through the reeded glass as the poor dog flung his head from side to side, paw against jaw, trying to get it out of its teeth. No sooner had he finished that one, the duo were back for another.

"I'll bring *King Crimson* next week," John said, stepping over the writhing dog on his way out.

"What the bloody 'ell does 'e think 'e looks like? And who's that woman in bed wiv 'im? Wot's that all about?"

Cyril was watching the news. John and Yoko were hosting their Bed-In for Peace at the Amsterdam Hilton. As far as Cyril was concerned, modern music was getting out of control and becoming a bad influence. George Harrison had been arrested for drug possession, Jim Morrison for exposing himself on stage and *The Who* were deliberately smashing up their equipment *for a laugh*. It was invading the bungalow too. Heavy metal spelt anarchy in the front room. Maureen and John had been in residence there rather too much lately and Ricky had lost a molar.

Inflamed feet had signalled the end of Cyril's factory cleaning job. Florrie was convinced it was the new stretchy fabrics that socks were made of that caused his allergic reaction, rather than the factory floor, but what was done was done. She turned her attention to her husband's teeth in a bid to raise his profile. Impressions had already been taken and Cyril was destined to have all his teeth removed in readiness for a false set, *tout suite*. To take his mind off the impending pain he decided a visit to Smokey was in order.

One warm evening Maureen returned from the train to see Benny Hill through the lounge window brandishing a sledgehammer. It turned out to be Cyril wearing his boiler suit, his hair covered by an old brown felt beret and wearing a pair of Bert's old round glasses to keep the dust out of his eyes.

"Fought you'd be surprised," he said with a laugh on seeing Maureen's shocked face. "We've decided to 'ave a froo room. It's all the rage."

"A *what?*"

All that was left of the wall between front and back rooms was a pile of rubble.

"Idea is…" Florrie continued, her cigarette smoke mingling with the dust, "it's gunna be a froo room when we 'ave a party or summink. Rest of the time it's gunna 'ave a perspex partition."

Maureen couldn't decide which sounded more ludicrous - the parties or the perspex, but within minutes she was filling the wheelbarrow with rubble and trying to manoeuvre it through the kitchen to the back door. In a couple of days it was all over. The two rooms were much the same, except that now there was a see-through wall between them.

"Mmm" Florrie purred admiringly, "much more light in the back room now. It's the effect of a froo room without 'aving to be one."

"Tell me I'm seeing things," John said as he slumped, deflated, onto the settee in the front room. As Maureen shut the door the whole screen wobbled and creaked. Florrie had positioned the television beyond the divide, with its back against the perspex, which meant that sitting in her chair she could now watch it - or Maureen and John by just lifting her chin slightly.

"I can see I'm gunna have to save up for a car," John mumbled under his breath.

In early summer they joined 100,000 other Flower Power seekers in Hyde Park to watch Eric Clapton, Ginger Baker and Steve Winwood performing for the first time as *Blind Faith*. It was amazing. One of the first free concerts to be held there, everyone seemed happy with the new line up apart from a few die-hards calling for the return of *Cream*. Maureen found herself in awe - the venue, the atmosphere, the excitement building from the minute they exited the tube at

219

Piccadilly, carried along in a sea of people heading into the park.

Donovan was on when they arrived, not that they could hear him from the back, but it didn't matter. It was just *being there* that was so special. As she surveyed the scene, she found it hard to take it all in; a mass of seething bodies many of them topless, were spread out as far as the eye could see. Some dancing, others writhing, swaying or squirming to the music. There was an overpowering reek of marijuana in the air. It was hot, heady and very hippie. John wore his frayed, red bell-bottom cords, fringed suede vest and tie-dyed frilled shirt, plus love beads and a homemade *peace and love* bandanna round his head. Maureen had left her bra in the drawer at home and was wearing a Mexican peasant blouse she'd picked up from the market in The Cut, behind Waterloo Station, and her gypsy-style long skirt purchased from BIBA's new shop in Kensington High Street. She felt light and liberated despite a heavy medallion necklace and chain belt.

As they'd left for the station, Cyril had felt the need to impart some words of wisdom. "Yanks are to blame fer all this," he said, nodding in their general direction. "Got no morals, been too liberal. It'll be betta now that Nixon's President. 'E'll sort 'em out. Trustworthy bloke I reckon. You can believe wot *'e* says."

As summer got underway, it did seem that the world Cyril was used to had spiralled out of control. He'd listened on the radio to the last ever episode of Mrs Dale's Diary at the same time as Soviet cosmonauts were enjoying a stroll in space. The Manson Family cult had gone on a killing spree, murdering movie director Roman Polanski's pregnant wife, Sharon Tate, and four others in chilling circumstances at their home

220

in Beverley Hills, California. Then the scenes of gay abandon at the Woodstock festival caused more upset than the withdrawal of the half penny.

Things weren't much better for Florrie, shocked by the needless and suspicious deaths of Judy Garland in a hotel room and Rolling Stone Brian Jones in a swimming pool, she was even more taken aback when Brit, Ann Jones, defeated Billie Jean King in her favourite *Wimpleton* final. Florrie concluded that, unless her daughter was taking this *Pill* that the Daily Mirror was going on about, she was going to be disgraced by an unwanted pregnancy any day now.

What a to-do.

Seventeen

Ricky

"Hard to imagine, isn't it?"

Maureen, John and his parents were standing in the front garden of John's house, staring skywards at the moon.

"Reckon I can see them - just by the Sea of Tranquility - over there." John's Dad, Trevor, was waggling his finger in the air, laughing.

They'd stayed up late to watch Neil Armstrong announce to 720 million distant earthlings that 'The Eagle has landed!' Having been rooted to the television for hours they'd gone outside with their drinks to toast the astronauts and by this time it was so late that there seemed little point in going to bed.

"Stopping for breakfast Maureen?" John's Mum, Hazel, asked matter-of-factly. Maureen enjoyed her time at John's house. His parents were easy going, modern in their views and general outlook on life, and, thankfully, sat in the front room. John was the eldest of three and yet Hazel was pregnant with number four. There'd been a brief moment when it looked like both sets of parents might meet, but Florrie was so horrified at the pregnancy news that she scuppered the plan, much to Maureen's relief. Apparently, having another baby when your oldest child was already eighteen smacked of bohemianism.

"What reason shall I give my Mum and Dad then?" John said, needing help.

"Something about leaving it till after the baby's born... better for your Mum. Will that do? Or, of course you could say that they will have absolutely nothing in common. That my Mum would be too embarrassed to look at your Mum and that my Dad will give them his life history before the drink cabinet's been opened."

Maureen stopped for breath. John stood up and dragged his feet across the carpet. *"One small step for man, one giant leap for mankind* - not for Cyril and Florrie evidently."

"No, Disraeli Drive will need a few more orbits yet."

"There she is, over there," Maureen said, pointing. John's eyes followed the finger, but it was clear he hadn't a hope of picking out Maureen's Grandmother from amongst the circle of white-haired elderly ladies seated around the room. Dot was now in a Council-run care home. She shared a room and therefore had only a few precious things of her own around her. Ethel had decided the time had come as her mother was no longer able to walk anywhere and was becoming extremely

223

lonely in her flat. "I know why I'm going, but I can't imagine what Bert would say," Dot had said philosophically as she'd left.

Maureen was pleased to see her Nanna looking very smart in her favourite navy dress with white spots. She had her shoes on, not slippers like the rest, and also a brooch and necklace. Only her hair was different. Gone were the long strands, painstakingly rolled and held in place with combs. Now it was short and permed and looked like everyone else's in the room. She could see that her grand-daughter had noticed.

"Much easier for the 'airdresser 'ere to do," she said unconvincingly. "Pull up a couple of chairs in front. Nowhere else to go I'm afraid. 'ow are ya both?"

"Fine Nanna. Did you hear men have landed on the moon?"

"I 'eard a few of 'em saying so this morning, but I wasn't sure wevver to believe it or not. You 'ear some fine old tales in this place. I get more sense talkin' to the canaries. They remind me of Aunt Lil's. Do you remember, Mo? She kept 'em on the windowsill. 'Ad 'em durin' the War as a warning if Gerry tried to gas us."

Maureen smiled. "Wonder if she still lives there?"

"Doubt it," said Dot screwing up her nose. "She's probably in somewhere like this."

Aunt Lil wasn't a relation at all; she was Dot's next door neighbour (the other side to Miss Payne). They'd been friends for thirty-odd years and lived through many a black-out.

"Yer Nanna's still got all her marbles," John said as they left. "It must be hard to be in there with all your faculties intact."

Maureen sighed as she reflected on how much everything had changed in just a few short years. Ethel had sorted out her Mother's belongings and cleared the flat. Cyril had complained, but not over-loudly, as it meant he didn't have to get involved. Maureen was given an empty locket full of teeth marks (her own included) which endless children had bitten into whilst lying in Dot's arms, plus a half sovereign, dated 1915, which Bert had put away on the day of their wedding. She'd also had Dot's tortoiseshell hair comb, a couple of china figures from her dressing table and a boot hook from her Victorian childhood. That was all that was left of the past, but important to Maureen nonetheless.

"No surprise this's all we got" sniffed Florrie, holding up the battered locket when the booty was being unwrapped. "Nuffink of any value comes this way. It's a bit different from the diamond Elizabeth Taylor's been showing off. Richard Burton paid over a million quid fer that sparkla. She just 'as t'say what she wants and 'e gets it. S'pose that's what true love does fer yer", she shot a wistful look towards Cyril who was tenderly fondling his Big Boys.

"I've 'ad to make do wiv Smokey Fishman's specials all me life". Knowing she was wasting her time, Florrie lit a fag and put the kettle on.

"What a load of rubbish..."

Cyril was draining the last dregs of his third Pale Ale which he reckoned was essential after the first airing of *Monty Python's Flying Circus*. Maureen had suspected this response and as there was no way she was going to sit through it with her father rattling the perspex, she'd watched it at John's.

"So you liked it then, Dad."

Cyril's sneer summed his feelings up perfectly. Nothing much on television suited him these days, except for the news, weather and shipping forecast.

Consequently, the Troubles in Northern Ireland gave rise to an hourly rant. In August, three days of serious rioting between the RUC and Catholic residents on Derry's Bogside resulted in seven dead and hundreds injured, along with scores of homes and businesses being burnt out. Thousands of mainly Catholic families were driven from their homes as the British Army was deployed to 'restore order'. Peace lines were being drawn up to separate the two sides. Cyril was of the view that things would never be any different and that 'we should just let them get on wiv it'. "Born into battle," he declared. "Kids don't know no difference and when they're not fightin', they're marchin'."

"How did the new job go?"

For a second Cyril looked like a rabbit caught in the glare of car headlights. He wasn't used to his daughter changing the conversation so quickly. Not that it made any difference to his mood.

"It's madness, if ya really wanna know. Tiny little boat 'avin' to get close enough to get 'em on safely. Plus I'll be out in all wevvers, low tide and 'igh tide. Bloody dangerous tryin' to keep the boat still, and if there's an accident, it'll be my fault, you wait."

"Night Dad..." "Here we go again," Maureen muttered under her breath as she turned to leave.

One of Cyril's new acquaintants at the Lord Tennyson had told him of a job that would suit him at the Merchant Navy College just up the river. They had a training ship - the *Worcester* - moored nearby and needed a qualified waterman to operate a small motor boat ferrying cadets and teachers to and from the shore. Cyril had once again gone off for his interview full of enthusiasm. Florrie was a bit worried about 'first impressions' as her husband was only wearing the bottom set of his new false teeth. Apparently the top set

226

made him feel sick, so they sat in a jam jar of Steradent on the bathroom windowsill. Inevitably his top lip was gradually sinking in and rested under his bottom lip. It didn't exactly inspire confidence as it caused a problem with phonics, 'th' sounds in particular. Thankfully the *Master* was more interested in him being a competent rower rather than raconteur, so gave him the job on condition of passing a medical.

As a potential employee of the Inner London Education Authority his medical examination was scheduled to be carried out on the ground floor, of all places, the GLC. Maureen was forced to take an early lunch one day to hold on to her Father's smalls while he took a satisfactory deep breath in a tiny cubicle. Given a clean bill of health, he left there intent on restoring his rightful place in society. Unfortunately his first day on the job didn't live up to expectation.

It's a pity really because he admired the *Worcester* and knew a lot about her history. Many's the time Maureen would hear how dangerous the Thames tides and heavy river traffic used to be – prompting the introduction of competency exams. This in turn created a need for pre-sea training for officers in both the Royal and Merchant services, which was met by the Admiralty lending the *Worcester*, a fifty gun frigate, to the new Thames Marine Officer Training School. There had only been eighteen cadets at the beginning, but by 1920 their numbers had swelled to around two hundred. To meet the growing need for places, Ingress Abbey, at Greenhithe, was purchased, providing a permanent shore base. Cyril had worked as an apprentice, and then a qualified lighterman, during the Worcester's heyday. Passing it almost daily, he would watch the cadets securing the ropes and climbing the rigging. But by the 1960's, the decline in British shipping had reduced the demand for nautical training which is why he was convinced the *Worcester* would eventually end up getting scrapped. This new job could be short lived, and after the experiences of his first day, all feelings of sentimentality had gone out of the window.

Unlike her Father, Maureen enjoyed going to work. The downside was having to get up really early to sort out her hair flicks and make-up. Once on the train though there were always people she knew which made the journey into London pass that much quicker. Her hours at the GLC were strangely decreed as 8.45am to 4.51pm and what actually went on in the Intelligence Unit was something of a mystery, although the end result was the publication of the department *Bible* called the 'Annual Abstract of Greater London Statistics'. A lot of her time was spent taking bits of paper around the complex of corridors linking the various units. If she was lucky she'd be asked to help with sample surveys around the London boroughs or collect data from Government Departments, which meant finding her way around the Capital armed with her trusty A-Z. Other times she'd be proof reading, answering phones, photocopying, filing and typing – on a manual typewriter which shook the adjoining table when she hit the carriage return. Her office companions were all very different, their conversations often illuminating, and, as her horizons began to widen, she found herself joining in the banter and enjoying herself.

Getting home around 7.30pm however, meant there was less time to see John, especially as he was now attending night school. He'd recently become a trainee systems analyst at the cement factory. More qualifications were required. Maureen struggled to understand what computers were all about and assumed that John's work must be similar to what went on in the GLC's massive *computer suite* - men in white coats pressing buttons on huge grey juddering, swirling

228

machines churning out reams of flimsy paper with tiny holes on the sides. The *suite* seemed to take up about half the 3rd floor and she'd be issued with a trolley to shift boxloads of paper up in the lift to her own floor for people to rip off chunks and pore over. They made brilliant doorstops.

John's Dad had taught him to drive. He'd passed his test and he and Maureen bought a little, blue, second-hand Mini for £200. When you were in it, it felt as if you were almost touching the road and the vibrations made your teeth chatter. But it was better than being on the back of the scooter, plus you could have a conversation and not get helmet hair. Maureen had got herself a provisional license and been out with John a couple of times, but once Cyril got to hear of it he found a million reasons why she shouldn't pursue learning. "It'll kill yer Mother," was a popular one.

Nothing had really changed. They still didn't see much of their daughter, yet made a fuss about virtually everything she did. Providing she and John were at the bungalow for Sunday tinned tea, they seemed happy.

"So ya still fancy 'im then? Saw ya snoggin' in the back row at the pictures."

It was Lorraine again, ringing Maureen at work.

"Did you like *Butch Cassidy and the Sundance Kid* then? We really enjoyed it."

"Didn't go a bundle on the ending, but I enjoyed the bit with the bike. Can't stop humming *Raindrops keep falling on me 'ead*. Anyway stop changin' the subject. Yer' out wiv 'im all the time now, so it must be serious."

"So far so good."

"'Ave yer done it yet?"

"Lorraine! I'm *at work*. Actually I'm about to leave

229

to get the train home."

"Yes or no?"

"I'll ring you later."

"I'll take that as a yes then. Bye."

The journey home was more unpleasant than usual. There were fewer carriages so Maureen had to stand most of the way. It was raining heavily which meant no one was inclined to open the windows. You could hardly see through the choking cigarette smoke and hanging on to the luggage rack meant getting poked by commuters grabbing their umbrellas at every stop. Wet and weary and finally reaching her front door, she battled through the porch only to hear her Father holding forth as usual.

"I 'ave to pick 'em up as soon as I see 'em waiting at the end of the jetty. Most of the time there's just one. I get 'alf way across and look back and guess what, another bugger's appeared! Come 'igh tide they gotta jump down inta the boat. Low tide they gotta scramble up slippery steps. It's a bloody nightmare keepin' the boat alongside too. Wot's more, I get no fanks most of the time. Only the Chief makes a point of saying it, but no one else."

Florrie was at the sink, cigarette in hand, looking out of the window at the driving rain, supposedly listening to her husband. Cyril never showed any interest in anyone else's business. Florrie made a stab at it, but rarely got beyond asking her daughter how busy the train was.

This particular night Maureen sensed something was wrong as she hung up her wet coat. The tension seemed more intense than usual. Wandering into the back room to give Ricky his customary stroke, she was surprised to find he wasn't on his chair, or by the fire. Thinking he must be finishing off Cyril's dinner somewhere she wandered around looking for him. It was then that she noticed his bowls missing. She looked up at the hook where his lead always hung, but it wasn't there either. Nor was his winter coat. That's when it dawned on her. Head spinning, she turned to her Mother, but Florrie continued staring out the window, inhaling deeply. Cyril pretended he wasn't there.

When Florrie finally looked round, her face was ashen and she was trembling. She shot a glance at her daughter and then lit another cigarette. The first drag caught her in the throat and she coughed violently. Maureen decided she had probably been chain smoking for most of the day, judging by the number of cigarette butts in the ashtray. But it served to confirm the worst. Ricky was gone.

Feeling the tears welling up behind her glasses, Maureen ran out of the room and grabbing her wet coat dashed out of the house mumbling something about having to be at John's. It was still raining. As she circuited the block, tears streaming down her face, a thousand questions ran through her mind. Had Ricky been run over? No, no, she'd have been told that. Was he ill? For sure he wasn't the fittest of dogs. His teeth were bad, which made his breath smell, he was grubby and badly in need of a haircut, but he wasn't even ten, so he was hardly old. Had he been to the vet before... an ulcer or something? He'd never eaten proper dog food, just all that sugar. Why didn't they *say* something? She can't just have got fed up with him? Had she? She often said he was becoming a bit of a nuisance. Oh no, she can't have... She's had him put down... today... without any warning. How could she? He was my dog too... What other answer could there be?

John opened the door to find a bedraggled Maureen standing there crying. He asked her what had happened, but she couldn't make the words come out properly. It was to take half an hour before she'd calmed down sufficiently to make any sense.

"What I can't get over," he said scratching his head, "is that Ricky was really *her* dog. How could she be so callous? Anyway, who the devil was Davy Crockett?"

Oblivious to the question, Maureen carried on rambling. "She can't have done it lightly. Must have taken a lot of soul searching for her to go, especially on the bus, knowing she was going to come back empty handed. He would have been so excited going out with her too. Bet she was planning it. Not a word. Not even a sign. It's like he never existed."

"And Davy Crockett?"

"Sorry John. Davy was a cat we had till I was about five. Lovely friendly tabby, I used to push him around in my pram. He disappeared too. I was told the gypsies had stolen him. I was suspicious of Molly and Jim in the Public Bar for years."

"Doubt that's what happened to Ricky," John replied with a shake of the head.

There were no answers. Maureen knew it. And there never would be. They were never going to say anything about it, because that's just the way they were.

John walked her back, intent on asking where Ricky was, but he, too, chickened out once he got inside. He'd had enough experience of Cyril and Florrie's unique behaviour to know better. They were watching *The Golden Shot* through a thick fog of cigarette smoke, *Bernie's Bolt* being lined up on the target - up a bit, stop, down a bit, stop…fire!

John kissed her goodbye on the doorstop, obviously relieved to be returning to his warm, friendly house. Maureen went to bed, but not before finding a photo of Ricky sitting on his bench behind the bar of the

Victory. In this one he was wearing the giant bow-tie that Bert had made him with flashing red and green lights (port and starboard) at either end. He knew he had to stay still so as not to disturb the wires connecting the lights to the battery attached to his collar. Fifteen minutes like this got him his own bag of smoky bacon crisps.

Eighteen

They Get Everywhere, Don't They

Florrie had her feet up, reading the headline in the News of the World out loud to Maureen. "The Beatles 'ave definitely disbanded. Paul announced it last night. I reckon it's all that Japanese woman's fault."

Maureen was about to answer when her father's rasping tongue invaded their peace again.

"Florrie, where are ya?" He was back from the Lord Tennyson.

Florrie sighed, put down the paper and crossed her arms in anticipation of whatever was about to come.

"You won't believe what I 'eard in the pub," he said, barging into the room. "Full of it they were."

Florrie stared at him until he started to look uncomfortable. "Whatever you 'eard, they certainly took their time telling it to ya. Yer dinner's been in the oven for hours. Still that's 'ardly new."

Cyril turned to Maureen and raised his eyebrows, unsure what the fuss was all about, and then sat down at the table in expectation of being fed.

"It's 'ot," Florrie growled, plonking a steaming plate in front of him. By now, whatever it was bore little resemblance to what it had been, the gallon of gravy it was originally floating in having been reduced to the consistency of treacle.

Maureen continued watching the news footage of the recent rock festival where a seething mass of 600,000 invaded the Isle of Wight. Expecting 20,000 who had paid £3 for the three day event, the vast number of extras broke down the barriers and climbed a hill overlooking the stage which gave them a perfect view for free. Residents talked of disruption and anarchy. Festival-goers raved about the brilliant atmosphere and amazing performances. As much as Maureen would have loved to have witnessed the incredible line-up, the snaking queues for the toilets, hundreds washing naked in the sea and sleeping in potato sacks lined with polystyrene, were scenes she was glad to have avoided.

"Bloody 'ell, you sure this dinner's been cooked enough? Looks like summink outa *Quatermass*." Cyril's jaw was churning like a propeller. "Sit down. I've got loads to tell ya... go on, over there." A waving fork signalled to his wife to sit in the other chair. "And turn that rubbish down, Sook. What a God awful noise. Hey, isn't that that geezer Hendrix who took all them drugs and snuffed it?

"Yes Dad, this was his last performance, just a couple of weeks ago."

"Wondered why that din was on the news. Anyway first bit of *important* news is that they've shut the old Seamans' Mission Church and sold the *Thistle*. That's the end of Bawley Bay. And, if that's not enough, the end of Queen's Street's being demolished. That's all the 'istory gone. In one fell swoop!" Cyril slammed down his knife for emphasis.

Maureen had read about all this in *The Reporter*, but hadn't dared tell her Father. The *Thistle* was the last remaining Bawley boat and the houses being torn down in Queen Street were the former homes of the last shrimping families.

"But the icin' on the cake...you ready for this, Florrie? Cyril continued, "It's official. Gravesend's got its first Indian Pub landlord. The *Lime Hoy*. The Lime Hoy, Florrie - where you worked... where we met. The bleedin' Lime Hoy. Indian, can ya believe it? Where

235

are ya Enoch? It's startin'."

Maureen kept very quiet. The dust still hadn't settled since the election the previous week. Cyril had been very out of sorts on the day due to the opinion polls predicting a third term for Labour. The voting age for teenagers had been reduced in March from twenty one down to eighteen, meaning that Maureen could vote for the first time. Cyril had escorted his daughter to the polling station, the entire way giving her the benefit of his knowledge on where to put her X. He was none too pleased when he discovered her vote had nullified his. Thankfully, for the maintenance of peace and quiet in Disraeli Drive, Ted Heath was the surprising victor over Harold Wilson, ending six years of Cyril's personal misery.

"So, 'ave you told them wotsisname's coming then?"

Lorraine and Maureen were trying on satin hot pants in Etam.

"It's Errol, and no, I haven't plucked up the courage yet. Thankfully, he's staying at John's, so that's a relief. I reckon popping in for a cup of condensed milk tea in Disraeli Drive will finish him off. Do you think these will really catch on? I look ridiculous!"

"Oh I don't know…"

Lorraine was going through all sorts of contortions trying to see what she looked like from behind. "I quite like them. Does my bum look big in these? Apparently they're gunna be all the rage. Not sure I could wear them to work though."

"My Dad would have a fit if I wore them. Not that I would, I don't think they're for me."

Maureen couldn't get them off quick enough. Lorraine was now trying on a pair with turn-ups, walking up and down the changing room to see how they felt in action.

"So, will you tell them he's black - Errol I mean?"

"I'll have to. Can't risk throwing in *that* kind of surprise. Are they comfortable?"

"Mmmm, not sure. My thighs are rubbing together."

"Maybe that's why they're called *hot* pants."

They both burst into fits of laughter, causing the curtains on the other cubicles to twitch. By the time they got outside they had tears streaming down their faces.

Errol was from Detroit. He had come on a six month secondment to the GLC. Not knowing a soul, Maureen had felt quite sorry for him, and besides he was good fun. John had been up on the train a couple of times and joined them in the pub after work. A few pints down the line one night they had rashly invited him to sample the delights of Gravesend. In the cold light of day they were struggling to think what those might be.

"So, you've remembered that I'll be bringing Errol back with me tonight?" Maureen asked her Mother, about to drop the bombshell.

"Yeh, yeh I remember." Florrie sounded irritated. "You've said it several times now. But I can't understand why you don't want any tea. I got the large-sized Fray Bentos steak and kidney pudding 'specially."

"Sorry Mum, we're going for an Indian. Errol wants to sample the local food. Look, there's something I need to tell you and Dad, about Errol…"

"Oh don't tell me, 'e's queer. I might 'ave known it. It all makes sense why 'e's made friends wiv you."

"No Mum," Maureen replied quickly, determined not to be sidetracked. He's black. Bye, see you later."

"I 'ope yer not implying that we're *racial preduced*," Florrie shouted after her daughter.

"Warn Dad, will you?" Maureen shouted back as she ran for the bus.

"You will act normal, won't you?"

Florrie was giving Cyril the once over.

"Gi'us a chance. I'm late cos I've been watchin' 'em bringin' the stuff up the river for the Flood Barrier. It's gunna be bloody impressive, they've got…"

"Not now Cyril, no time."

"Alright I get the message. I'll 'ave a wash and change me clothes. What time's Ghandi comin'?"

"I intend to make this black man feel at home. If you can't be civil you'd betta keep yer mouff shut. Besides he won't be 'ere long."

"So you keep promisin'." Cyril slammed the bathroom door.

Maureen and Errol entered the air lock, her key proving unnecessary as Florrie had seen them from her vantage point behind the nets at the window. Determined to display the utmost hospitality, she opened the door and lurched forward. They collided in the doorway knocking over the geraniums. Maureen could see soil flowing over the top of Errol's shoes.

"Er, hi there," he said in an unmistakable American drawl.

Still intent on creating the best possible impression for a foreigner entering her domain, she grabbed Errol's hand in both of hers and pulled him bodily over the threshold.

"Do you want to go to the toilet?" she asked in a tone usually reserved for small children. Maureen wished the floor would swallow her up.

"Er, no, not right at this time," Errol replied in a slightly frightened voice.

"Only we want you to know," she continued somewhat poshly, nodding for extra emphasis, "that we're happy for you to use it."

Errol broke free and, clearly embarrassed, busied himself with returning the soil from his shoes to the flowerpot.

"I'll get us a cuppa then. You won't say no to a slice of Battenberg I trust?"

With that, Florrie headed for the kitchen.

Of course Maureen had forewarned Errol, but this greeting had exceeded her wildest expectations. She whispered her apologies and tried to comfort him with news of John's anticipated arrival time. Errol surveyed the glass walls and doors in disbelief. "What is a *cuppa battenberg*?" he whispered back, the confidence visibly draining from his face. You wait, thought Maureen. That's nothing. A freshly-washed Cyril will no doubt introduce you to his rollocks and point at his Big Boys with his wanky finger.

Errol didn't stay long, but he did go to the toilet.

After only a few months in the care home, Ethel rang to say that Dot had been taken to hospital. Nobody seemed sure what was wrong, but they were doing some tests. John was quick to respond once he got the message and dropped Maureen off so she could keep Cyril abreast of the situation. Like at the Home, every elderly lady on the ward looked much the same, but thankfully she spotted her Aunt talking to the doctor and, following their gaze, realised that the dishevelled heap in the bed was her Grandmother. She looked very disorientated and was having trouble holding herself up

"Mum," Ethel whispered in her ear, "we need to get you over to the X-ray department. You're goin' to 'ave a scan."

Dot nodded and let the nurses get her into a wheelchair, while Ethel explained to Maureen that the doctor now thought she'd had a mini stroke as she'd lost the control of her left side.

"OK Mum, we're off, hold on tight."

Ethel and Maureen took turns pushing the heavy chair through a maze of corridors.

"Not sure she's gunna come back from this," puffed Ethel. It was hard work and Dot wasn't reacting to anything on the way.

"Can you hear me Nanna? We're nearly there."

Dot's head was resting on her chest and listing to the right. Maureen took over the pushing and shook the wheelchair gently just to check she was conscious.

"If I'd known this was gunna 'appen so soon, I wouldn't 'ave put 'er in the 'ome." Ethel was feeling guilty.

"You weren't to know, and anyway if this had happened in the flat, she might have fallen down the stairs and lain there for ages."

"S'pose so. Look there's the arrow. We go through that door."

Inside, there were long queues at every desk. They joined one of them and resigned themselves to the wait. Maureen bent down to straighten her Grandmother up and tuck in her trailing blanket. Sensing Maureen's closeness, Dot lifted her head and opened her eyes.

"They get everywhere, don't they," she said, her eyes darting left and right before the weight of her own head got too much. Maureen wasn't sure what she meant initially, but on surveying the queues realised that it was mostly made up of turban-wearing men and sari-clad ladies. Consistent to the end Nanna, thought Maureen. She squeezed Dot's hand, which made her smile.

Dot never made it back to the home. She died three weeks later after another stroke. Ethel took over the funeral arrangements which turned out to be a large family affair at her house. Maureen seemed to be the only one aware that her parents were being included in the gathering for the first time in twenty years. She watched Cyril talking easily to his few remaining aunts and uncles and there were several jokes about the similarity in looks between him and his male cousins. The ice was melting between brother and sister too. Dot'll be pleased, Maureen thought. It was as if the last piece of the jigsaw representing her childhood had finally fallen into place and she was closing the lid on the box.

"So d' ya reckon you'll get engaged if you 'ave an 'oliday then?"

Maureen was talking on the phone to Lorraine on one of those rare occasions when Cyril and Florrie were out together.

"Oh Lorr, you know I don't really want to yet, we're ok just jogging along." Privately, Maureen's heart sank at the thought.

"You might think it's ok to jog along, but I've 'eard John's all for it. He told Rob, who told Chris, who told me."

"Oh, God, he's been talking about *our future* quite a lot since his baby brother was born."

"What d'ya mean? 'E doesn't want you to 'ave a baby surely?" Lorraine almost sounded excited at the prospect of a scandal.

"No, not yet, but he keeps saying how he loves to look after Simon and how he wants one just like him. Well, four actually."

"And you don't want that then?"

"I don't know what I want. That's the problem."

"Well I think yer mad. You could do a lot worse, you know. John's a great bloke. If I was in your shoes I'd be getting that ring on me finger and settlin' down in one of them new 'ouses out at New Willow Green."

The more Lorraine went on, the more Maureen felt trapped. Details of her weekly routine spun around in her head. Watching TV on a Friday with John's family, shopping on a Saturday with a car ride to a nice pub, then on Sunday John would play football in the morning, tinker with the car in the afternoon and turn up with grease under his fingernails just in time for their tinned tea. It wasn't greatly exciting but it went without saying that it would all be unbearable without him. For once she was pleased to hear Cyril's booming voice as he tried to get his key in the door.

"Gotta go, Lorr, they're back"

"Bloody State of Emergency. That's 'ow important dockers are. I told ya it would come to this."

"Wot about me own state of emergency?" Florrie snapped back. "That didn't seem to bovver ya!"

It turned out that Cyril had gone on the bus with Florrie to stock up with food in case the shortages predicted during the National Dock Strike happened. Panic buying was already wreaking havoc at Tesco's, the aisles resembling a rugby scrum, headscarves and handbags flying. It was all too much for the mild-mannered Cyril who'd abandoned his wife at the condensed milk shelf and headed off to the Victory Public Bar to hear what was going on, first hand, from Curly's brothers.

John managed to arrive just as temperatures were rising and found himself being co-opted into rearranging the teetering tower of toilet rolls in the hall.

"Let's go back to my place and look at the holiday brochures my Dad's got," he whispered. "Simon's scuppered *their* plans for this year. I've heard about a place called Benidorm. My boss went there. Loads of brand new giant hotels right on the beach. So new in fact some haven't been finished yet…. I can afford it

242

now I'm working."

John's job at the new Blue Circle cement works was going well. The place was huge - believed to be the largest of its kind in the world. Even Cyril was impressed. They made their excuses and retreated to the sanity of Nightingale Avenue, where Maureen stared at pictures of people lying on long stretches of sand outside huge white blocks with the occasional cement mixer scattered between the flower beds. Everyone looked bored to tears, or perhaps it was how she imagined herself in that situation. Having suffered sunstroke in Jersey and being positively scared to death of swimming pools (thanks to Cyril) her interest wasn't sufficiently sparked to make a decision. *Pull yourself together* she told herself. *You're never satisfied. Poor bloke's trying his best to add some excitement.*

"I'll leave it to you," she said diplomatically, "I'm sure you'll pick the right one." It was hard to resist the temptation to add that one page looked much like the next. No sooner had the weight of the travel brochures been lifted off her lap, than they were replaced by the spring edition of the Freemans catalogue. "Have a look in there and sort yourself out a bikini," John's Mum helpfully suggested. As a home agent she probably sensed a sale.

"I've booked it!" John announced a couple of days later. "All we need now are passports."

Unfortunately, Cyril was listening.

"What, d'yer wanna go abroad for. I can assure yer, yer won't like it. In fact yer'll be desperate to get 'ome!"

"Have you been to Spain then, Mr Cooke?" John replied, seemingly unaware that he was treading on dangerous ground.

"Near as damn it, my boy. 'Ad a few Spaniards in

me pub. Never got on wiv 'em. Always wantin' onions in their cheese rolls!"

"Wot's more," added Florrie as the doors to her new musical cigarette dispenser flew open at the touch of a button, "you won't be able to eat the food you know - it'll all be foreign."

"'Ope yer not goin' on one of 'em new Jumbo 747 planes," Cyril continued. "Right fiasco that's turned into. I saw it on the news. All the suitcases fallin' off the conveyor belts, just like our old bottle shunter in the pub. Airports can't 'andle all the extra luggage. And what about that Concorde eh? I always said getting into bed wiv those Frenchies was askin' fer trouble. Look what that de Gaulle done in the War. Cleared off to Britain, leavin' 'is country in the lurch... we look after 'im, put the biggest bloody invasion force in 'istory togevver to kick the Nazis out of France, and 'ow does he fank us, eh? Says we ain't fit to be parta Europe! We bloody *freed* Europe so as he could go 'ome, didn't we... bloody cheek."

"I think we might have touched a few nerves there," John remarked as he parked the car at the top of Windmill Hill.

"Believe me; we escaped in the nick of time. Harold Wilson usually comes in for it after the Common Market. We got off easy."

"I take it your Dad's never been abroad then?"

"Only Scotland," sighed Maureen.

Nineteen

Holidaytime

"Got some news yer'll be pleased about."

Cyril was tending his melons. Afraid that their own weight would cause them to drop before ripening, he'd come up with an ingenious plan to support each fruit in a pair of Maureen's old tights. And very fetching they all looked too.

"Seein' as yer got a couple of days off work before yer holiday, fought you and yer muvver could get the bus up to Greenhithe ta see what I 'ave to do fer a livin.' Watch them toffee-nosed teachers come down the jetty one by one. Bet yer'll be able to see the next one 'iding in the bushes wating till I've cast off before 'e appears. Yer need to know what I 'ave ta put up wiv."

"Will we get to go on the Worcester then?" Maureen was hopeful of some incentive.

"No. Yer not important enough fer that. Just sit on the grass from a distance and keep an eye out. Bring a sandwich if yer like"

"Woopedy doo," Maureen mumbled under her breath.

"Anyway, that's not the real news I wanna tell ya. Yer Mum wants a kitchen-come-diner. It's *where it's at* apparently. Drawn up some plans. Yer'll get a bigger bedroom out of it."

Maureen took off her cardigan, the heat in the lean-to making her head spin, and looked at Cyril's scribbles.

"I don't understand, where..."

245

"Know what yer wonderin'. But I'm gunna knock down the wall between the kitchen and yer bedroom, and *voylar*, there's yer kitchen-come-diner."

"Then I'll have no bedroom at all!"

"Gi'us a chance. All part of me plan. The back room'll become yer bedroom. I'm gunna rebuild yer wardrobe in there. Then we'll be using the front room to watch telly in. Bit daft 'avin' that settee doing no good."

Maureen and John had long since given up playing records in the 'goldfish bowl', but the idea of having a bedroom on the other side of a perspex partition was horrendous.

"That means I'll only have two real walls, one of which has a doorway in it. How am I supposed to get any privacy?"

"*Privacy*," Cyril mocked. "Who d'ya fink you are? Queena bloody Sheba. Anyway fer yer information, yer Mum's been ponderin' over the perspex." He was sounding confident. "She's gunna put up curtains. I'm taking me annual leave while yer on 'oliday, so the work'll all be done by the time yer get back."

There was obviously no more to be said as he bit into a fresh tomato, its seeds and juice running down his chin, before strolling off to the garage. Maureen pictured him enjoying a secret pale ale in the *New Victory*, clipboard in hand, refining his plans for the demolition of her bedroom.

Thanks to the burgeoning package holiday business, a massive development was taking place at Luton Airport. John and Maureen were sitting in a large marquee, which served as a temporary departure lounge, perusing the Court Line brochure. Its aim seemed to be persuading passengers that the flight was the fun part of the holiday.

"The plane's a BAC 1-11", John read. "Wonder if ours'll be the pink/rose/magenta combo or the light green/medium green/forest green one? And listen to this: *The all-over colour designs are in keeping with the holiday feel-good factor.*' Bet you won't feel too good after a few too many *cuba libras*."

"What on earth are they?" Maureen asked.

"Bacardi and coke. I've learned how to ask for all our drinks in Spanish."

'Impressive', she thought.

"Here we go," he said, pointing at the departure board, "we're heading for the pale violet/mauve/purple Halcyon Skies."

They were, in fact, heading for San Antonio, Ibiza, courtesy of Clarkson's holidays, the whole two weeks, including full catering in a three star hotel, costing £52 each in late summer. Once on the plane the alcohol flowed liberally. For many this was their first flying experience and a spot of Dutch courage was needed. Maureen watched the flight attendants, in their trendy Mary Quant uniforms, really earning their money that day.

"I can see a sandwich in there," John said excitedly as he began excavating the pre-packed spam salad from the seatback in front of him.

"Top section's for us," Maureen interrupted, pushing his hand away from the lower shelf. They were experiencing *seat back catering,* a whole new concept of cheap-and-cheerful package holidays. The pre-packed meals were loaded into a small two-shelf compartment in the seatback facing each passenger. It saved galley space and reduced the workload of cabin staff as they no longer had to handle trays. The outward salad was on the top shelf, with the return sandwich below. The latter contained a pellet of dry ice under the plastic food container, the idea being to keep it fresh on

247

the round trip. To prevent outbound passengers from consuming both meals, locks were installed, though they were clearly proving a poor deterrent against the more determined travellers.

Spontaneous clapping broke out as they landed, and several of the passengers appeared to be wobbling down the steps. Further chaos occurred as they then tried to find the right coach from the dozen or so waiting, engines running. All afraid that they'd be left behind in this strange land, suitcases were being trampled underfoot.

Having settled into their room, the happy couple dutifully attended the *meet and greet* session in the Granada ballroom. The Clarkson's Clan representative told them about all the optional trips that simply couldn't be missed - watching a bull fight, flamenco dancing, horse displays, boat trips, and sightseeing trips - with meals and as much as you could drink all included.

"Let's do the flamenco dancing," John said, knowing he'd be pushing his luck suggesting a bull fight. "Bit of authentic Spain and all that."

Having planned and booked their *extras* itinerary, they could finally relax and get on with the whole business of following the traditions expected of a summer sun holiday. They soon picked up the essentials –

1. Place your towel, on a south facing poolside lounger, before breakfast.

2. Liberally coat yourself in oil, and remember to turn when your skin starts to sizzle.

3. To avoid a scrum, be early for the lunch buffet and not flinch when tasting the chilled gazpacho for the first time.

4. Think carefully about your souvenir choices. Do you really want that cute stuffed donkey with its ears

popping out of a straw hat?

5. Try to scratch discreetly when your skin starts peeling in a hot disco.

On the *Flamenco Demonstration* evening, Maureen and John got on the coach and circuited the resort, picking up more Clarksonnaires all eager for a fun night out. The atmosphere was already electric. Arriving at a large barn, they parked alongside several similar coaches and headed inside. Horizon, Global, Cosmos, and some other tour operators whose names Maureen couldn't pronounce, all had their own long table where the food kept coming and the *sangria* kept flowing. After the statutory vigorous dancing demonstration, with much hand clapping and stamping of feet, everyone was *very* much in high spirits. It was now that the real purpose of the evening got underway. This was the drinking competition in which you volunteered to 'drink as quickly as you can from a yard of ale without drowning'. Egged on by the tour reps, and accompanied by the strongly rhythmic flamenco music, willing victims from each table drained a long glass tube which required precision tipping to win. The rivalry between tables was intense. John became quite proficient at it, a shame really as by the third yard he'd passed out in the toilet. The waiters, mumbling something about *Yobbos Ingleses*, dragged him out into the night air, only to witness him being violently sick over the *agaves*.

Maureen sat with him on the wall listening to the crowd singing *Y Viva Espana,* praying for the coach to start up. Sadly, things went from bad to worse, when a crowd of Los Yobbos decided to perform a mock bull fight in the adjacent barn. Distracted for a moment, she missed John falling backwards into a bed of succulents. If nothing else, it sobered him up rather quickly.

Trouble was, she now had to spend most of the night yanking spikes out of his bloody back with her eyebrow tweezers.

Such highlights aside, the holiday was an overall success. Maureen loved being abroad. She found the huge skies and twinkling seas beautiful and never tired of hearing the crickets chirping in the bushes during warm late-night walks. She particularly liked it on the days they hired a vespa scooter and rode around the island taking photos of the scenery. Stopping for drinks in tiny hilltop villages, you could watch the real islanders going about their daily lives and savour being away from all the other holidaymakers.

On one of these expeditions, John took advantage of the quietness as they were sitting outside a café. He had ordered a bottle of Cava and after popping the cork, poured out two glasses of the gently fizzing nectar.

"So what do you think about us getting engaged then?" he said, handing her a glass, clearly intending to raise a toast to themselves.

The soundtrack from *Love Story* should have filled the air at that moment. Maureen and Lorraine had sobbed their way through it at the Majestic. It was so tragic, *so* romantic. *Love means never having to say you're sorry*, a distraught Ali MacGraw had said to Ryan O'Neal, her love overflowing. Somehow the current scenario didn't quite match up. Try as hard as she might, Maureen just didn't feel like Ali.

"Sorry John, not now. Maybe one day... I'm not sure we're..."

"You always say that. Look we love one another don't we? And we're having a lovely holiday. I can't see why we can't go back engaged. It'll be something to remember and my Mum and Dad would be so pleased."

"I'm just not ready to get married yet and I don't

want to be engaged for ages beforehand. Can't we leave it till my 21st? I'll definitely be up for it then."

"Alright, next year it is," he sighed, raising his glass.

Maureen struggled to lift hers to meet his.

As they pulled up outside the bungalow on their return Maureen began to experience her usual sinking feeling.

"Oh Lord," John said, staring at the front garden, "not another rockery."

"Wall must be down," Maureen replied, a note of trepidation creeping into her voice. "You coming in with me?"

Struggling to prize herself, her suitcase, a sombrero and bottles of Mateus Rose out of the Mini, she could feel her throat drying up. If ever she needed support, this was the moment.

"No thanks," John replied, keeping the engine running. "I want to stay feeling high after the holiday for as long as I can. Ring you later."

With that he drove off.

With no hope of getting her belongings through the front door, she headed past the new rockery, round the side to see what had become of her bedroom. Such was the volume of bricks and rubble extracted during the various demolitions that Cyril had already built two substantial rockeries, with waterfalls and pond, between the garage and the lean-to. This left only a tiny patch of grass for his home-made seats which resembled giant wooden toadstools, painted pillar box red with white spots. The view from the back door was not dissimilar to the mural scene on the Victory yard wall.

"Adios amigos!" Cyril yelled, spotting her first. "You'll be sayin' mucho grassyarse when yer see yer new bedroom. Come on in."

251

With that, Cyril flung his wife a tea towel whilst he, waggling his index fingers on his head - hornlike - headed the towel out of Florrie's hands. "Ole!" they both shouted in unison. It had clearly been practiced.

Maureen swiveled round to see what was left of her tiny bedroom. A drop leaf table and two chairs stood where her bed had been and what remained of the wall previously holding up the built-in wardrobe bore signs of significant nail, bolt and screw damage. There were even bits of purple psychedelic wallpaper adhering to them.

"So, are ya glad t'be back?" Florrie didn't wait for an answer. "Was it 'ot? Bet yer didn't like the food. Tell us all about it later. Come'n look at this now."

Maureen poked her head around the door of her new room.

"So, 'ere's the wardrobe, rebuilt on this wall. We got rid of the table and Joey's old cage. Full of dust it was. I've put up these lovely green flowery curtains against the French doors. You'll be able to open 'em in the morning and say 'ello to yer Dad weighing 'is melons on the uvver side. I've put up red curtains in the front room against the perspex - 'ung 'em up *that* side so I can open 'em as soon as you're awake. See, it's very cosy; you can 'ardly notice the walls are gone."

"What d' ya reckon then?" said Cyril fishing for compliments.

"I can't really take it all in…" Maureen spluttered.

"Knew you'd like it, plenny of that *privacy* you wanted," he responded with a contented nod. "Oh, and by the way, yer bed's pushed right up against the gas fire, so don't get any daft ideas about lighting it. Whole lot'll go up."

Resisting the temptation to say what was really on her mind, she bundled her things into the new bedroom, closed the door and hurled her case onto the chair.

252

Feigning jet lag, she made an excuse to go to bed early.

It wasn't long before her thoughts turned to John and why she kept putting him off. It was all so confusing. She loved him, didn't she? But he was the only person she'd ever been out with, so how could she be sure? The truth was, she didn't really know what it was supposed to feel like. John didn't seem to have any doubts himself. He'd saved her from going insane, but was that why she had stayed with him? Surely not. He was kind and generous and would do anything for her. According to Lorraine, he was all she could ask for. Her parents had accepted him, which was not to be sniffed at. Florrie always seemed to be expecting 'news' every time they neared another milestone. On the other hand, Aunty Ethel had told her *not to settle with the first one. Even if you come back to him in the end, try out a few others first.* But what if I break it off with John and then no one else ever asks me out again? Can I take the risk? I'll go mad if I'm stuck here. Oh God, that can't be right reason to stay with John. Am I just using him then?

Her head throbbing, she wondered whether Cyril was right about her getting above herself. Perhaps it would all be well by the time she was 21? Somewhere around that point she must have fallen asleep.

The next morning, being Sunday, Florrie was champing at the bit to open the curtains in the front room. Meanwhile Cyril had been waiting impatiently in the lean-to, listening at the French doors until he too could hear Maureen stirring. Deciding he could hear a cough, he flung them open and barged in through the closed curtains.

"I didn't wanna 'ave to tell ya this, but I think yer Mum's trying to gas me."

Maureen sat up in bed trying not to laugh, all dreams of getting back to normality being dashed in a flash. Her Father had been getting more and more eccentric of late. Too many of those ferry journeys between the *Worcester* and the shore in bad weather, she thought. Water on the brain, probably.

"It's this North Sea gas stuff they're sendin' us - it's stronger. She's been turning on the rings and then not lightin' 'em. Only just managed to save meself, not just once neiver. 'Ad to fling the kitchen door open lotsa times." Cyril felt the shock overcoming him and sat down on the bed.

"Oh Dad, surely it was just an accident."

"No, it's no accident. It's deliberate I tell ya."

Suddenly the curtains flew open behind Maureen's head and seconds later Florrie appeared with a look of scorn on her face. Hearing noises coming from the back room she'd initially imagined the worst… John must have got past security and be in there - but on hearing the last bit of Cyril's tale of woe, disgust turned to vengeance.

"You're not *still* going on about the gas!" she raged at her cowering husband. I told ya, the draught from the door keeps blowing it out."

"That's what you say now. They've brought in the quickie divorce, you know, if you wanna get rid of me that much!"

Florrie raised her eyes to the ceiling and clenched her fists. "What is all this Cyril? It's like that car crash you said 'appened. Made it sound like one o' them *Evil Ken Evil* bloke's stunts… how many cars you fly over, eh?"

Norman, carpenter on the *Worcester*, had been giving Cyril a lift to and from work. One treacherous morning, according to Cyril, they had been in an accident where the car spun round several times and he'd had to be cut free by the fire brigade.

Not waiting for a reply, she tore on; "As it 'appens,

I saw Norman drop you off that day. Car looked right as nine pence to me."

"That's right, woman. Bring it up again, why don't ya? I'm not stoppin' 'ere for this. Gunna go and pollenate me cucumbers".

Cyril's exit left Florrie perched on the end of Maureen's bed telling her how she was convinced her husband was going round the bend. The more she talked, the less her daughter heard. It wasn't just Cyril. The place was a madhouse, and it wasn't going to get any better.

In fact it got a lot worse. The TV became the sole provider of entertainment and company for Florrie. She gradually stopped going to the Tennyson with Cyril and, having nothing else in her life besides her job, she watched just about everything now in glorious Technicolor. Being the other side of the perspex, the TV was always very loud, which meant Maureen found herself condemned to listening to her Mother's particular favourite *Wednesday Play* whilst Cyril would be watering his plants in the lean-to, refusing to watch such 'dirt'. He never gave it a chance, missing some important gritty dramas such as *Cathy Come Home* which caused outrage over the nation's homeless families. How strange, Maureen thought. Her Mother could endlessly watch films and plays about *real life* but never talk about her own.

"'Ere Cyril, come quick!" Florrie screeched through the perspex. Her husband was dozing on a deckchair in the lean-to, making the best of an hour of January sun.

"Bloody 'ell woman, what's up now?"

"Valerie Barlow's been electrocuted wiv an 'airdryer. Look, 'ouse is on fire. Pity it's not in colour."

Both Cookes became glued to the screen, entranced by this dramatic episode of *Coronation Street*. Having now got used to a colour set, they had to watch *this* action in black and white because ITV staff refused to work the new equipment after a dispute over pay. It had been going on for more than two months, Christmas included.

Without Dot to visit and no colour TV, Christmas had become even more unbearable. Cyril didn't bother with the polystyrene stars - the edges having curled up in the rain the previous year. He spent most of the time at the Tennyson, Florrie asleep in the chair and Maureen at John's.

"What d'ya reckon on that then?" Cyril said as he put the phone down on Maureen's birthday, the day before New Year's Eve.

"You sure she's got the right number?" Florrie responded, with a mixture of amazement and sarcasm. Maureen couldn't believe her own ears. It was Ethel on the phone inviting them to her house to see the New Year in.

"Let bygones be bygones eh? Be churlish not to go now she's made the first move. We could go in John's car. Tight squeeze but it's not far." Cyril had made his mind up.

Maureen and John already had plans for New Year's Eve, but they dropped her parents off on the way. Maureen hadn't seen her Father look so cheerful for ages. He was even wearing his knitted beige waistcoat.

"Whatatodo…"

Florrie crashed in through the back door, out of breathe from trying to get some bread for tea. "'Ad to walk in the end, bus crew wouldn't take the new coins."

"Same 'ere," nodded her husband, having just got back himself. "Took bloody ages to get a pint. "It's all them *pees*. Gi'us shillin's an' pence any day."

Maureen's peaceful Saturday afternoon was brought to an abrupt end. The Cookes had just had their first practical experiences of decimalisation. Everyone was up in arms about rising prices, and 'galloping inflation' had become the tabloids' favourite buzz phrase. Even the Ford workers over in Dagenham had downed tools over price hikes at their vending machines.

"Now we're all 'ere, we can tell ya our news, Mo… we're goin' on an 'oliday!" He was brandishing a leaflet. "Yer Mum and me, Effel and Fred. We're goin' to an 'oliday camp. Pontins at Camber Sands. Right next to Dungeness. Be able to winkle out me old mate Curly. Dunno what I'll do about the food. Won't bovver Fred of course, 'e'll eat anyfink'. Anyway, it'll be our first 'oliday together in twenny-odd years. Will you remember to water me Big Boys?"

'Hope you'll be able to keep the peace with your sister', Maureen thought, 'a week's a long time…' As there seemed to be no suggestion of her having to join them, she sensibly booked a week off work to coincide with the Pontins escapade. Not that she told them. She simply fancied a break on her own away from them and the arguments. What's more, she was heartily fed up with commuting. The trains were often packed, delayed or cancelled during peak hours. There were often bomb scares as the Northern Ireland troubles escalated. In August, British security forces detained hundreds of paramilitary suspects in Long Kesh prison. It was the beginning of internment without trial and twenty died in the ensuing riots. By September the toll reached 100 with the death of a fourteen year old girl caught in crossfire between British soldiers and the IRA. Life in the Capital got that much more difficult as a result. On a number of occasions she found herself caught up in

257

police attempts to evacuate Waterloo station and when an IRA bomb exploded in the restaurant at the top of the Post Office Tower, Maureen decided that it was better to stay and come home later. There were always some GLC friends ready to go for a drink or a meal and indeed one of her fellow commuters, Pauline, was happy to stay late too, so she always had a friend to travel with.

"Don't make any plans after work on Friday," John said one day. "We've got free tickets to see Bruce Forsyth at the London Palladium."

The expression on his face said it all. They would both have rather gone to see *No Sex Please, We're British* but it wasn't worth the aggravation being lectured to later by Cyril about the evils of the permissive society. By this time Maureen's father had become a fan of Britain's self-appointed guardian of the nation's morals, the blue-rinse filth crusader, Mary Whitehouse. For her, the declining standards in the British media had to be countered lest the commercial exploitation of sex and violence corrupted the young and ruined the Nation. So, when 50,000 people attended a *Nationwide Festival of Light* mass rally against permissiveness, in Trafalgar Square, Cyril was mightily impressed. For him the fight-back had started.

Maureen and John took their free seats in the front row of the dress circle. Up went the curtain and on came The Tiller Girls, dancing in formation, followed by *Brucie* who, in inimitable style, got the show underway with a few appalling jokes before introducing Scotland's Kenneth McKellar direct from the White Heather Club, complete with pipers, drummers, kilts and bagpipes. Half way through, the stage was set for *Beat the Clock* – a game in which members of the audience had to complete ridiculous tasks to win prizes.

"Put up the house lights," ordered Bruce. "Right, are there any newly-weds in the audience?"

No response.

"Alright then, what about engaged couples?"

"That's us," said John excitedly.

"No it's not," Maureen whispered a little too loudly.

"That couple there, in the front row, yes you…"

Maureen froze. Brucie was looking straight at them.

"Engaged or not? Aren't you *sure*?" he mocked, sensing an opportunity to gain a laugh at their expense.

"Almost," said John, "we've been going out over three years."

"Good enough for me!" said Bruce. "There's an usherette behind you. Follow her and join us on the stage."

The audience stared as John and Maureen, and a lady with an array of ice creams and a torch walked up the aisle and out through a rabbit warren of corridors. Maureen was speechless. She couldn't decide if the public announcement of their engagement was more humiliating than what was about to happen to her on the stage of the London Palladium.

Bruce and Anthea Redfern met them in the wings. They looked incredibly *orange*. Maureen noticed that the low neckline and underarms of Anthea's long dress were caked in hastily-applied make up.

"Just follow me and we'll all get a laugh," said Bruce.

The next ten minutes or so were, without doubt, the most excruciatingly embarrassing moment of Maureen's life. The game involved lying on a bed, jumping up when the alarm went, pretending to make breakfast, ironing and kissing John goodbye when he 'went off to work' - all against the clock. There was much rushing around the stage, pushing and shoving and dropping props.

"Do this and it'll be funny… pretend to be cross now… push me out the way, etc…" were thrown in here and there by the hosts for added effect. Then, if all that wasn't bad enough, Maureen had to sit on Bruce's knee, Anthea on John's while they all sang *If you were the only girl in the World*. The orange rubbed off onto Maureen's dress and John's shirt. He was also plastered in red stage lipstick which proved extremely hard to get off. For being good sports John got a Rael Brook shirt modelled by a girl wearing little else whilst strutting around the stage. Maureen got some cheap perfume. There was also an *all girls together* moment when Anthea presented her with a rolling pin. The usherette was waiting to escort them back to their seats and gave them a free ice cream. People in the surrounding seats stared at them for quite some time.

"Can't believe Lorraine's got in there first!" John said indignantly. Maureen was on the phone to him having just been shopping with her friend. They'd stopped for a cup of coffee in British Home Stores when Lorraine broke the news of her engagement.

"Didn't seem much point 'anging about, so we done it on Firework night. What d'ya reckon on this shirt?"

"Nice… erm, blimey Lorr, how long've you been going out?"

"Six months. You sure about this shirt? You don't think it looks like it needs ironing?"

"No, it's cheesecloth, meant to look like that. So did Chris get down on one knee then?"

"Do me a favour, course not. I said d'ya wanna get engaged and 'e said alright then. What about this Tank top?"

"*Lorraine*! You've got no doubts then, seeing as it's only been six months?"

"No Mo, I'm not you."

Twenty

Happy New Year

Maureen's 21st birthday turned out to be a memorable occasion. Cyril and Florrie decided there should be a party, which had all the makings of a bizarre event right from the outset. For a start Maureen had to get ready ridiculously early to allow plenty of time for the perspex partition to be opened up. Cyril had his concerns as it was the first time he had attempted it. "You finished yet?" he kept complaining. "Gotta take a shufti at it all."

He needed to follow his clipboard instructions for the great dismantle and it was a miracle that something didn't go horribly wrong. Anyway, that done, chairs borrowed from Horace next door were placed round the perimeter of the room and cushions plumped up to conceal the identity of Maureen's bed.

Deciding what to wear amid the chaos wasn't easy. In the end she decided on her new long jersey skirt which had eight panels of pink flower print. This was topped with a chiffon purple blouse with huge see-through long sleeves and finished off with pink suede platform shoes. Her hair, still long, was permed now, to look *naturally* curly. (It still needed rollers, but only on hair wash nights.) She noticed that her Father was again sporting his beige knitted waistcoat - it was destined to be a good night. His wife had a new paisley patterned shift dress from C&A in Lewisham which had giant patch pockets. Maureen was amazed to see her Mother's exposed knees, short skirts having finally been accepted in Disraeli Drive. Shame really, because maxi skirts were now the *in* thing.

Florrie had gone for the very height of sophistication in her choice of party food. Sausage rolls had stood the test of time, but were now joined by bridge rolls filled with tinned salmon, replacing boring old sandwiches. However her *pièce de rèsistance* was grapefruit halves wrapped in tin foil, peppered with cocktail sticks containing cheese and pineapple chunks. Then there were tiny silverskin onions on sticks which she'd discovered could now be obtained in a variety of colours. All-in-all they made the table look very festive. Someone at the Co-op had told her about crudités and dips, but the nearest she got to them were chunks of celery with Primula cheese spread squirted in the grooves. Deciding these looked a little lacking, she sliced up a couple of saveloys and dotted them around the plate. For afters, trusty Birds Trifle Kit came into its own - jelly, custard powder, sponge fingers, instant whip topping and decorations, all in one box. Just what the doctor ordered.

On the drinks side, Cyril was impressed when John told him about Watney's Party Seven - a seven-pint tin of Watney's tried-and-tested *Red Barrel* bitter, costing 59/9d.

"Betta 'ave two of 'em, then," he said, "and get some of that Martini so we can 'ave it … *any time, any place, anywhere.*"

That set Florrie off, who couldn't resist singing the jingle aloud whilst mimicking the Martini girl reclining by a tropical pool, with a cool breeze flowing through her hair and a tray of iced drinks at her elbow. The 'liberated woman's drink of choice,' its suggestive catchphrase went totally over Florrie's head.

The final touch was the musical cigarette box which she'd filled with Players No 6, her new favourite. She'd watched Doreen – Jack's niece in *Get Carter* - smoking them on the screen when she went to see Michael Caine at the Majestic and been taken in by the advertising blurb telling her that *People like you are switching to No. 6.* It took a lot for Florrie to change the habits of a lifetime and she certainly wasn't about to stop smoking because of health warnings. Changing to the 'number one' brand had more to do with its smaller size - and therefore lower price - than the filter being better for you.

John brought his new Phillips portable cassette player and his *This is 1970* and *1971* tapes. "This party's gunna be *groovy*," Cyril yelled, adding to the embarrassment by doing his version of the *Twist*. He insisted on having the Dansette record player warmed up for when the *oldies* started twitching and already had his two Des O'Connor LP's, *Careless Hands* and *Dick-A-Dum-Dum* dusted and ready to drop. John's casual remark that the two record titles perhaps oughtn't to be put together was completely lost on Cyril.

At the appointed hour the guests started arriving at Chez Cooke, which, in the case of Cyril's relations, was the first time they'd crossed the threshold. There was Dot's remaining sister *Friday* and family, Bert's youngest sister Daisy, who'd come from the East End to stay with Ethel, Ethel herself and Fred, and their children and grandchildren, Uncle Charlie (frisked at the door for meths and matches) and lastly, Florrie's sisters, Mavis and Maud and their husbands. Outsiders included John's parents and four of Maureen's friends: Lorraine and her, now, fiancé Chris, Rob and Pauline - in fact only people who'd already been exposed to Cyril in all his glory. She'd thought better of inviting any of her new friends from the GLC. They wouldn't have understood.

Once proceedings were underway, Cyril presented

Maureen with a hand-made, four-foot tall wooden yale key coated in yacht varnish. Florrie gave her an electric sewing machine. There was a tearful moment all round when Maureen was told that half the money for this had been put aside by Dot when she realised she wouldn't live to see her granddaughter reach twenty one.

As Maureen opened the rest of her presents it became clear they all followed a similar theme - pillow cases, towels, table cloth and napkins, indeed everything for her 'bottom drawer'. Florrie had prompted all the guests to expect an announcement, so by the time the last present was opened Maureen was feeling sick. It was possibly the jolt she'd needed, as, by now, she was absolutely certain she couldn't go through with it. Not just the announcement, the whole marriage thing. It was one of those defining moments when you know you haven't got any choice any more. You just have to tell the truth and face the music. So she decided to tell John quietly there and then.

Not really being able to do much else, he got somewhat drunk. As the evening drew to a close there was an air of expectation, the guests hovering with their near-empty glasses. One by one they gave up, downed the last drop and bade their farewells. John left propped up by his parents. Lorraine, last to leave, shook her head in dismay.

Maureen put on *Dick-a-Dum-Dum* to break the silence as they tidied up.

"Aunt Daisy's still lookin' good, 'aven't seen 'er fer years," Cyril said, shaking the beer tins and checking for dregs.

"You've 'ad enough fer one night," Florrie snapped. "Everyone liked the coloured onions. Didn't seem keen on the *crudits* though. Can't say I'm surprised."

Maureen looked at her parents. Predictably they said nothing about the anticipated announcement. The tidying finished, everyone went off to bed, Maureen to hers, *sans* perspex, curtains or privacy. Her head was spinning. As she lay there in the dark she wrestled with her conscience, yet somehow she knew she'd done the right thing. A weight was lifted off her shoulders.

Getting up early, she went to Nightingale Avenue to see how John was.

"I was hoping I'd got it all wrong somehow, seeing as I was drunk, but from the look on your face you meant it, didn't you?" He was looking decidedly grey.

"I'm sorry John, but if we carried on it would be for all the wrong reasons. We don't know where we're going or what else there is out there for us... neither of us has really been out with anyone else."

"Speak for yourself. I know where *I'm* going; I just always assumed you'd be going with me. Bloody great New Year this is going to be."

As the bitterness crept in, the conversation started going round in circles. "What is it you're looking for anyway? Or have you already found it? You've met someone else, haven't you?"

Maureen stared at him for a minute. "No there isn't anyone else, John. I think I'd better go."

He remained silent. As she headed for the door, she realised she knew what she *didn't* want out of life, if not what she did.

When she got back Cyril was rehanging the perspex doors, picking up tiny onions and cocktail sticks as he was doing so.

"Well, that's a turn up fer the books. One minute yer gettin' married; now it's all off. So 'ave yer been leadin' 'im on all this time? Bet 'e's 'appy. What was it then? When 'e got drunk and fell in a cactus, Eh?"

Maureen said nothing.

"Yer'd betta come wiv us down the Tennyson

265

tonight, what wiv it being New Years Eve."

For a second Maureen longed to be back in the Victory - balloons, talc and all.

Over the next couple of weeks things moved quickly. Maureen and Pauline had often joked about sharing a flat together so as to get them off the commuter treadmill. Now Maureen was deadly serious and was greatly relieved to discover her friend was too. They both scoured the Evening Standard as soon as it came out and rushed off to look round available flats after work. Despite stiff competition they found a room to share in a flat in Putney. Perfect for their jobs near Waterloo.

Maureen told Florrie about her intentions. She explained that she was fed up with commuting and that she needed to put some distance between herself and John. Her Mother appeared to listen but didn't make any comment, or ask any questions. All she said was "What do ya want fer yer tea? 'Ad to chuck yer chop away again seein' as yer so late."

When she told Cyril about the flats she'd looked at, and where they were, he just looked straight through her and continued complaining about his one man ferry service. By now he was of the opinion that the teachers at the College were deliberately playing games with him by only appearing on the jetty one at a time.

"It's a conspiracy. That's what it is. A bleedin' solo service I am. Back and forwards, back and forwards, all I do all ruddy day. No chance of another job, not wiv over a million unemployed. Worst it's been since the Thirties. And anuvver bleedin' state of emergency now. Miners' ain't gunna stop strikin'. You wait; it'll only get worse now we're in the *Common Market*."

"Anyway," Maureen said, turning back to her Mum, "we're signing on the dotted line tomorrow, moving in on Sunday. Pauline's Dad's hired a van to take our stuff."

Florrie looked up at the kitchen clock as if to make sure she wasn't late for an appointment. She took her cigarettes and lighter out of her patch pocket, expertly flicked the lighter wheel with her left hand and lit up.

"So *they* know about it then?" she said dragging on her cigarette as she headed for the door.

"Who? Pauline's Mum and Dad. Of course they do. They're all for it. We…"

There wasn't time to finish the sentence, Florrie was gone.

Maureen initially took her parents' reactions as indifference. That is until the following Friday night when she arrived home from work. No one could have been more surprised than she was about what transpired. The house was very quiet. No television noise, nothing. Just Cyril, pacing up and down the hall. He was wearing a shirt and tie, reserved for funerals and he was running his yellow, nicotine-stained fingers through his Brylcremed hair.

Maureen hung up her coat sensing that something was very wrong.

"Right. Now you're in and behind closed doors, I'll tell the plain clothes policeman sittin' in his car outside that 'e's not needed."

Maureen's mouth dropped open.

"'E's 'ad 'is instructions to catch yer if yer bolted when yer saw me."

"Wha… what?" she stammered.

"So, I'm takin' it yer not gunna run, right?"

Maureen stared at the stranger before her, his eyes darting everywhere, unable to believe what she was hearing. She hadn't seen a car parked outside, nor was there any indication of anyone doing anything even vaguely police-like. So when Cyril went to the window and mouthed *you can go now* she became concerned for his sanity.

"Right. We need to talk. I've sent yer Muvver off t'stay wiv one of 'er sisters, in case she couldn't cope when she 'eard the secret yer obviously keeping."

"What secret? I don't have any secrets."

Maureen was staggered. Her Mother had hardly ever been to her sister's house let alone stayed.

"I'm doin' the talkin' now." Cyril's eyes were wild. He was making her sound like she was one of the scum he regularly threw out of the Victory.

"So what is it then, are yer *pregnant*? Assume it's not that boy you've been wiv for the past four years uvverwise yer wouldn't be runnin' away from 'ome. One of 'em GLC blokes is it? Eh? 'E don't wanna know now I s'pose. Runnin' away to 'ave an abortion are ya?"

"Dad I am *not* pregnant and I'm *not* running away from home. I'm 21, going to live in a flat…"

"Yeah, yeah, yer Mother and me 'ave 'eard all that twaddle. So must be drugs then. Getting 'em from London are yer? You'd better tell me what yer on. Yer Mum's been down the Doctor's already 'n the woman behind the desk, that Miss Jones, said there's 'elp you can get."

Maureen started to cry. Was this really what her Father thought of her? Was she really that despicable?

Hearing her mother's tell-tale cough coming from the bedroom, where she'd been hiding, just made it worse.

"See, yer provin' I'm right or yer wouldn't be gettin' so upset now the troof's comin' out, would ya!"

Suddenly Maureen snapped.

"I'm crying because you obviously don't know me at all. We live in this bungalow together, but we're

268

strangers, total strangers."

She ran into her bedroom before her father could say any more and slumped into the only corner that couldn't be seen through the glass door. It took all her strength not to run round the corner to John and say it was all a terrible mistake. She didn't move until she heard her Father go to bed, then she crept into hers not bothering to get undressed.

"Lord knows what they're gunna say," Cyril said, groping for the light switch in his bedroom, unsure where Florrie was hiding.

"Who yer talking about?" the voice came from near the window.

"Mr and Mrs Jenkins, Effel…and all the uvvers fer that matter."

As Maureen woke the next morning, the atmosphere was still decidedly icy. She turned on her radio for company. A report was just coming in about numerous casualties at a civil rights protest in Derry. Thirteen dead as soldiers opened fire on the crowd. Someone called it *Bloody Sunday*. 'Cyril's going to have plenty to say about that', Maureen thought. At least I won't have to listen to it though. She climbed out of bed and was crossing the hall when the phone rang. It was clear her parents weren't going to answer it, so thinking it might be Pauline she picked it up herself. It was Ethel.

"Yer'll be runnin' back wiv yer tail between yer legs, won't take long," she sniffed. "I just wanna know one fing though– did yer get us to give yer all 'em towels and stuff under false pretenses, so you could run away wiv 'em?" Her tone was just like her brother's. "I've been watchin' you. Yer've been plannin' this since you were seventeen."

"Aunt Ethel," Maureen answered wearily, "I haven't been capable of planning *anything*, until now, let alone when I was seventeen. I'll leave the presents on my bed."

As she replaced the receiver, Cyril and Florrie appeared out of their bedroom door and walked past her without saying anything. She watched them as they negotiated the air lock, closed the porch door and disappeared out of the front gate.

Pauline's Mum and Dad had hired a van to move the girls' stuff up to Putney. They had helped sort out the paperwork and, unlike her own parents, were full of encouragement for the new adventure. Everyone laughed as a human chain was formed to pass Maureen's belongings around the side of the bungalow - there was no way they were going to risk going out the front.

"Should have got a bigger van," Pauline's Dad said as he bundled the last of the stuff on to the roof rack. "Where are your Mum and Dad? Aren't they going to wave you off?"

"Doesn't look like it," Maureen replied. "Seems they don't approve."

"Probably think you're going to have an orgy every night," he joked.

"Already done that, apparently," she mumbled as she closed the door and walked away without looking back.

"All in? Right, let's go. Next stop Putney," laughed Pauline's Dad, his free hand flicking through the pages of his map.

They drove into the centre of Gravesend passing Sudan Street where Maureen caught a glimpse of the underwear factory, its steps not half as high as she remembered. Woolworths seemed a blur as they turned onto Hamilton Road, the traffic lights outside the Victory changing to red as they approached. For a moment it seemed as if time was standing still. Winding down the van window she could hear the Toby Ales sign creaking gently in the wind and picked out their ghostly reflection in the uneven green tiles. Then something on the upper floor caught her eye. "It's open… the window's *open*," she stammered.

"What did you say?" Pauline asked, turning her head to locate the source of Maureen's surprise.

Maureen pointed silently to a net curtain that was flying out of her old bedroom window and flapping in the wind.

"Didn't you say you lived in a pub once? Gosh, was it that one? Looks dead grotty. Bet you were glad to move away from that."

The lights changed. Maureen's eyes followed the open window until the Pub disappeared from view. As the river rose up in front of them she fought back the tears and prayed the assorted rivercraft would prove enough of a distraction to ward off any further questions for a while. Pauline's Mum and Dad chatted happily about their holiday on a cruise ship out of Tilbury and how they were planning an adventure on a barge next year. But Maureen wasn't really listening. Her thoughts in turmoil, she felt a deep sense of sadness – a hollowness - about John, her parents, the past that was slipping away in front of her eyes. She was too numb to cry.

Perhaps it was the fresh air, but as they left the cement dust behind and hurtled up the A2, she started to feel light-headed. At first, she put it down to not having had any breakfast, but then realised it was excitement. Heaven knows what her future had in store, but she was sure about one thing - she wasn't going to go back 'with her tail between her legs' as Aunt Ethel had predicted. This was a new start and she was determined to make the most of it…….

271

Lightning Source UK Ltd.
Milton Keynes UK
UKOW03f2103260314

228911UK00004B/201/P

9 781910 162149